14-99

TRUANCY

TRUANCY

The politics of compulsory schooling

Pat Carlen, Denis Gleeson
and Julia Wardhaugh

Open University Press
Buckingham · Philadelphia

Open University Press
Celtic Court
22 Ballmoor
Buckingham
MK18 1XW

and
1900 Frost Road, Suite 101
Bristol, PA 19007, USA

First Published 1992

A catalogue record of this book is available from the
British Library.

Library of Congress Cataloging-in-Publication Data

Carlen, Pat.
    Truancy: the politics of compulsory schooling/Pat Carlen, Denis
Gleeson, Julia Wardhaugh.
        p.   cm.
    Includes bibliographical references (p.   ) and index.
    ISBN 0-335-09615-8   ISBN 0-335-09614-X (pbk.)
    1. School attendance.   2. Compulsory education   3. Education and
state.   I. Gleeson, Denis.   II. Wardhaugh, Julia, 1960–
III. Title.
LB3081.C29 1992
371.2'95--dc20   91-43050
                                                                                    CIP

Typeset by Gilbert Composing Services, Leighton Buzzard, Beds
Printed in Great Britain by Biddles Ltd, Guildford and Kings Lynn

CONTENTS

ACKNOWLEDGEMENTS

We would like to thank the following:

The Economic and Social Research Council (Award No. R000231010) for a grant of £65,323.

Keele University for providing us with the accommodation and resources necessary for the completion of the project.

The staff of a variety of legal, welfare and education agencies who devoted time and energy to helping us with the project – in particular education welfare officers, teachers, social workers and residential care staff, juvenile justice staff, magistrates, education psychologists, child psychiatrists, psychiatric social workers, police and probation officers.

Members of the Birmingham police force, Dr Roy Hullin of Leeds University and the staff of the Gorbals Truancy Project, Glasgow, for their kindness in meeting with us and discussing their various approaches to dealing with school non-attendance.

Anne Musgrave, project secretary, for her hard work in transcribing taped interviews, typing fieldnotes and coping very efficiently with the management of the project; also for her great patience in word-processing the whole text.

We would like especially to thank the forty young people, and the ten sets of parents, who gave their time to speak to us about truancy and the education, legal and welfare systems.

AUTHORSHIP

All empirical research for this book was conducted by Dr Julia Wardhaugh.
Authorship of the book's different sections is attributed as follows:
Introduction by Pat Carlen; Chapter 1 by Denis Gleeson; Chapter 2 by Julia
Wardhaugh and Pat Carlen; Chapters 3 and 4 by Pat Carlen and Julia
Wardhaugh; and Chapter 5 by Denis Gleeson.

ABBREVIATIONS

BTEC   Business Technician Education Council
CHE   Community home with education
CPVE   Certificate of Pre-Vocational Education
CTC   City technology college
CYPA   Children and Young Persons Act 1969
DES   Department of Education and Science
ERA   Education Reform Act 1988
ET   Employment Training Programme
GCSE   General Certificate of Secondary Education.
HMI   Her Majesty's Inspectorate
LAPP   Lower Attaining Pupils Programme
LEA   Local education authority
LMS   Local management of schools
MSC   Manpower Services Commission
       (replaced by Training Commission and now the Training Agency)
NCC   National Curriculum Council
NCVQ   National Council for Vocational Qualifications
NTI   New Training Initiative
ROSLA   Raising of school-leaving age
TA   Training Agency
TRIST   TVEI Related In-Service Training
TVEI   Technical and Vocational Education Initiative
YPA   Young person's accommodation
YTS   Youth Training Scheme

INTRODUCTION

This is a book about absence: absence from school, absences of legitimacy, absences in official discourses and absences of mind. It is also a book about ownership: of absences, of time, of tutelage and of education. Most immediately, it is about all those young people who, for one reason or another, do not attend school. Constituted within nineteenth- and twentieth-century political, legal and ideological discourses on compulsory schooling, these young persons are variously called truants, school phobics or non-attenders. Among the cognoscenti of officialdom they may be designated 'sad', 'deprived' or 'bored'; or, alternatively, 'a ratbagging lot', 'knowing little bitches' or 'the sump'. These are the erstwhile or putative pupils who perenially gave meaning to the term 'opting out' well before the 1988 Education Reform Act applied it to schools electing to remove themselves from local authority control. And these too, are the youngsters upon whom the combined but often cross-eyed gaze of a myriad of interlocking state agencies – schools, police, education welfare, probation, social services and juvenile courts – is perpetually directed in an aura of suspicion and uncertainty. For if they do not go to school, what do absentees from school *do*? Who is responsible for them? How can their absences be construed? We pose all of these questions (plus a few more) and, in describing the economic, political, legal and ideological conditions which make such questions both possible and impossible, we will also both recognize and deny their inevitability. But first, a few paragraphs about the socio-political conditions pertaining at the time when the research upon which this book is based was undertaken, during the period October 1988 to July 1990. They were, of course, an admixture of both those conditions and discourses which *effected*, and those which are *effects of*, the 1988 Education Reform Act.

Unravelling all of them in the fullness of their continuities and contradictions obviously cannot be essayed now; in any case, Chapter 1 focuses in greater depth upon certain dimensions of the present education scene's discursive past. Here we will just outline some of the more immediate intermixes of economics, politics and (predominantly conservative) ideologies which helped fashion the 1988 Act.

How the Tories got their (1988 Education Reform) Act together

In 1979 when the first Thatcher (Conservative) government came to power, de-industrialization was already in process. 'By 1984 the service sector accounted for 65 per cent of the workforce. In the fourteen years to 1985, over four million manufacturing jobs were lost' (Morris and Griggs 1988: 9). But, contrary to right-wing Tory ideology, the high unemployment levels of the 1980s were 'generated not by failures in the state education system, but by shifts in the national and international economy' (Bash and Coulby 1989: 7). Even before the international oil crisis of the mid-1970s triggered cuts in public expenditure, the state education system had become the butt of an onslaught of criticism: from the right-wing Black Papers, a series of ill-informed critiques of progressive education methods; and from the popular press with its sensationalist and (again) ill-informed attacks on comprehensive schools, teachers and Labour-led councils. Then in 1982 Keith Joseph became Education Secretary. Brian Simon, Emeritus Professor at the University of Leicester, charts what happened next:

> [I]t was with the appointment in 1982 of Sir Keith Joseph, Thatcherite monetarist guru, that the attack on the schools – and on local authorities and especially on teachers as a profession – really got underway.... During his period of office the schools and colleges were systematically allowed to deteriorate in terms of buildings, maintenance and equipment, to levels not previously known. At the same time a consistent and ruthless thrust towards centralised control ... wrenched the heart out of both local authority – and teacher-led initiatives.
>
> (Simon 1988: 25)

The legacy of Joseph, together with the 1984–7 industrial action taken by an alienated teaching profession in dispute with the Government about pay and conditions of service, resulted in both a popular and (Tory) Government belief that something must be done about (state) education. Once the teachers' dispute had been 'ended with a pay settlement and a new teachers' contract being imposed by the Government and enforced by the Teachers' Pay and Conditions Act 1987, [the teachers' unions] were in no position to resist the attack on the education professionals which the 1988 Act presaged' (Maclure 1990: vii). Our main concern right now is only with those two major elements and effects of the Act (and the events and debates leading up to it) that, we consider, are most relevant to an understanding of why unauthorized absences from school, and the responses to them, currently take the particular forms that they do.

Structural elements and effects of the 1988 Education Reform Act

Centralization and the downgrading of teachers

Several studies looking for the cause of truancy argue that schools have failed pupils and that one cause of unauthorized absence is pupil alienation (Grunsell 1980; Reid 1986; Holmes 1989). A more recent phenomenon is *teacher* alienation and shortage, with one teacher in seven changing jobs each year (*Guardian* 18 September 1989) and with many pupils in junior schools in large cities (especially London) having to be sent home from, or refused admission to, school because of recurring teacher shortages.

Teacher alienation and shortage have stemmed from several interrelated factors: the near contempt for the profession expressed by Keith Joseph and his successors at the Department of Education; the concomitant cuts in education expenditure and poor conditions of work; the rabid bad-mouthing of the teaching profession and comprehensive schools by the tabloid press; the undermining of the ideal of comprehensive (i.e. equal opportunity) education by the Tory determination to legislate for increased privatization and status-differentiation for schools; the unreasonable and onerous demands made on an underpaid and demoralized profession by DES officials bent on steamrolling through a government-imposed National Curriculum for which the schools were ill-prepared and under-resourced; and an increase of central direction and surveillance which has removed from teachers much of their professional control and discretion in relation to the method, pace and content of teaching, leaving them merely 'to "deliver" the curriculum' (Simon 1988: 147). Add to all this school-and-teacher-bashing, unprecedentedly high rates of youth un-employment and a Prime Minister whose anti-intellectualism and disservices to education earned her the distinction of being the first of its prime ministerial ex-students upon whom Oxford University refused to confer an honorary doctorate, and it may well be thought that the proper question to be posed by this study is not why a few children truant but why, indeed, the overwhelming majority continue to go to school at all.

Regulation and the ascendancy of the curriculum

'Regulating what?' you say. And before we go any further in this exploration of law, education and social control, it may be as well to make some definitional distinctions: between education and schooling, and between social control and social regulation. Defining 'education' and 'schooling' will introduce into our discussions three more conceptualized elements of social structure informing the analyses of the following chapters: class, gender and race. Discussing the distinction between social control and social regulation will also involve raising a key issue in the depiction of the relationships between law, education and social control; that is, the relationship between criminal justice and social justice in general.

When in this book we talk of education we refer to all those processes which develop a person's emotional, mental and physical capabilities. By schooling, we will be instancing a more specific process: the training of pupils by teachers according to a curriculum and with always an overt, and often a covert, agenda of ways, means and ends. Thus it will be assumed that education can occur as a result of, without or despite schooling, and that schooling can variously involve education and/or its opposite – the stunting or limitation of emotional, mental and physical capacities. Throughout the book we will, in fact, see how the degree of education received via schooling is mediated by class structure, gender differentiation and racism – and, as we have already seen, by the prevailing political economy and dominant educational ideologies.

Our overlapping definitions of 'social control' and 'social regulation' distinguish between form and substance. By 'social control' we refer to all those informal and formal institutions (including law and education) born of a recognition that, because of scarcity of material, spatial and temporal resources, limitations necessarily have to be imposed on individuals' freedom of action. By 'social regulation' we refer to all the mechanisms (including law and education) employed to enhance the likelihood of social control modes achieving particular economic, political and ideological ends partial to the interests of a dominant regulatory class, gender and/or race at the expense of those bearing the brunt of the regulation.

The foregoing distinctions are important simply because we do not wish our writings to be infused with overarching and global assumptions about any essential function of education in society. In particular we would not wish it to be thought that we conceive of education as being always – already for the reproduction of a capitalist social formation. Instead, the analyses that follow are shaped by a project that seeks to deconstruct the combination of socio-political-legal conditions that fashion specific instances of contemporary educational control and regulation in Britain.

So why couple regulation with the ascendancy of the curriculum? We do so because the imposition of a National Curriculum was one of the central features of the 1988 Education Reform Act, an Act which blatantly excluded the private education sector from having to meet the demands of the curriculum imposed in the state schools and which allowed for increased privatization and elitist differentiation between schools.

Schools have been placed in the market place and their accountability mediated by the test of consumer preference. [But the] 1988 Education Act has ... secured the principle of market competition in the provision of education, with the secretary of state controlling and directing the terms on which the market operates.

(Ranson 1990: 104)

Thus teachers in the private sector retain their professional autonomy to decide what should be taught and when, while those in the state sector are being reduced to what Hargreaves (1989: 59) has called de-skilled educational technicians. Likewise, the 'key stages', the 'attainment targets', the 'programmes of study' and the 'assessment arrangements' are all to be used to regulate the content of study and rate of learning of those in the state schools, while those whose parents choose to use their superior wealth and power to send them to fee-paying schools will be taught by teachers still able to exercise their professional judgement about what should be taught and when. The exclusion of, on the one hand, all social science from the list of national topics and, on the other, all business studies, adds credence to a suspicion that the reported comments of a senior official at the DES in the early 1980s might well reflect the way in which the Tory establishment responsible for the 1988 Act perceived the links between education and the regulation of social mobility and social unrest.

We are in a period of considerable social change. There may be social unrest, but we can cope with the Toxteths. But if we have a highly educated and idle population we may possibly anticipate more serious social conflict. People must be educated once more to know their place.
(DES official, quoted in Ranson 1984: 241)

A history of educating people to know their place is offered in Chapter 1, which deconstructs the political economy of the legislation governing compulsory school attendance from 1870 onwards. Here, we will turn to the other set of socio-legal conditions informing the manufacture of 'truancy', 'school phobia' and 'unauthorized absence' from school – the criminal law and the folklore responsible for the governance of youth and the rise of the juvenile delinquent.

Regulating youth

Criminal law, juvenile justice and welfare

The core of the present-day nexus of youth regulatory agencies, comprised of schooling, criminal law and welfare, has existed since the mid-nineteenth century, although then (as recently in the 1988 Education Reform Act) the main concern was more with regulating the children of the poor than it was with containing the delinquent excesses of the offspring of the rich.

By 1866 magistrates could commit to industrial schools children who were vagrant, who were said by their parents to be incorrigible or who were associating with criminals and prostitutes, so that they could be resocialised or reformed.... By 1894 over 17,000 children from the 'perishing classes' were held in industrial schools compared with a mere 1,400 delinquent children in the reformatories.

(Morris *et al.* 1980: 5)

The beginning of the twentieth century saw the introduction of the probation and borstal systems and in 1908 the Children Act initiated a separate system of juvenile justice with the juvenile courts being given 'both criminal jurisdiction over the offender and civil jurisdiction over the needy' (Harris and Webb 1987: 9). The process of collapsing the distinction between delinquent and neglected children was begun

by the Report of the Departmental Committee on the Treatment of Young Offenders (1927) which averred that, there being no distinction between neglected and delinquent children beyond the fact that the former condition led to the latter, there could not exist any justification for dealing with them separately. Hence the Children and Young Persons Act, 1933, abolished reformatory and industrial schools, creating the approved school system in their stead.

(Harris and Webb 1987: 16)

As far as young people were concerned, the rehabilitationist penology which had developed in England at the beginning of the twentieth century reached its zenith with the 1969 Children and Young Persons Act (1969, CYPA). Thereafter the notions of 'the deprived' and 'the depraved' were selectively and differentially invoked or conflated to form an increasingly coercive and widening disciplinary space for the regulation of guilty and potentially guilty (i.e. 'at risk') youth (see Collison 1980: 158; Cohen 1985). By the time of the 1969 CYPA, local authority children's departments had been in existence for over twenty years and statutory links had already been established with both education departments and the juvenile justice system. The fundamental concern of this regulatory nexus was not so much with the 'sad' or 'bad' child, but with the 'pathological' family.

Criminal law, welfare and the pathological family

The dominant mid-nineteenth-century discourses which emphasized that juveniles became morally depraved because of the twin effects of poverty and lack of parental control were gradually displaced in the twentieth century (and particularly after 1945) by discourses that bemoaned the primary role of pathological families in producing delinquent children (see Home Office 1946,

1949, 1965, 1968). In 1980 Mike Collison made a telling comment on the way in which these discourses relating juvenile crime to 'bad families' had resulted in the provisions of the 1969 CYPA, which put on trial *all* families with children in trouble:

> The CYPA 69 recognizes the need for a wide-ranging investigation prior to court appearances, privileges social work as a major co-ordinating agency, and prescribes that the family situation should be the source of knowledge of the case. If one member of the family is in need of care or before the law, then this becomes the condition for the right to intervene in the social management of all familial relations ... the displacement of responsibilities and the extension of concepts of interest has put the family on trial through the mechanism of the social inquiry report.
>
> (Collison 1980: 60)

Indeed, it is arguable that the development of the personal social services has always had the policing of working-class families as one of its primary functions (Meyer 1977; Hall *et al*. 1978; Donzelot 1979). Since the mid-1870s, school attendance officers – originally known as 'school board men' and nowadays called educational welfare officers (EWOs) – have been employed to visit homes in the process of enforcing 'the legal requirement that parents ensure the regular attendance of their children at ... school' (Wardhaugh 1990). And with official discourses putting the emphasis on truancy as pathology (rather than on truancy as law-breaking), it is not surprising that a series of researchers have teleologically located the cause of unauthorized absence from school within the pathology of (predominently poor) families, designated pathological partly *because* of their truanting children (Hodge 1968; Davie *et al*. 1972; May 1975; Tibbenham 1977; Farrington 1980; Fogelman *et al*. 1980; Reid 1982, 1987). Yet, despite the emphasis on the 'pathology' of truancy, the criminal justice system has routinely provided enforcement back-up to the 'child-saving' agencies – by fining or imprisoning the parents (1944 Education Act), by placing children under supervision orders or by removing persistent school absentees from their homes and placing them in local authority care (Children and Young Persons Act 1969).

How youngsters who don't attend school are differentially processed according to typifications of class, gender and race, so that some tread a predominantly welfare path of social regulation while others are responded to more punitively, will be among the issues addressed in Chapters 3 and 4. The rest of this Introduction is primarily concerned with two tasks. First, with deconstructing some contemporary and intermeshing networks of social control. The argument here is that the present day regulation of unauthorized absence from school is but one disciplinary mode among the many constituents of a spreading transcarceral complex designed to keep troublesome populations in their place. Second, with arguing that given the recent governmental fostering of economic, educational, fiscal and welfare conditions antagonistic to the interests of working-class youngsters, it is likely that for the foreseeable future a sizeable minority of young people will continue to be sceptical of the official rhetoric which proclaims that compulsory schooling is equally in *everyone's* interest.

The transcarceral complex and the regulation of youth mobility

In the years immediately following the implementation of the 1969 CYPA the number of juveniles removed from home into residential care or penal custody increased alarmingly. More recently there has been a decrease both in the numbers taken into local authority care (Department of Health 1984, 1987) and in those awarded custodial sentences (Home Office 1989). Yet as the 1988 Green Papers *Punishment, Custody and the Community* (Home Office 1988a) and *Tackling Offending: an Action Plan* (Home Office 1988b), together with their White Paper successor *Crime, Justice and Protecting the Public* (Home Office 1990), indicated, governmental decarceration discourses have not been predicated upon any diminution of punitive rhetoric. Rather, the phenomenal costs of imprisonment and residential care are to be reduced by transcarceral policies designed to ensure that the pains of imprisonment are brought into – and sometimes enforced by – the 'community' (usually, the family). Already a range of competing 'packages' and 'programmes' of leisure-time surveillance and supervised activities have been developed by social work agencies anxious to 'sell' their non-custodial schemes to the courts. And, despite the effective decriminalization of truancy by the Children Act 1989 (not fully implemented until 1991) there is extensive and up-to-date evidence that a young person's school attendance record will continue to be of prime importance in influencing the outcome of criminal proceedings (see Brown 1989, and Chapter 4 of this book) and employment opportunities. But in times of high youth unemployment it is not enough to keep tabs on those deviant teenagers who call into question the educational system's legitimacy by not going to school. It is also necessary to maintain the levels of motivation of those who *do*:

> Many young people were, until recently, prepared to trade their obedience for qualifications. But once there are very few or no jobs at all available for school leavers, and once a few qualifications can no longer guarantee employment... the existence of these qualifications can no longer be relied upon to secure classroom consent or effort.
>
> (Hargreaves 1989: 54)

Instead, pupils have to be motivated to achieve, and the only achievements allowed them are the 'normalizing' (Foucault 1977) assessments of a schooling tied to increasingly hierarchical and elitist curricular differentiation. 'Community' normalizing devices, which variously regulate potentially disruptive pupils at one extreme and delinquent or dissident youth at the other, may well be conciliatory controls masking increasing levels of inequality.

The new assessment-led system of dispositional adjustment, of generalized inclinations towards institutional and social loyalty ... has been grafted on to an increasingly differentiated and divided curricular system. ... The development of common motivational dispositions within a differentiated curriculum works to adjust young people to their social fate and, through complicated systems of credit accumulation and modular study denies them access to an overall grasp of the processes, structures and mechanisms by which such differentiated adjustment is achieved. ... Horizons are not just shortened, but limited too (a modular step by step curriculum, for a modular scheme-by-scheme life perhaps?). Through the use of pupils' profiles, processes of negotiation and target setting, institutional loyalty and adjustment are secured. ... Assessment-led strategies of curriculum reform ... look as if they might well be adjusting many pupils to their failure. ... To many, the patterns of common assessment ... appear to meet the principles of comprehensiveness. In fact, they may well be the opposite – a method of gaining and reinforcing pupil consent to newly developed structures of curricular differentiation.

(Hargreaves 1989: 57–8)

However, and as Hargreaves (following Habermas 1976) points out, in addition to the demoralizing effects of school-leaver unemployment, there may be a second cause of motivation deficit, the 'erosion of existing cultural supports as the state intrudes more and more into community and family life and existing bonds of loyalty and association are weakened'. A third may be emanating from the attack made on the life-chances of youngsters from less affluent homes by swingeing economic cuts and a decade of increasing inequality of income and wealth (Walker and Walker 1987). Government determination to minimalize the role of state welfare provoked cuts in benefits under the 1986 Social Security Act (implemented in April 1988) and the 1988 Housing Act, which aggravated the pains of youth unemployment still further. In August 1990, Labour Party research (Labour, 1990) revealed that local councils suffering punitive rate-capping (i.e. disproportionate loss of government grant as a result of setting the new community charge (poll tax) above a government-defined limit) had been forced to cut education expenditure by £36 million. Widespread resistance to payment of the poll tax may have been indicative of an increasing deficit of legitimation which will continue to subvert both 'normalization' strategies in the schools and disciplinary processes in the courts and the 'community'. One outcome may be a rise in levels of unauthorized absence from school.

Book's structure and main arguments

The purpose of this Introduction has been to sketch some interrelationships between dominant economic, ideological and political conditions and discourses shaping schooling and juvenile justice during the time we conducted the study of non-attendance at schools in an area of the North Midlands (Norwest). In the rest of the book we will show how the effects of the historical continuities and contradictions in ideologies of education and youth control manifest themselves today, both in official responses to absence from school and in the views of compulsory schooling held by absentee pupils and their parents.

The detailed arguments based on the research findings are to be found in the ethnographic analyses of Chapters 3 and 4, with Chapter 3 unravelling the inter-agency responses to truancy in Norwest and Chapter 4 exploring the worlds of some targeted truants together with their own and their parents' views on schools as they have known them. Chapter 2 details the research methods employed in the empirical investigation while Chapters 1 and 5 place the politics of compulsory schooling in historical and contemporary perspective.

The general arguments based on the research findings are:

1 That in Norwest most illicit absence from school is effectively regulated by in-school sanctions and EWO supervision.
2 That in Norwest certain truants are targeted for harsher sanctions and that such targeting is informed by stereotypes which discriminate according to typifications of class, gender and race.
3 That in Norwest contradictory inter-agency responses to targeted truants result in the further alienation of determined truants and their parents.
4 That persistent non-attenders and their parents may be so cynical about the disjunction between the promised benefits of schooling and the actual living and educational conditions on offer to them that they are prepared either passively to ignore or actively to resist all attempts to compel effective school attendance – even when such resistance results in penal sanctions.
5 That despite the continued existence of a very small minority of school-age children determined not to attend school, the ideal of compulsory schooling for all has to be upheld as being a prerequisite for eventually achieving the ideal of education for all.
6 That schools cannot by themselves remedy the gross economic and educational inequalities which presently make schooling appear so irrelevant to a minority of young people.
7 That full implementation of the Education Reform Act 1988 with its National Curriculum and local management of schools is likely to result in increased numbers of alienated teachers, alienated children, impoverished state schools and illicitly absent pupils.

1

TRUANCY AND COMPULSORY SCHOOLING: A SOCIO-HISTORICAL ACCOUNT

The class is a small society.... Indeed it is certain that an undisciplined class lacks morality. When children no longer feel restrained, they are in a state of ferment that makes them impatient of all curbs, and their behaviour shows it even outside the classroom.... A class without discipline is a mob.

(Durkheim 1961)

Background

In the late 1980s and early 1990s issues associated with school non-attendance have attracted considerable media hype and attention from politicians, employers and others concerned about declining standards in the nation's schools. A feature of this familiar concern equates poor standards of discipline and behaviour in home and school with other forms of social and economic malaise, principally those linked with low economic growth, rising crime and anti-authority attitudes among the young. Even after a decade of Conservative education reform those seeking to account for the continued decline in educational and economic performance have identified new ways of explaining what has gone wrong - in particular, rising levels of truancy reflecting a breakdown in family, education and work discipline. According to some protagonists truancy has now become so widespread as to confirm yet another 'crisis' of schooling, one largely overlooked by the educational establishment (Stoll and O'Keefe 1989). Elsewhere, in a speech to the 1987 Conservative Party Conference, expressing concern about rising levels of truancy, the Secretary of State for Education Kenneth Baker argued that pupils '"bunk off" because they are bored with school'.

Although subsequent reports from Mr Baker's department at the time (DES) do not endorse this view (e.g. Elton Report 1988) there can be little doubt that school non-attendance occupies a prominent position in the list of what is seen by government to be the failures of comprehensive education. Yet, notwithstanding the 'discovery' of truancy by the agencies mentioned above, it will be argued in this chapter that far from constituting a 'new' crisis, issues concerning school attendance are part and parcel of the history of compulsory education. In other words compulsory education and school non-attendance constitute two faces of the same coin: it would be inconceivable to imagine otherwise where education for all is required by law. Hence, this chapter considers the two interrelated aspects of this phenomenon. The first concerns a socio-historical account of compulsory education as it is mediated by the relations between family, law and economy. Here, questions regarding whose interests state education serves, and the juxtapositioning of *education* versus *schooling* are considered. The second concerns the relatively recent status of mass secondary schooling and shifting definitions of its role as changing historical, political and economic conditions alter its relationship with parents, pupils and the world of work.

Introduction

Although school non-attendance is synonymous with the historical preconditions of compulsory schooling, it is not within our brief here, nor within our expertise, to provide a definitive history of compulsory education. What we seek to do is draw attention to historically recurring themes associated with order, authority, discipline and control, which interrelate family, education, law and economy, but which often remain obscured in conventional accounts of the schooling process (see Abrams 1982). Ostensibly, the history of schooling and its relationship with industrialization is one of an evolutionary process of enlightenment, from the initial stark struggles to ensure nineteenth-century school attendance through to the more popular forms of education characterizing late twentieth-century developments. Yet in reality the expansion of mass popular education, which has involved the progressive separation of traditional family, education and productive functions, has both complemented and contradicted capitalist development, most recently reflected in debate regarding 'crisis' in the transition and transmission points between family, school and work. For Reeder (1981) it seems ironic that a debate on education and industry should arise in a country whose economic and social development is historically bound up with the provision of compulsory education (Wiener 1981). Paradoxically, after a century of educational reform designed to get young people into schools, out of factories and away from the inimical influence of parents and employers, growing gaps have been discerned between family, education and economy. It is equally ironic that recent curriculum and school development (TVEI, CTCs, TECs, Work Based Learning, Enterprise and other initiatives) has seen almost the reverse – seeking to get young people back into factories, places of work and under the influence of employers. Concern about such matters has been expressed in different ways by prime ministers of different parties:

> I am concerned on my travels to find complaints from industry that new recruits from the schools sometimes do not have the basic tools to do the job that is required.... There is concern about the standards of numeracy of school leavers.... There is no virtue in producing socially well-adjusted members of society who are unemployed because they do not have the skills.
> (James Callaghan, extract from speech at Ruskin College, October 1976)

> We want education to be part of the answer to Britain's problems, not part of the cause.... And in the inner cities – where youngsters must have a decent education if they are to have a better future – that opportunity is all too often snatched from them by hard left education authorities and extremist teachers. Children who need to be able to count and multiply are learning anti-racist mathematics – whatever that may be. Children who need to be able to express themselves in clear English are being taught political slogans. Children who need to be taught to respect traditional moral values are being taught that they have an inalienable right to be gay. Children who need encouragement – and so many do – are being taught that our society offers them no future. All those children are being cheated of a sound start in life – yes cheated.
> (Margaret Thatcher, extract from speech to
> Conservative Party Conference, 1987)

Since the current economic crisis broke in Britain in the early 1970s, state policy-makers have become increasingly preoccupied with foreign competition and the apparent threat falling educational standards pose to economy and society. In the Labour Government-initiated Great Education Debate (1976–9), which followed closely on the heels of the recession, problems of political economy in the form of economic decline, unemployment and industrial unrest became transposed as crises in education. At one level progressive and anti-industrial attitudes in education were blamed for failing to deliver relevant, up-to-date basic vocational skills in the curriculum while, at another, indiscipline in the work force was seen to be inextricably linked with lack of parental control, truancy, bad behaviour and incompetent teachers. A central tenet of such debate, which has since informed a decade of Conservative education reforms, is that declining standards of discipline and behaviour, both within and outside education, have undermined economic progress as well as the education reform process itself.

Despite prevailing concern expressed about declining standards, rising indiscipline, incompetent teachers, outmoded curriculum and mounting truancy, such issues are not new. While it may come as a surprise to those agencies who appear to have recently discovered such flaws in our educational system, it is our argument here that these issues are part of a historical debate that has its origins in eighteenth- and nineteenth-century conceptions of schooling, and beyond. Thus, for the purposes of this chapter, research and policy which are premised on 'discovery' of declining standards of literacy, behaviour and non-school attendance is questionable precisely because of the level of analysis from which they begin is inadequate. According to McCulloch (1991), awareness of the historical context of education should help policy-makers at least to avoid 're-inventing the wheel' and, at best, to understand the complexities and problems involved in curriculum reform. It may also allow greater understanding of alternatives to the approaches and prescriptions that currently dominate the policy agenda.

What this chapter seeks to do is provide a socio-historical account of the background to school attendance, juxtaposing various historical, sociological and policy perspectives on the changing relationship between state, family, economy and schooling. The chapter is divided into five main sections. The first deals briefly with the rise of compulsory schooling, focusing on the earliest attempts to 'school' working-class pupils, separating family, school and work; the second emphasizes the strategic role of the family in delivering state education policy, with particular reference to women, welfare and the law. Following the third section, which deals with the effects of war on changing expectations of school–work transition, the final two sections address contemporary issues of policy and practice from the 1944 Education Act through to the 1988 Education Reform Act. In different ways these sections chart the expansion of mass secondary education as a recent phenomenon, its relations with government, family, economy and society and, finally, its subsequent impact on the lives and expectations of young people. In various ways the chapter questions certain prevailing myths regarding the links between compulsory education and school non-attendance: that truancy is necessarily school-related, an easy option or a feature of faulty working-class socialization. It is argued that there was no golden age of schooling against which modern judgements about standards make sense, and that many of the contemporary issues most complained about (anti-industrial attitudes, truancy, indiscipline etc.) have their origins in historical and structural contradictions that have always characterized the beleaguered relations between state, family, education and economy. It is to such issues that we now turn.

The rise of school attendance

Early beginnings

Before the establishment of compulsory education by the 1870 and 1880 Education Acts, schooling was largely provided by churches, religious orders and philanthropic organizations for the poor and very wealthy. The regimes, such as those in the Dame Schools, were often harsh and brutal, and the curriculum in both Sunday and day schools was largely devoted to religious and moral rescue. With variable pupil attendance, lack of teacher training, and inadequate resources and facilities, what teachers were able to do with pupils was limited. Large classes, often taught in a single hall or room, using rote learning, verse and catechism, supported by a monitorial system of teacher–children, came to represent a model of schooling with eschewed present day notions of education. Moreover, the prevailing mechanism of funding both school and teachers' pay on the basis of a system of 'payment by results' accentuated the crucial importance of pupil numbers and their levels of attendance. As Rubenstein (1969) points out:

> Teachers had the strongest incentive to establish and maintain high rates of attendance. Irregular attendance was of course a source of both apathy and rebellion against the attempted discipline of the classroom. But, more important, until the end of 1883 teachers' salaries in London directly depended on good attendance, as the Revised Code of 1862 intended that they should. Children who did not attend school for a prescribed period each year could not be examined and hence could not earn government grants. In September 1883 over a fifth of the total salary of an assistant teacher and over a third of the salary of a head teacher depended upon his share of the grant. In subsequent years, while salaries were fixed, the total grant continued to depend on the number of children in average attendance, and this system lasted until after the end of the Board's life. If average attendance dropped schools were regraded, and this meant a reduction of head teachers' salaries.

Although the Newcastle Commissioners Report of 1861 did not fully find in favour of the system of payment by results, it concluded that there was a need to tighten up on the payment of grants, to stabilize inspection and to focus attention on more able as well as less able students. According to Paterson (1989) the new code was a means of re-enforcing and extending the regulation of schools through increased inspection and through rationalization of the system of grants being paid for buildings, training pupil-teachers, teachers' salaries, books and apparatus. In so doing it influenced the pattern of compulsory schooling that was to follow in the 1870 Act, which in principle exists to this day, shifting the financial focus from the means of schooling to its results.

Attendance at school for all children from the age of five to the current statutory leaving age has been compulsory since the Forster Education Act of 1870. While the 1870 Act stipulated that no child under ten years of age could be employed, and that parents had a statutory obligation to ensure their children's attendance, the legislation was widely interpreted then as it is today. Although school boards were expected to oversee the 1870 Act's provision, this was mainly organized by school attendance committees, who appointed school attendance visitors, whose duties largely concerned dealing with non-attenders.

Such visitors, often referred to as 'the school board men' or 'truant catchers', were hampered in their task by a relaxed attitude towards attendance on the part of landowners and industrialists, whose respective livelihoods were undermined by compulsory legislation for school attendance. Moreover, a prevailing view held by magistrates at the time was that particular categories of young person would gain more benefit from working in the home or factory, principally if it relieved the state of otherwise supporting families in need. Perhaps not surprisingly, evidence indicates that girls, who were more frequently absent than boys, were more likely to be involved in undertaking household, child-care and domestic duties. It was mainly boys whose school non-attendance openly defied authority, attracting the surveillance of the despised street visitors, whose task it was to search the streets and open spaces for them (Green 1980). For girls who remained within the confines of the home such surveillance was rare although in some instances baby rooms were provided in schools where infants could be left while their brothers and sisters attended classes. Green (1980) reports of twelve such rooms which were opened in London schools: 'one advocate from the school board, putting the advantage of baby rooms before the Cross Commissioners in 1887, was accused of opening the way to socialism.' According to Digby and Searby (1981), by the early 1900s while 88 per cent of those under twelve were on school registers, only 72 per cent were in average daily attendance. Local factors such as the poverty of the neighbourhood, availability of juvenile employment, weather conditions, domestic duties and alternative amusements maintained a lively truanting problem (Turnbull 1987).

So, although the 1870 and 1880 Education Acts made school attendance compulsory, empowering local education authorities to prosecute parents and remove children from the home into truant schools, reformatories and later 'care', the guidelines regarding how local authorities were to control and enforce the legislation remained open to interpretation. Thus, school boards were, as LEAs are today, free to enforce school attendance as they liked and to choose their own officers. As Green (1980) points out, these officers were in turn reliant on their LEAs for a definition of their duties and for approval of their methods. Despite subsequent changes in legislation affecting education, LEAs and the young person, little has changed to alter this pattern of provision or the collection of data regarding school non-attendance. The question arises, that if compulsory legislation and changing patterns of provision did not necessarily secure school attendance into the twentieth century, what did?

Winning hearts and minds

'My misfortunes all began in wagging, Sir; but what could I do exceptin' wag?'
    'Excepting what?' said Mr. Corker.
    'Wag, Sir. Wagging from school.'

'Do you mean pretending to go there, and not going?' said Mr Corker.
'Yes Sir, that's wagging, Sir.... I was chivied through the streets, Sir,
when I went there, and pounded when I got there. So I wagged and hid
myself, and that began it.'

(Dickens 1848)

It is commonly assumed that the 1870 Act, which empowered compulsory
education for the first time, represented a long-overdue response to emerging
industrialization. Yet as Johnson (1976) has pointed out, capitalism and
manufacture were already well established in England before 1870. However,
increased levels of capital investment in technology, manufacture and workplace
in the mid to late nineteenth century focused particular attention on the
problem of how to manage working class resistance to innovation and change.
Disraeli's (1867, quoted in Paterson 1989) remark that 'The Working Class
Question is the real question, and that is the thing that demands to be settled'
did not simply refer to issues of adult suffrage. Rather, it referred to over one
hundred years of agricultural and industrial worker insurrection over pay,
conditions and trade union rights. Despite the repeal of the Combination Acts
in 1824, the effects of Chartist resistance and struggle against new forms of
capitalism resonated well into the late nineteenth century. Increasingly time
and work discipline, management and factory organization rendered obsolete
traditional divisions of labour and control of workers based on 'gentry
paternalism' (Thompson 1963). Thus, if the impetus of Chartist activity and
struggle described the making of a new working class, it equally posed the
problem for capital of managing such a potentially volatile working class. In
other words the English working class in its making posed the question of how
the consent of the majority was now to be won (Thompson 1967; Johnson
1981).

This consent was not easily achieved. In the Potteries region, for example,
Wedgwood's earliest attempts in the late eighteenth and early nineteenth
centuries to reform familial, working and social life of the pottery workers by
scientific factory management, education and discipline met with strong
resistance. The potters' devout regard for 'St Monday', drinking, festivals and
sports was the very antithesis of Wedgwood's new model capitalism based on a
rigorous, rational and closeted system of work, training and schooling.
Commenting on the irregular work rhythms which continued on the older pot
banks into the mid-nineteenth century, Thompson (1967) writes

Although the custom of annual hiring prevailed, the actual weekly
earnings were piece rates, the skilled male potters employing the children,
and working, with little supervision, at their own pace. The children and
women came to work on Monday and Tuesday, but a 'holiday feeling'
prevailed and the day's work was shorter than usual, since the potters
were away a good part of the time, drinking their earnings of the previous
week. The children, however, had to prepare work for the potter (for

example, handles for pots which he would throw), and all suffered from the exceptionally long hours (fourteen and sometimes sixteen hours a day) which were worked from Wednesday to Saturday.

This is followed by another observation from an old potter:

> I have since thought that but for the reliefs at the beginning of the week for the women and boys all through the pot works, the deadly stress of the last four days could not have been maintained.
>
> (Thompson 1967)

Like other areas of England by the middle of the nineteenth century, this area saw a changing division of labour, the introduction of fines, bells, clocks, money incentives, 'preachings and schoolings', the suppression of fairs, sports and holidays, and the imposition of new labour habits and time discipline (Thompson 1967). Although such developments did not go uncontested, with the potters insisting on their 'potters' fortnight'[1] and family groupings working together in the factories, resistance against time, factory discipline and schooling gradually became one of struggle about it. According to Johnson (1976) the absence of coherent legislation, despite the impact of the 1870 Act, meant that working people used schools in an instrumental fashion, drawing from them only relevant skills, such as literacy, and withdrawing children from school once these skills were secured. In this respect Johnson argues there is no reason to believe that children in the nineteenth century were any less creative in their forms of resistance within school than children are now. What is important to recognize is the way in which Chartist and Owenite models of education (1830–50s), based on the notion of 'really useful knowledge' and not schooling, initiated more formalized state intervention. It was the Chartist model of education as self-determination that attracted suspicion from the authorities, who associated it with political radicalism, socialism, strikes and insurrection. Equally, this suspicion was reinforced by Owenite and Chartist rejection of the earliest attempts by philanthropic and religious educators to establish schools, removing children from the home in preparation for a religious education, citizenship and work (Simon 1960). Such resistance, combined with the prevalence of child labour, reinforced state and church pressure to reclaim children from the errors of their parents' ways. This was achieved in a number of ways, not least by the birth of the 'child-saving movement' (Platt 1969), involving public discussion about morals, family responsibilities and child neglect, temperance concern over drinking, and post-Malthusian debate regarding the links between poverty and the sexual habits of the poor. Equally it was achieved with the discovery by the middle class of urban dereliction, poverty and crime in cities, which were fast becoming dangerous places, breeding grounds of disease, ignorance and neglect. According to Platt (1969) one solution was for the emerging new middle class to initiate substitute controls for those which had previously regulated deviance in small-scale society but which, at the same time, maintained myths about close-knit rural values (Durkheim 1972).

> The child-saving movement was not so much a break with the past as an affirmation of faith in traditional institutions. Parental authority, education at home, and the virtues of rural life were emphasized because they were in decline at this time. The child-saving movement was, in part, a crusade which, through emphasizing the dependence of the social order on the proper socialization of children, implicitly elevated the nuclear family and, more especially, the role of women as stalwarts of the family. The child-savers were prohibitionists, in a general sense, who believed that social progress depended on efficient law enforcement, strict supervision of children's leisure and recreation, and the regulation of illicit pleasures. What seemingly began as a movement to humanize the lives of adolescents soon developed into a programme of moral absolutism through which youth was to be saved from movies, pornography, cigarettes, alcohol, and anything else which might possibly rob them of their innocence.
>
> (Platt 1969)

Even before the rise of the child-saving movement in England, the earliest attempts to initiate a bill to support universal education in 1819 failed to gain parliamentary support. In later debate, John Stuart Mill (1848, quoted in Paterson 1989) argued the case for compulsory education, saying that such provision was a duty of the state both to the children and to the community (Sutherland 1973). Despite the political push for universal state education in the early to mid-nineteenth century, it failed to gain momentum for a variety of reasons. At one level, non-established religious groups feared denominational inspection from the established Church. At another, aristocratic and industrial interests felt schooling would threaten the supply of cheap labour. Although the radical influence of Benthamism and the philosophy of utilitarianism were waning by the late 1830s, they had already become a fundamental component of middle-class common sense. (Johnson 1976). Following the earlier influence of Smith's *Wealth of Nations*, 'enlightened self-interest' became a key concept in public debate on education. According to Finer (quoted in Paterson 1989)

> Any Benthamite was automatically an educationist, since his philosophy depended on the perfectability of society through the free play of its members' enlightened self-interest.... Education was desirable because it prevented juvenile delinquency and mendicancy, because it increased a labourer's skill, productivity, and earning power; because it prevented the growth of criminal classes; and because it led the workman to realize his true interests lay not in Communism or Chartism but in harmony with his employers.

Importantly, this view resonated strongly with nineteenth-century reformers, philanthropists, Fabians and key experts in government departments, among HMI, Poor Law Commissioners, factory and public health inspectorate, the prison service, the police and the medical profession, who all advocated a national system of compulsory education. Although such experts did not constitute a united movement their views represented two possible kinds of politics embedded in 'a populist, anti-aristocratic radicalism, or an alliance with reforming politicians to "change the people"' (Johnson 1981: 88). Thus, even though the movement for educational reform came from different sources and divergent ideological persuasions, it emphasized the common goal of transforming working-class belief, attitude and behaviour. In Paterson's (1989) view, schooling was seen as an important means for achieving this end.

> It should be emphasized that this transformation was to be structured from the perspective of these 'experts' with their shared aims and interests, and not, for example, from the perspectives of Chartism, Owenism or trade unionism, all of which were advocating national provision of schooling at this time. The strategies of the experts in advocating state intervention into schooling were not simply concerned with the provision of something which was lacking ... there were schools already in existence. State intervention was to be aimed at correcting that which was already present.

Yet as we have seen in both policy and practice, securing popular support for compulsory schooling was not a straightforward process, but involved struggle and resistance in the historical relations between state, law, family, church, schooling and industry. A central feature of this tension involves the competing rights of access to children's socialization by agencies beyond the family, seeking to secure less parochial and more universal forms of social and economic allegiance.

Family and schooling

A crucial feature of the historically recurring debate about how education should best respond to the needs of industry and economy is the role of the family in that debate. Compulsory school attendance by law has, for example, always been of historical interest for the ways in which the state secured economic access to the family, principally by protecting children from economic exploitation by their parents. In this respect nineteenth-century education and factory legislation were significant in altering the traditional 'property rights' of parents over their children, in favour of closer state surveillance, monitoring and control. However, such state intervention and access to the family were not secured by legislation alone, but by ideology, involving compelling arguments as to why formal compulsory education existed in the interest of the child, the family, state and nation. Correspondingly, education could not be entrusted to the traditional family alone, since the hidden agenda of universal education was to construct a new social order which would facilitate the organization, division of labour and discipline of the new workforce. Hence a principal feature of the compulsory element of schooling was not simply the legal enforcement of attendance, but the separation of child from home and school from work, with the emphasis of school and teacher on preparing children for work and citizenship. Here, compulsory education has operated as an effective ideological device both to exert social control and to separate off key elements of the family's unitary productive function. Thus, although children were still regarded as their parents' property, parents now had to conform to certain standards of child-rearing practice which could be inspected, and were held accountable if need be in law. But parental support for educational reform was still needed. How was this to be achieved?

According to David (1980), state regulation of the family–education couple reserves a special place in its attention for women's position. Since the nineteenth century, for example, the state has taken over more and more responsibilities for the type, length and quality of schooling, including responsibilities for health, welfare and citizenship education. Nava's (1984) view is that via women moral, hygienic and budgeting norms were to be diffused into the families of the working class as a means of securing allegiance to education reform. However, to do this it became essential to change the granting of aid from charity and philanthropic sources to state support: 'the order of priorities led to reflect this concern to reinforce family autonomy. Children came before the elderly, for beyond childhood there was the whole period of maturity' (Donzelot 1979). This paradox of state support for the family–education couple represents the institutionalization of self-reliance, most recently expressed by David Waddington, then Home Secretary (1990), as 'making parents more responsible for their children' in the fight against crime and in improving overall standards of education, discipline and morality. Increasingly, the state has redefined the family–education couple to have a social and economic purpose, emphasizing the importance of both the schooling process itself and economic efficiency. In this respect mothers, in their traditionally conceived role as home-makers and carers, have been historically targeted by health, welfare and educational campaigns, a position reinforced within the sexual division of labour of the curriculum and by the specific recruitment of women into the teaching profession at primary school level. Moreover, the earliest provision of child-care benefit, clothing allowances, grants and special payments to women reflects their central role in and responsibility for delivering state education policy, in particular ensuring their children's attendance at school. Thus, it is within these progressive arrangements of education and welfare reform that failure to comply signals faulty socialization, which, in turn, legitimates surveillance and sanction of family activities. As we will demonstrate in the chapters that follow, this has grave implications and consequences for women in the family and also for the differential ways in which young male and female school non-attenders are defined and processed in the system. According to Fitz (1981) such young people are caught up in highly discretionary legal processes; discretionary in that discipline and treatment are meted out in a legal process not safeguarded by some of the guarantees of the 'fair trial' embedded in the adult criminal legal process. Moreover, as Casburn (1978) discovered in her research on the Hackney juvenile court, an 'enmoraling' process can be seen to operate (Erben and Dickinson 1983): although girls are brought to the courts less often than boys, they receive stringent care and supervision orders for offences for which boys on similar charges are merely fined. In this respect, the way courts and the supervision process constitute themselves as moral guardians, particularly when handing out dispositions to female offenders, reflects the traditional social division of labour in home, school and curriculum.

Certainly a notable feature of the emerging curriculum (1870–1918) was its gender-specific orientation, which extended and formalized existing differences in the treatment of boys and girls, largely in terms of anticipating their future social and occupational roles. Although for both boys and girls the prevailing diet emphasized the Three Rs, by the early 1900s the sexual division of labour in the curriculum was between handicraft, workshop instruction, woodwork and metalwork (trade labour for boys) and domestic arts, cooking, cleaning and clothing (domestic labour for girls). This division was confirmed in the 1918 Education Act, which raised the school leaving age to fourteen and redefined the education of the adolescent as 'the workman in training and the little wage earner' (Fleet 1976). In other important respects the specific recruitment of women teachers in the elementary sector provided continuity in the emerging feminized relationship between the family and education couple (David 1980; Purvis 1981). While in the early part of the nineteenth century men dominated the ranks of elementary classroom teaching, this situation dramatically changed in the late 1890s and early 1900s. By the beginning of the First World War women numbered over 70 per cent of the staff in elementary schools. According to Steedman (1988) the social contract of teaching as a version of motherhood, epitomized as 'the feminization of a trade', was in practice a form of control more effectively worked on a woman (teacher) to woman (mother/child) basis. In reality then, the feminization of teaching was not primarily concerned with mothering working-class children. In questioning Fredrich Froebel's (1782–1852) analogy of the ideal teacher as a 'mother made conscious', Steedman (1988) argues

> that the reality cannot match the prescription because it is impossible for teachers to mother working class children. The prescribed act of identification with the children implies a further and harder one *with the children's mother* [our emphasis], 'that dark young woman with tousled

hair and glittering eyes' playing out a travesty of motherhood in her cellar dwelling.

If concepts such as 'mothering and nurturance' were established as official prescription for women teachers, in practice it was what the teacher through her feminism came to represent as a role model in the eyes of children and their mothers that was more significant. According to Steedman this may go some way towards explaining the position of working-class children in school, and the theories that have evolved to explain both their and their parents' inadequacies.

Another area concerns the targeting of women in the family for support and social investigation. Crucial to building a healthier and better-educated society has been a high level of intervention in family and child-rearing practices at a number of levels along the medical-hygienic-education axis. State sponsorship of the family is, for example, premised on the inability of most, if not all, families to fulfil the vast array of functions expected of them. Consequently, over time, the family has become bounded by a number of normative and corrective agencies, social work, education, welfare, social security, medicine, judiciary, largely concerned with the preservation and protection of children. The 'wardship complex' referred to by Donzelot (1979) is premised on a process of social investigation, which legitimates points of intervention in the family in 'cases' where lack of hygiene, unhealthy nurturing and absence of control arise. Invariably, the process of investigation occurs via the ideology of 'care' (supervision), rather than by repression (prison), and is ostensibly designed to assist families through supervision, support programmes and visits. According to Hodges and Hussain (1979), what social investigation and survey does is to filter out 'hard cases', i.e. those who cannot be brought into line by progressive preventive social work methods and who necessitate the use of penal and legal methods. Increasingly the court is being used as a source of last resort, with the children's court historically representing:

> the junction point of the various social work practices; it is the privileged area for registering the inter-relationships between the practices – penal, education, psychiatric – which come to bear on the child and the family.... The juvenile court represents not only a displacement of the scope of the judicial but also a transformation in the value of familial authority.
>
> (Hodges and Hussain 1979)

Although under the terms of the Children Act (1989) school non-attendance is no longer a principal criterion for care orders or court appearance, it remains a sensitive indicator of proper parenting. In lifting the 'threat' of court action, in an attempt to decriminalize truancy, the Act has reinforced the progressive tariff of preventive social work practice, which has become an ever more prevalent, yet unaccountable, medium for gaining access to the family. In this respect a close association intersects the family and school, which makes it possible to translate problems children encounter at school into problems in their families. According to Prout (1988) it is an association that can cause fear among mothers. Prout's (1988) study shows that mothers' perceptions of their children's health is closely linked with their perceptions of teachers' reactions to their children's school non-attendance. Their fear is that an unhealthy child may be seen as inconsistent with good mothering, the phrase 'normal healthy child' being much used by mothers in the study to describe their children, with the implied opposing notion 'not healthy – not normal – damaged by bad mothering'. In, particular, Prout found mothers to be anxious about what teachers would construe from the frequent absence of their children from school, a view confirmed in interviews with teachers, who did seem to hold negative images of children who were frequently absent, and of their mothers. Such mothers were, for example, likely to be seen by teachers as over-anxious, over-indulgent and not encouraging the type of 'backbone' and independence expected in their children (Wells 1990). This study, in questioning the pre-vailing view of primary school teachers' progressiveness (see Sharp and Green 1976), also points to the tension which underlies the family–education association when things are apparently not 'normal' – in which case they must be abnormal. This thin dividing line characterizes much prevailing political dogma and debate in education, concerning child rearing practices, child-centred learning, disruptive behaviour in the family, sex education, parental attitudes towards educational attainment, and their children's attendance at school. Moreover, such an association has influenced the 'making and taking' of problems in social and educational research (Seeley 1966; Ingleby 1972, 1976), defining the parameters by which psychiatrists, psychologists and sociologists review the 'causes' of educational failure, largely in pathological terms ('subnormality', 'maladjustment', 'retardation', 'less able', 'underachievement', 'special'), which themselves legitimate the experts' rights to intervene in family affairs.

Thus, the very process through which experts gain access to care for and support families in need confirms the inability of these families to be self-reliant, which in turn further marginalizes their position. A key concept in relation to school non-attendance is 'maladjustment', since it defines problems of parenting and the parameters that allow counsellors, social workers, teachers, education welfare officers and others access to the family. In common parlance this is legitimated in terms of getting at the *cause* of the problem (the relation between child and parent), *defining* it (as excusable or not as the case may be) and finding a *solution* (i.e. re-integrating the young person into mainstream schooling). Ostensibly, this process is a supportive, caring and educative one; in practice, it is often less straightforward, often involving previous school exclusion orders, court investigation of family circumstances and proceedings connected with related 'misdemeanours'. Yet, paradoxically, the law ensuring that parents enforce their children's school attendance is contradictory and confusing.

Essentially, the 1944 Education Act reinforces earlier coercive intent clauses in school attendance legislation. In the doctrine of strict liability, a succession of unaccounted-for absences is recorded and may, for example, be considered as evidence of truancy. According to Holmes (1989), clauses 36, 37 and 40 of the 1944 Act oblige parents to ensure their children's attendance and, at the same time, presuppose that if parents fail to do so and are punished, the child may be shamed into school attendance. Elsewhere the 1969 Children and Young Persons Act reinforces the control principle, assuming that a child not receiving continuous full-time education is automatically in need of care and control. Thus, for a number of reasons, education reform, legal factors and case law judgments can make parental enforcement of their children's school attendance problematic. Grenville (1988), for example, has given attention to the difficulties parents can face in law when attempting to enforce their child's attendance. She refers to the 1944 Education Act, which provides parents with no independent powers to ensure that their children attend school; moreover, zealous punishment by parents may render them liable to criminal prosecution under the 1969 Children and Young Persons Act (now replaced by the Children Act), and the criminal law offence of false imprisonment. In addition, changes in matrimonial, domestic, care and adoption cases since the late 1960s – which determine that access is the right of the child, not the parent – also reduce parent power in law. Referring to the Gillick judgment of 1985, Holmes (1989) quotes Lord Scarman's submission regarding children's rights: 'Parental right yields to the child's right to make his own decisions when he reaches sufficient understanding and intelligence to be capable of making up his own mind on the matter requiring decision.' Significantly, this judgment may allow fifteen-year-old pupils legitimately to stay away from school to revise for public examinations, or to follow a prescribed course of study which parents may or may not support. Following on the Children Act (1989), partly in response to the Cleveland enquiry, school non-attendance is no longer deemed the basis for making a care order but, instead for a supervision order and intermediate provision. However, the Children Act (1989), while it seeks to ascertain the views of parents and children, hitherto ignored, does not alter or amend compulsory school provision in the 1944 Education Act, particularly with regard to parental responsibility for their children's school attendance. Moreover, it does not clarify how a child is to be brought back into the classroom even when another person or a local authority assumes parental rights, supervision care or control (Grenville 1988).

In other respects, the progressive raising of the statutory school-leaving age (ROSLA), from eleven to fourteen to fifteen and sixteen (1972), has extended the time-scale of parental responsibility for young adults at a difficult time in their social, intellectual and emotional development. The point here is not simply that the law has not kept up with the changing status of young people in society, or that it is ambiguous, but that beyond defining legal access, rights and duties within the family, it fails to provide independent support mechanisms for families 'in trouble' to ensure effectively their children's education or school attendance.

The law places parents, families and children in a double bind (which does not, however, stipulate children's rights, duties and obligations): on the one hand it requires parents to ensure their children's attendance at school while, on the other, paradoxically, it provides the child with legal protection from its parents. In the circumstances, therefore, it would seem ironic that some leading experts in the field should advocate new penalties to enforce school attendance via the family. Reid (1985, 1987) has argued that fines imposed on parents should be collected directly from child benefit. 'In cases of non-condoned absence which are proven the education welfare officer would be required to sign the family allowance book to verify the fact' (Reid 1987: 210). Elsewhere, Berg *et al.* (1988) regret the replacement of court appearances with supervision and intermediate methods of dealing with school non-attendance: 'it was the fact that going to court, and the implications of that which appeared to get them back to school, rather than any other particular procedure.... Casework might have had a positively deleterious effect on school attendance and committing criminal offences.'

There is, however, no strong evidence that the discipline and punish model effectively works; if anything it is more likely to amplify deviance by confirming the delinquent identities of families via court appearance and what follows. In other respects getting 'them' back into schools at all costs, via a system of fines, withdrawal of benefit and court orders, ignores broader questions about what *they* are being sent back to, and why young people truant in the first place. Getting pupils back into school by dictat may ostensibly have a short-term impact on school attendance but this may have little educative effect in the long term for pupil, school or society. Such coercion masks a deeper frustration felt by various agencies, such as educational psychologists, social workers, magistrates and police, none of whom have defined responsibilities for returning young people to school. Although in theory they all work together in an 'inter-agency' function to provide care, support and supervision for non-attenders, none view school non-attendance as their historical province. Thus, according to different agencies school non-attendance is not their concern: to some critics in social services and education welfare departments, for example, if schools were more effective and responsive, truancy would not be a problem. Similarly, there is ambivalence on the part of schools towards social workers and EWOs, whose support role is often criticized for being inconsistent and transitory. In the policing and legal anomalies that follow from such ambiguities inter-agency 'blame' becomes superimposed on non-attenders themselves, whose 'nuisance value' reinforces busy agencies' reactions to them and their parents. In practice, social and welfare services have more pressing cases than school non-attenders to deal with: however, a combination of legal, political and media factors ensures that truancy remains firmly on the inter-agency agenda even though such agencies can do little to resolve it in law, and parents, teachers and even courts frequently turn a 'blind eye' until 'problems' are brought to their attention.

Essentially, the point being made here (and further explored in Chapters 3 and 4) is that the social processes of investigation, care and support are part of the 'problem' of school non-attendance and not its solution: following such processing few school non-attenders return to mainstream education, which, ostensibly, is the main purpose of the exercise. In saying this our purpose is not to discredit the professional activities in which teachers, EWOs, social workers, psychologists, LEA officials, police and magistrates are engaged. Rather, it is to emphasize a criticism which professionals themselves make about the futility of 'policing' families (see Chapter 3) in circumstances where 'structural' constraints, such as poverty, unemployment and homelessness, often render simplistic solutions to school non-attendance highly problematic. We will return to this issue in due course. For the moment it would seem important to emphasize two interrelated points: the first concerns the paradoxical way in which state regulation of the family has emphasized self-reliance and the second concerns the inversion of child-centredness as a means of infantalizing young people's relationship with the state, economy and schooling.

Although in the contemporary context parental responsibilities and relations between family, education and economy have significantly altered, the laws and social expectations governing nineteenth-century legislation and control still hold. The term 'truant',[2] for example, was invented with the introduction of nineteenth-century compulsory education; and as with such other nineteenth-century terms as 'childhood' and 'adolescence', society has been faced with two major problems. According to Musgrove (1964) these problems are how and where to accommodate young people in the social structure, and how to make their behaviour accord with the specifications. He writes, 'for two centuries English society has been involved in the problem of defining and clarifying the concept of precocity' (Musgrove 1964). Thus, by withdrawing adult status from young people in the family, principally through the factory and education acts, nineteenth-century society effectively distinguished young persons from children on the one hand, and from adults on the other (Aries 1973). In so doing the transition from childhood into adolescence and onwards via youth into adulthood has become a matter of public interest, reflecting the interface between family and the state's right to police the various relations between family, law, education and work. As Aries (1973) notes, 'everything to do with children and family life has become a matter of worthy attention. Not only the child's future but his or her presence and his or her very existence are of concern; the child has become a central concern in the family.'

If at one level child-centredness reflects a healthy interest in the well-being of the young, at another it represents a social construct, which defines and separates off 'children', 'adolescents' and 'youth' from adult society. In placing children and young people at the centre of the family-education debate, this both legitimates public access and rights over them, and renders parents more accountable for their children in law. Should children, adolescents or youth, in other words, fail to conform to their labels, i.e. by 'behaving like adults' (or children), such precocity is seen to confirm their deviant status. One is reminded here of Margaret Thatcher's 1987 remarks pertaining to children, 'who need to be taught to respect traditional moral values' and who are at present 'being taught that they have an inalienable right to be gay'. Although contemporary rhetoric associates child-centredness with progressiveness in education, this only has meaning if parents and children accept their defined roles, duties and responsibilities (and there is some doubt about this), in acceding to received morals and wisdom, linked with expected levels of behaviour, discipline and school attendance. If the 'norm' suggests that this makes societal sense, it ignores the reality by which 'child-centredness' becomes inverted (i.e. a stick to beat young people with) in circumstances where wider indications of social breakdown (such as delinquency, common crime, truancy, indiscipline and unemployment) can be blamed on the family and young people themselves.

According to Stronach (1989), 'blaming the victim' had become a recurring theme in education and social policy in the 1980s, one which has personalized Britain's economic failures in relation to perceived inadequacies in the young. Citing a number of policy statements and documents, from the New Training Initiative (1981) through to the White Paper (1986) on *Education and Training*, Stronach argues that the case rests on an economic assumption that recovery depends on improved motivation and skills, principally among youth.

> Both the problem and the solution are personalized by the White Paper in terms of the individual attributes that young people lack. Indeed, personification extends to rival countries as well – 'determined', 'educated', 'trained', 'strongly motivated'. Presented in these terms, the person is invested with a tremendous agency in terms of the nation. She is responsible, and all the mediations of natural resources, investment policies, class, gender, racism, organisational structures, and historical legacy, fall away. There is a similar tendency towards personification in academic debate on the connections between the economy and education – except it is the qualities and attitudes of the worker that are excoriated.
>
> (Stronach 1989)

Stronach's reference to *she* is pertinent here to the way in which the MSC sought to market its new 'vision' of the YTS model worker in the 1980s and 1990s taking on foreign competition. Following an extensive media campaign, featuring representatives from major companies (and the England football manager), the MSC attempted to revive the flagging fortunes of YTS by appealing directly to parents and employers to support the scheme. One means of doing this has been to place youth centre stage while, at the same time, eliciting responses of nationalism.

> Watch out Japan, Here comes Tracy Logan. Tracy Logan is a typical British sixteen year old, leaving school this year. But to Japan, and our other international competitors, she's a big threat.... Tracy will be spending the next two years learning how to take trade away from them for a change.
>
> (MSC advertisement for the new two-year YTS,
> *Guardian* 28 January 1986)

The threat or promise of Tracy bringing about general economic recovery is revealing for the question it poses regarding the role of school-leavers in the process of economic growth or decline. Here, the irony of Tracy as Britain's economic answer to Japan has to be measured against a decade in which schools, parents and young people have been criticized by government for their anti-industrial attitudes. However, it is important to recognize that 'blaming the victim' does not take place in a straightforward way or go uncontested by those on the 'receiving end'. As we argue in later sections of this chapter relations between family, education and economy are not functionally determined or clear cut: much depends on what is meant by schooling and where the child fits in (or not as the case may be) to its processes, and what is meant by education. 'Does schooling maintain, select for, apprentice to, correspond with, prepare for, feed into, replicate, reproduce or mirror the dominant class relations and structure of society... or, is its "function" to enlighten, challenge, control, innovate or sustain?' (Hall 1981).

For Illich (1971) in his *Deschooling Society* the existence of schools produces its own demand for more schooling, independent of the needs of either learners or the education process itself. 'In schools we are taught that valuable learning is the result of attendance; that the value of learning increases with the amount of input; and, finally, that this value can be measured and documented by grades and certificates.' Yet, if this provides a particular definition of schooling, it is not necessarily passively accepted by pupils, who resist and struggle against such apparent determinism (Willis 1977). According to Bourdieu (1976) and Bernstein (1976), the school–society relationship is best understood as a set of continuities and discontinuities which do not sit easily with either 'func-tionalist' or 'reproductive' theories of education (see Althusser 1972; Bowles and Gintis 1976). For Bourdieu (1976), to view education as simply a mechanism which allocates people into heirarchical positions on the basis of merit, or which mirrors or services the cognitive and affectual skills demanded by the labour market, is to 'refuse to see that its relative autonomy enables it to serve external demands under the guise of independence and neutrality' (Bourdieu and Passeron 1977).

Although clearly education fulfils various 'functions', reproductive and otherwise (see Bowles and Gintis 1976), this should not obscure sight of the ways in which people act in institutions and society, and construct knowledge of the world (Willis 1977). If this is not understood there is a danger of viewing families, pupils, parents, teachers and others as passive recipients of economy, society and school itself; a position that does not stand up to close scrutiny in the 'real world', where people conform, deviate, challenge, participate and engage with state apparatuses (Erben and Gleeson 1977). Thus, in agreement with Paterson (1989), our view is that schooling is as much about the *production* of the individual and social normality as it is about reproduction. If this would seem to oversimplify the complexities involved, it is not our intention here to conceptualize the school–family–society relationship in abstraction. Rather, we seek to explore the nature of the relationship with those historical, policy and contemporary issues that have given shape to the schooling process. This, again, returns us to the matter of 'responsible parenting', and to issues relating to the transition between school and work – in particular, to the question of what schools are for. It is to this aspect of the contemporary debate about education policy that we now turn.

Effects of war and after: what are schools for?

From the arguments presented so far it is apparent that mass schooling and attendance at school are relatively recent phenomena, evolving gradually from the turn of the century to the watershed of the 1944 Education Act. Moreover, the effects of two major world wars and a depression in the period 1914–45 seriously undermined the establishment of a coherent system of education and training for all in the UK, including consistent patterns of school attendance. At the same time, the dislocation of war had important effects in generating new questions about what schools were for, particularly in relation to their social and economic objectives.

As we have observed, before the First World War school attendance remained a contentious issue, despite the legislative framework established between 1870 and 1910. Part-time and half-time schooling for children nearing school-leaving age in mill towns, potteries and other industrial areas largely explained high levels of school non-attendance. Similarly, seasonal fluctuations in agriculture seriously affected school attendance across the spring and summer months, particularly at harvest time. Moreover, in the period up to the First World War, high unemployment, low wages and poverty made many families reliant on child labour, which in turn depressed adult wages still further. Although school attendance in this period remained low the First

World War had a dramatic influence on family life and its relation to the economy and schooling. At one level, war wages among men and women from soldiering and the war effort improved living standards and expectations, enabling many parents to pay the fees required for attendance at secondary school. Following the dislocation of war and its aftermath, the 1918 Education Act sought to restore the economy by investing in closer policy links between family, education and employment, notably via trade training. The Act fixed the school leaving age at fourteen, abolished exemptions from schooling below that age and provided financial support to schools and parents, including scholarship provision. It also emphasized partnership between parents and state in socializing children and adolescents into adult society. In so doing, it set in place penalties and sanctions to be imposed on parents and young people who did not cooperate, with particular reference to school attendance. However, irrespective of such threats, popular demand for schooling increased well into the 1920s, based partly on its perceived value in the labour market, notably in connection with skilled training, and partly in relation to the impetus of post-war reform.

Such optimism was short-lived with the onset of the depression and the Second World War. Cuts in budgets in this period prevented the planned extension of nursery provision education and part-time education across the fourteen to eighteen age range. Throughout the 1920s and 1930s financial stringency failed to support the impetus of the 1918 Act, although the Hadow (1926) and Spens (1931) Reports did have the effect of securing grant aid for separate provision for grammar, technical and modern schools, by examination at eleven. Following on from the Spens concept of 'parity of esteem' (between technical, modern and grammar schools), the Norwood Report (1943) reinforced the principle of tripartism, replacing the grouped subject examination of the school certificate by a single subject examination, which led the way to O and A level examinations. It was not, however, until the 1944 Education Act, which established continuity of provision from primary (five to eleven) into secondary (eleven to fifteen), with FE (fifteen to eighteen) as a non-compulsory element, that the ground rules of mass participation in secondary education were established. In particular, the 1944 Act initiated secondary education for all, but with selection by examination at eleven (11+) designed to stream pupils by ability (measured in terms of types of mind, i.e. academic, practical and general), which corresponded to the three types of school, grammar, technical and secondary modern. Although the word curriculum is not mentioned in the 1944 Act, the Act reinforced the spirit of tripartism, assuming that equality of opportunity would be achieved as pupils found their natural level of ability (practical versus academic). It was also assumed that 'parity of esteem' would exist between the different levels of ability and the types of school which overlaid them.

Despite the limitations imposed by tripartism, the 1944 Education Act embodied changing definitions of education and work, incorporating 'new' concepts – equality of opportunity, career, social mobility, occupational choice, transition between school and work – terms previously not extended to the majority of the population. In a variety of ways the effect of two world wars and a depression had a significant impact on the pattern and provision of education, expectations of schooling and school attendance, not least in raising new questions about the social and economic aims of schooling. If in the period from 1850 to 1930 schools more or less confirmed geographical, social and economic origins (and destinations) of young people, that was intended to be changed with the passing of the 1944 Education Act and new expectations that education should challenge rather than reflect such determinism. Apart from the minority of pupils who gained scholarships to grammar schools before the 1944 Act, a form of social mobility more akin to escapology than equality (Roberts 1984), prevailing school structures mirrored marked class, regional and occupational differences. In this period, expectations that schooling for all should fulfil broader social, economic and educational ambitions, notably in promoting educational opportunity, social mobility and industrial efficiency, were barely considered. As Britain returned from the devastation of two world wars and a depression, cracks in its social and economic infrastructure became more apparent – particularly in relation to the decline of empire, the effects of increasing foreign competition and low productivity – rendering the pressure for educational reform great. This, coupled with women's and men's experiences of working and fighting in war, increased popular demand for social and economic improvements in housing, education, health, welfare and job opportunities. Thus, in the decade following the Second World War a major era of corporatist reconstruction took place, primarily targeted towards New Deal type investment in education, housing, welfare, nationalization, full employment and regional development.

The central importance of the Education Act 1944 in this programme of wider reform should not be underestimated either in relation to the new educational concepts being brought to bear, or in the way it redefined the relations between education, economy and society (Halsey *et al.* 1960). In coordinating previously disparate patterns of educational reform, the Act secured the central role of the state in defining the part education was to play in the emerging pattern of post-war reconstruction. A striking feature of this new order was the way it equated the interests of the state with those of the individual as one and the same thing (Crowther Report 1959). This, in turn, influenced both the content and the form of educational policy and debate in the post-war period, in which individual, national and economic progress were seen to be the product of a partnership between family, education and economy.

The process was not a straightforward one. By the mid-1950s it became apparent that the tripartite system had failed to provide equality of opportunity or parity of esteem (Banks 1955). It was also apparent that increasing numbers of pupils, parents and employers viewed the secondary modern as a low status, indeed less able, track. Elsewhere, a growing body of evidence (Glass 1954; Floud *et al.* 1956; Halsey *et al.* 1960) indicated that the 11+ was a poor measure of assessment and educability, disadvantaging working-class pupils whose failure rate was disproportionately higher than their middle-class counterparts (Douglas 1964, 1968; Musgrave 1965; Banks 1971). In other respects too, those working class pupils who did pass the 11+ exam and went on to grammar schools were, for economic, cultural and social class reasons, more likely to drop out early, confirming earlier concerns about high levels of wastage generated by tripartite structures (Jackson and Marsden 1962). However, it was not simply the evidence linking tripartism with working-class under-achievement that captured the imagination of government and policy-makers; concern was also expressed about the ways in which tripartism arbitrarily separated off types of pupil and types of knowledge. As P. Brown (1991) has observed, the failure of the tripartite system to generate equality of opportunity was particularly acute in the 1960s, because a shortage of skilled labour was placing increasing demands on the educational system to tap the 'pool of ability' that was known to exist among working-class youth. Indeed, this was anticipated by the DES and various cross-party Parliamentary Select Committees in the 1950s and 1960s, who advocated support for comprehensive schooling on the grounds that a broader and more integrated form of education was more compatible with a rapidly expanding labour market and the flexible skills demanded in it. According to P. Brown (1991), 'a further indictment of the tripartite system came from middle class parents who were acutely aware that failing the 11+ was a life sentence, particularly if one could not afford to send one's child to a private school.'

Strange as it may now seem, such diverse criticism dominated education debate from the mid-1950s to the late 1960s, and had a marked influence on the development of comprehensive education (Halsey *et al.* 1980; Gray *et al.* 1983). Although such development was often *ad hoc* and piecemeal, with LEAs interpreting circular 10/65 in many different ways, it captured the imagination of a majority of politicians, parents, employers, teachers and others. At the time, the commitment of both Labour and Conservative governments to post-war reconstruction, fuelled by economic growth, led to a new optimism about schooling and the opportunities it offered in providing skills for an expanding labour market. In contrast with tripartism, comprehensive education was seen to reflect more accurately the changing nature of British society, in being less divisive and in accommodating a broader intake of pupils than the selective system. For many advocates of comprehensive education, 'mixed ability' grouping was at the time seen to be synonymous with the increasingly heterogeneous nature of British society itself (Wright 1977). Thus, in a period of economic expansion and skill shortage, Labour and Conservative governments viewed investment in 'human capital' as the most effective mechanism for sustaining economic growth; both arguing that industrial competitiveness was best served by opening up opportunities for educational and economic advancement which allowed the most able to rise on the basis of talent, rather than patronage or background. This concept of the meritocracy was premised on the view that the changing technological base of production, skill and industrial investment required a broader cross-section of talent and ability than had previously been recruited into the occupational structure(s) or provided by private education. In important ways comprehensive education was seen to legitimate the twin objectives of increasing educational opportunities and economic efficiency while, at the same time, drawing on as wide a pool of talent as possible.

If in the early days of comprehensive education reform indiscipline, pupil alienation and school attendance were acknowledged as pressing problems (Musgrove 1964; Rubenstein and Stoneman 1970; Hargreaves 1982), such issues did not dominate the policy agenda; the main task being how to reorganize schooling as quickly as possible to ensure that pupils both attended school and benefited from the new opportunities afforded by comprehensive education. In this spirit of reformist optimism perennial concern about working-class under-achievement, including early leaving, truancy, school non-attendance and problems in the transition from school to work, were viewed as remediable – almost hangovers of the last vestiges of tripartism and selection. Although mounting social science evidence indicated that comprehensive schools contained within them tripartite structures (Eggleston 1965; Ford 1969) and that essentially working-class pupils still got working-class jobs (Banks 1971; Willis 1977), such factors represented a challenge to rather than an indictment of the comprehensive school (Hargreaves 1982). Despite numerous and recognized contradictions in the links between family, schooling and work, particularly in relation to pupil alienation from schooling, supporters of comprehensive education retained faith in the power of schooling to overcome inequalities in education. At the time, what was called for was a greater investment in more appropriate forms of guidance, counselling and careers development, backed by a new curriculum, including innovative approaches to student-centred teaching and learning (mixed ability), 'new' maths, 'new' science, 'new' humanities and so forth, which would make schooling a more relevant and democratic process. In this respect the setting up of the Schools Council in the late 1960s in anticipation of ROSLA, and investment in Education Priority Areas to counteract the worst effects of urban poverty, were welcomed as signs of positive discrimination in support of the school reform process (Halsey 1972). If research at the time questioned the extent to which schools could compensate for society (Bernstein 1971), there remained a strong commitment among supporters of comprehensive education that such schools did make a difference, particularly in challenging social differentiation and divisiveness (Reynolds 1976; Halsey 1980; Reynolds 1985). Given the contradictions that often underlay objectives associated with social mobility, equality of opportunity and economic efficiency, comprehensive education was seen to work – as long as investment in education, full employment and an expanding economy remained intact.

In reality, comprehensive education development did not proceed undisputed or in such a straightforward manner as we have so far described. For the greater part of its development comprehensive education was hampered by under-investment, invidious comparison with the grammar and private sector and haphazard growth and development (Simon and Rubenstein 1969; Hargreaves 1982; Simon 1988). In other respects, legal wrangles over reorganization (Tameside) and right-wing pressure over apparently falling standards dominated the agenda of comprehensive education reform. Cox and Dyson (1969a,b) and others (Cox and Boyson 1975) complained of the impact of progressive reform on school attendance, discipline and reading levels, drawing attention to the infiltration of 'trendies', 'egalitarians' and assorted 'lefties', all of whom were trying to manipulate education for ulterior motives. Such writers pointed to the *causes célèbres* of Risinghill Comprehensive and William Tyndale Primary School, whose respective heads were sacked for 'imposing' progressive regimes (Berg 1968; Auld 1976). Both cases had significant reverberations throughout the educational world in the late 1960s and early 1970s, epitomizing to a hostile press all that was dreaded about progressive practice. Hall (1977) refers to Risinghill, Tameside and Tyndale as 'trigger events' demonstrating in practice what is denied in theory, '. . . that the ideological balance in education and the ideological forces outside are inextricably linked'. Moreover, evidence from the USA (Coleman 1966; Jencks 1972), indicating that liberal reforms of the 1960s had been misdirected, was reinterpreted by the New Right to fit the British context.

In different ways Coleman (1966) and Jencks (1972) questioned the adoption of human capital theory, which carried the presumption that the abolition of poverty was possible through investment in the skills of the poor. What they sought to demonstrate was that schools bring little influence to bear on a child's achievement that is independent of their family, peers, neighbourhood, background and social class (Coleman 1966). According to Jencks (1972), major occupational differences may be discerned among people with the same amount of education, and there is no evidence to support a direct link between resource inputs and educational outputs. Although Jencks's political position is that if inequality is to be reduced then it must be attacked at source (namely the economic system and not primarily through education), this provided a convenient ideological rationale for politicians, in both the UK and the USA, to re-appraise liberal policies which supported investment in education for all. However, as Robinson (1981) points out, Jencks's counsel is against reducing the money spent on schools on the grounds that schools do make a major contribution to the quality of life (an issue taken up later in this chapter).

> The evidence presented in *inequality* seems to me to show that variations in family background, I.Q., genotype, exposure to schooling, and the quality of schooling cannot account for most of the variation in individual or family incomes. This means we must reject the conservative

notion that income inequality is largely due to the fact that men are born with unequal abilities and raised in unequal home environments. We must also reject the liberal notion that equalising educational opportunity will equalise people's incomes. The evidence in Inequality cannot carry us much further, even though it tries.

(Jencks, quoted in Robinson 1981: 169)

Notwithstanding such qualifications, researchers such as Jensen (1980) in the USA and Eysenck (1971, 1973) in the UK cited Jencks's work to bolster their claims regarding inherited ability and the need for selection. In doing so Eysenck, for example (see Cox and Boyson 1975, 1977), pointed to the way success is determined by IQ rather than school reform or other environmental factors, claiming that attempts to disband selection in favour of equality of opportunity, or mixed ability teaching, represent a form of romantic sentimentalism. According to Wright (1977), such misinterpretation of Jencks's evidence provides a spurious scientific legitimacy to the Black Paper writers' claims that the comprehensive experiment had failed. Cox and Boyson (1975, 1977) in support of Eysenck's views drew attention to a supposed national conspiracy against 'excellence' in which mixed ability, the abolition of selection and political education were linked with a wider breakdown in society, particularly in relation to pupil misbehaviour, indiscipline and rising truancy. Quoting evidence of such breakdown, Cox and Boyson (1975) claimed 'some 650,000 children play truant everyday from our schools and teachers flee from city schools because of lesson resistance and insolence by pupils.' In support of this argument, Boyson (1975) argues that 'where twenty five years ago it was the badly-behaved boy who played truant, it may now be the good boy who stays at home for his own protection' (quoted in Wright, 1977). If in the late 1960s the Black Paper writers did not capture the political agenda as they would have liked, by the time economic recession appeared in the early 1970s their writings were to assume greater significance – not least in providing a convenient explanation for why things had gone wrong. Signs of economic crisis became transposed as 'educational problems'; evidence of lowering standards of literacy, numeracy, behaviour, discipline and school attendance signalling a connection with poor economic performance, industrial unrest and rising crime.

Signs of crisis and beyond

The situation so far described, characterizing post-war investment and belief in education, dramatically changed with the oil crisis in 1973, followed closely by recession, the three-day week, miners' strike and fall of the Heath Conservative government (1974). However, the obvious signs of economic recession dogged the incoming Labour government, who oversaw a period of rising inflation, unemployment and industrial unrest throughout their period of office to 1979

(Finn *et al.* 1978). In this period, mounting concern about industrial conflict, youth unemployment, urban decline and growing crime rates fuelled consternation about declining standards of discipline and behaviour in both the family and the school. Almost simultaneously, a politically inspired debate about the purposes and practices of comprehensive education arose, prompting the so-called 'Great Education Debate 1976–9'. Although concern about the failure of schools to respond to the needs of industry achieved prominence in this debate it was, according to Atkinson and Rees (1982), the demoralization of youth linked with a collapsed youth labour market, urban disorder and apparently rising crime levels which most occupied government attention. If at the root of the 'crisis' was the way youth unemployment undermined the ground rules of schooling (interrupting the transition and transmission points between school, work and adulthood), there was also a law and order problem for the incoming Conservative government, in this case involving an excess supply of young people on the streets. Almost simultaneously, efforts were made by several ministers and police officers to increase police influence within schools and youth centres to tackle what Sir Keith Joseph described as rising 'community violence and disorder' (*Times Educational Supplement* 2 April 1982). Moreover, street disturbances in 1981 and 1985 intensified pressure to introduce conscription or, at the very least, to champion issues of law and order in schools by more effective community liaison, community service and policing.

By the mid-1980s the scale of police involvement in schooling was considerable, including organizing school quizzes, disco dancing competitions, cricket and soccer matches, involving sports and leisure coaching and supervision in youth clubs and community schemes, including the Duke of Edinburgh's Award Scheme (DES 1983). In addition to such 'policing by tracksuit' (Cashmore 1989), there was also sponsorship of holiday and play schemes, and weekly meetings and weekend camps which among other things provided training in various aspects of police work (Davies 1986). At this time concern about school non-attendance further encouraged police cooperation at the local level in respect of dealing with truancy and pupils suspended from school. According to Davies (1986), in Cheshire this involved getting heads to help police identify first- and third-year pupils, and police visits to where truanting pupils congregated, in order to take them home or back to school. Elsewhere, in Birmingham, North Wales and other regions, police patrols of supermarkets, cinemas and licensed premises became a regular occurrence, with HMI's 1983 survey indicating that 75 per cent of LEAs had regular contact between the police and the education welfare service, 'probably due in part to the fact that some of its members were formerly police officers' (DES 1983; Davies 1986).

Consequently, if, at one level, the Great Education Debate focused on the apparent failure of schools to ensure a proper fit between the vocational preparation of young people and the needs of the economy, at another it confirmed earlier criticisms of the Black Paper writers that Britain's economic decline was interlinked with a law and order problem; in particular the failure of progressive education reform to deliver high enough standards of behaviour and discipline. In explaining Britain's social and economic decline in terms of experiential and progressive forms of education, the Black Paper writers were able to equate declining standards of literacy, numeracy, behaviour and school attendance with lowering standards of discipline and morality in home, workplace and school. Significantly, the Black Paper writers provided a convenient ideological rationale for a Conservative election campaign seeking to bolster the message 'Labour isn't working', by *politicizing* truancy and related school problems as indicators of a more prevalent social conflict and malaise. However, in generating a 'moral panic' about truancy and poor standards of teaching, bias among left-wing teachers and disregard for basic skills in the curriculum, the New Right were able to legitimate their vision of alternatives with the appealing message of 'parental choice'. Although the views of the Black Paper writers had been earlier dismissed by liberals and socialists as reactionary, their subsequent advocacy of consumer-led schooling, national curriculum, opting out, vouchers, local school management, selection and assisted places has since found support from industrialists and a right-wing press anxious to blame schools for declining productivity and industrial unrest. If in the late 1960s and early 1970s the Black Papers were not taken seriously, by the late 1970s their ideas came to dominate the policy agenda, anticipating the 1988 Education Reform Act almost in detail. So, despite the political origins of the Great Education Debate, the debate itself did little to stem growing criticism levelled against both comprehensive education and the Labour Party; instead it confirmed suspicion that schools had failed society and that the experiment with liberal democracy and equality of opportunity was over (Hillgate Group 1986). However, according to P. Brown (1991), New Right criticism was careful not to dissociate itself from a belief in schooling itself.

> What they have criticized is the fact that its organization and content have been subordinated to liberal democratic principles of equality of opportunity rather than the 'national interest'. Therefore a faith in the school's ability to provide solutions to such problems has not been questioned. There is nothing wrong with investing in human capital (although it is believed that this should be organized through the operation of the free market rather than through a state monopoly of education) but that the education pupils receive must correspond to the requirements of their future occupational roles. The Right have argued that the comprehensive school has given the wrong medicine, in the wrong dosage, to the wrong children, and that this explained why a disproportionate number of school leavers are unemployed, and why so many of them are unprepared for the world of work.
>
> (P. Brown 1991: 93)

In order to retain faith in schooling while, at the same time, restructuring its basic principles along market lines, the Conservative government has since 1979 drawn heavily on the Black Papers' findings and recommendations. At the policy level this process was to prove relatively straightforward; by withdrawing level funding from LEAs and schools in favour of categorical funding for targeted projects (e.g. via the Department of Employment and MSC), government was able to wrestle control over schooling from LEAs and introduce an aura of competitiveness. In the decade following the 1981 New Training Initiative, through to the Education Act 1988 and beyond, successive Conservative governments have sought to bring about educational change by direct intervention, through a proliferation of initiatives, such as YTS, TVEI, TRIST, the Assisted Places Scheme, GCSE, CTCs, TECS, local financial management, national curriculum and much else, all designed to make schools and LEAs more responsive to the market place and consumer demand. Perhaps more importantly, what the Black Paper writers provided was the ideological rationale for such policy changes, premised on widespread evidence of LEA intransigence, declining standards of literacy and numeracy, attendance and discipline. Thus, in the troubled circumstances of the 1970s and 1980s, which saw cuts in education budgets, increased unemployment and rising disaffection with school among some pupils, creating a moral panic about standards in education was not a difficult task.

Further controversy surrounding comprehensive re-organization in the 1970s, followed by subsequent amalgamation, re-organization and teacher industrial action in the mid to late 1980s, did little to encourage public confidence in schooling. Almost simultaneously, such concern was picked up and played back via media coverage, portraying school non-attendance unequivocally as *truancy* (O'Keefe 1981). If one looks at newspaper headlines it is possible to see writ large something that is systematically disclaimed by politicians and employers, namely the crucial relation between schooling, economy and society: 'in the British case – the structure and kinds of education we are said to "need" and the needs of a capitalist economy in crisis' (Hall 1981). A notable feature of the 'news' about school non-attendance is, for example, the nature of its language, which evokes deep-seated concerns about order and control, proper parenting, the work ethic, crime and much else, reinforcing the 'suspicious state of isolation' in which the 'deviant' is viewed (Durkheim 1972). Media headlines, for example, titillate and sensationalize truancy, while adopting the moral high ground in 'fighting', 'battling', 'eradicating' and 'stamping' it out (*Evening Sentinel* 1 December 1988; *TES* 13 October 1989; *Guardian* 30 January 1990; *Observer* 4 March 1990). There is a certainty about such crusading rhetoric in the media and elsewhere, as in the 'fight' against crime, child abuse, drug addiction and alcoholism, which assumes a consensus about what the problem is, and what should be done about it. After all, who in their right mind would argue that truancy, crime, child abuse, drug addiction or alcoholism are a 'good thing'? The danger is that since the problem

Figure 1.1 Montage of headlines.

is taken as given, the search for causes, solutions and moral homilies comes that much easier. Consider, for example, two accounts, one advertising a TV series on truancy by TVAM in the *Guardian* (depicting a full page photograph of a police constable apprehending a schoolboy thief) and, the other a *Guardian* article about the same TVAM series.

> Missing Sums: Do you know what your children are doing today? Graph plotting? Map reading? Purse snatching? With 500,000 pupils regularly skipping school, we look at tomorrow's destitutes, drop outs and criminals.
>
> (Missing Out: the TVAM Truancy Report. Advertised in the
> *Guardian* 23 October 1990)

> *Ending the Game of Hookey* More than half a million children, research indicates, are absent from class at least once a week without acceptable reason. At least 200,000 are skipping school every day. The figures are disturbing but their consequences offer cause for greater long-term concern. A workforce that has been weaned on truancy is not best-placed to compete in the world economy.
>
> (*Guardian* 16 October 1990)

For our purposes what is interesting about such accounts is the way in which they lead on from a *statistic* (500,000 pupils regularly truant) to a *conclusion* defining truancy as *causally* related to 'destitution, criminality and poor economic performance'. Not only does this legitimate the moral stance taken on truants and their families, but it also pathologizes and sensationalizes school non-attendance in disproportion to the vast majority of pupils who attend school regularly. Although this point is acknowledged by HMI (DES 1989a), who portray issues of school non-attendance in more sober fashion, there is no escaping the fact that recent changes in the financial basis, funding, curricula and control of education have placed attendance firmly on the political agenda. Why should this be the case at the present time, and what is the 'official' explanation for this?

According to HMI (DES 1989a), in contrast with the low levels of school non-attendance in the nineteenth century, the situation towards the end of the twentieth century is more acute. In their recently published *Attendance at School*, HMI argue that 'technological progress is accelerating and the supply of school leavers is diminishing; more than ever society needs as many people as possible educated to the best levels of which they are capable.' The familiarity of such remarks, however, echoes the importance of school attendance in the national interest, as mentioned earlier. Ostensibly, school non-attendance is dysfunctional for a number of reasons: it impairs the value of education for attenders and non-attenders alike, adversely affects attainments and skills, limits post-school further education, training and job centre opportunities, and reduces the effectiveness of schooling itself.

A number of factors explain why this is the case. In the first place, recent categorically funded initiatives, such as TVEI, LAPP, COMPACTS and related work-based learning projects, have accentuated the importance of attendance and progression within and between school, college and work. Secondly, the emphasis placed on course work in GCSE development, modular programmes, active learning strategies, supported self-study and records of achievement stresses personal discipline and self-control. As if to reinforce this message, the HMI report 'Good behaviour and discipline in schools' (DES 1987) and the Elton Committee of Enquiry into discipline in schools (Elton Report 1988) point to the various ways in which disruption and non-attendance adversely affect school effectiveness and the reform process itself. Implicit in their recommendations for school reform is the acknowledgement that the two key elements of the Education Reform Act (1988), the National Curriculum and local management of schools (LMS), are contingent on increased levels of pupil attendance and parental support. There is, therefore, clear official awareness that the National Curriculum, with its emphasis on phased assessment and testing at four key stages (ages 7, 11, 14 and 16) places an additional premium on high levels of attendance, not least in *policing* the way national standards are monitored and appraised. This, linked with devolved local and financial management of schools, embracing greater consumer choice (parents) and units of resource (pupils) has sharpened competition between schools in attracting and holding on to pupils. In so doing, this has increased the divisive pressure on schools to publish examination results and improve attainment scores and attendance levels as they compete for survival in the market place. Yet, if as HMI claim, 'a school's attendance rate can be regarded as a significant indicator of its effective performance' (DES 1989a), what that term means in the present climate of rising unemployment, cuts in benefit, effects of poll tax, school closure and teacher shortage remains to be seen.

One inescapable conclusion is that under the aegis of improving standards, schools will be expected to turn the social control screw more tightly on pupil behaviour, thereby increasing rather than reducing the incidence of school-generated problems. The danger is that measuring school effectiveness in this way may reduce schooling to a narrow set of observable performance indicators, test and exam scores, attendance levels, dress, delinquency rates, incidences of vandalism, graffiti and 'bad' behaviour, at the expense of all else. According to Rutter *et al.* (1979), there are a number of factors open to modification by the staff of a school, which can more positively influence success in a range of areas, including public examinations, attendance, pupil behaviour and discipline. 'What distinguishes the successful from the less successful school', argue Rutter *et al.*, even allowing for similar resources, catchment and intake, '... is the notion of "ethos" generated by a challenging, caring, supportive, well-organised, stimulating and disciplined environment' (Rutter *et al.* 1979; see also Gray 1981; Reynolds *et al.* 1987; Mortimore *et al.* 1988). Yet despite the oft-quoted attribute of a good school, 'the elusive *ethos* felt but not measured, sensed but unseen' (Robinson 1989) remains unclear and difficult to pin down empirically. As Reynolds and Reid (1985: 195) point out, 'we do not have any real idea as to how the process factors actually generate outputs, which may be through effects upon peer group processes or upon individual self conception.' Notwithstanding such a disclaimer it is ironic that, in the 1980s round of expenditure cuts in education budgets, the Conservative government has fastened on to effective schooling and in particular ethos (rather than resources) as the best way of improving standards of behaviour, discipline and motivation in schools.

For Brighouse (1990), the debate about how to make schools more effective confronts two major obstacles: one relating to the market orientation of Conservative school reform and, particularly, the divisive influence of opting out, LMS, open enrolment, assisted places, CTCs and vouchers; and the other relating to the effects of deregulated government social and economic policies (unemployment, poverty, homelessness, cuts in benefit), which find their expression in communities, families and schools in areas least able to compete equally in the open market with all others. In acknowledging the competitive ethos of 'winners and losers' in this process, government has in effect pre-empted the definition of effective schools as those which survive and out-compete others in attracting and maintaining pupil numbers as their main source of funding. However, little thought has been given to the consequences of such policy, in circumstances where 'losing' is likely to have marked effects on school attendance, motivation and discipline. This brings into sharp relief ways in which school reform itself generates the very 'problems' it ostensibly seeks to address.

School, work and civic exclusion

Paradoxically, despite the apparent trend towards political centralism and control, there is in practice little sign of any coherent national system of education and training emerging. Indeed, one effect of the passage of legislation from the New Training Initiative 1981 to the Education Reform Act 1988 has been to destabilize systematic educational development in favour of disparate initiatives – YTS, TVEI, CPVE, BTEC, CTCs, assisted places, opting out and privatization – which reduce effective coordination of education policy and curricular balance across secondary and further education. In addition, far from reducing duplication and repetition in the system, government reforms have increased competition and overlap between various intermediary bodies (e.g. NCC, NCVQ, TECs), various courses (e.g. BTEC, CPVE, YTS) and various sectors (e.g. CTCs, grant-aided schools, comprehensives, FE, tertiary and sixth-form colleges). In curricular terms such haphazard development defies concepts of society, system or citizenship, making it all the more difficult to establish a coherent, comprehensive pattern of participation and attendance for all. Instead, educational provision now operates on the basis of delivering agreed national objectives, which are consumer-led and generated by employer demand, market forces, sponsorship and enterprise. In this respect, education for citizenship has little to do with nurturing the complex relationship between individual and society, and everything to do with sponsoring individuals acting in support of their own sectionalized interests. This is particularly noticeable in the ways government has targeted various educational projects to specific audiences – the assisted places scheme, CTCs, new grant-aided schools – and elsewhere, has conscripted the less fortunate into youth (YT) and adult (ET) training programmes, backed by changes in social security legislation, family income support and housing benefit. Moreover, the danger is that the disparate range of curricular and institutional reforms set in motion in the late 1980s and early 1990s is likely to reinforce traditional differences between academic, technical and general knowledge, a factor that was recognized as a blockage to social, political and economic progress in the 1950s and that has been a major source of conflict in education and society ever since.

The fundamental question being asked here is whether a decade of school reform, culminating in the 1988 Education Reform Act, has significantly redefined the objectives of schooling, improved school effectiveness or addressed changes in labour market conditions, job opportunities and the transition between school and work. This would seem crucial given the evidence that pupil responses to schooling are closely interlinked with their occupational aspirations, which in turn have an influence on motivation, discipline and school attendance. If all the government proposes in its package of reforms is yet another variation of schooling, but one which addresses neither the career or occupational aspirations of pupils, nor the limiting effect of inner-city decline and unemployment, those reforms will have limited effect. At present, there is little sign of education and training reform being linked with corresponding changes in work; as a consequence, the lack of a relationship between education, training and productive labour has led to initiatives based on the containment of youth, involving discipline, control and employer-led considerations above all else. In such circumstances, attempts to raise standards by placing education in the market place, alongside health and welfare provision, are unlikely to capture the imagination of families and schools marginalized by divisive government economic policy. This, according to Willis (1977) and others (see Jenkins 1983; Wallace 1987; Brown 1989), further limits any coherent understanding of the cultural and class influences that bear on pupil identification with school, which in turn affects their participation in or resistance to it. In contrast with earlier studies by Hargreaves (1967), Lacey (1970) and Bernstein (1971), which focused on counterculture in secondary schools (as a feature of selection and failure among working-class pupils), Willis points out that school counterculture is a cause, not a consequence, of educational failure. It is his argument that in their experience of schooling, working-class pupils draw on their working-class culture to challenge the ideology of the school, particularly in relation to humour, testing teachers and bending rules. This is, however, more than a symbolic interactionist account of pupils developing antidotes or survival strategies to schooling (Woods 1976, 1979). Rather, it concerns the way pupils produce and reproduce knowledge of themselves and others, in relation to success and failure, via their class position in opposition to school values.

Elsewhere, Corrigan (1979) argues that for working-class youth to accept success at school involves them in rejecting their class, a factor often overlooked in considering 'why working-class pupils fail'. However, Jenkins (1983), refutes the notion that working-class pupils collude in their own oppression, arguing more in line with earlier findings in the sociology of education that working-class pupils' rejection of schooling represents a 'cultural alternative' adopted by youth as a defence mechanism against school. In Jenkins's view, defining working-class culture and resistance in blanket terms is not satisfactory, since not all working-class youth in school rebel, and to define conformists or achievers simply as 'ear-oles' (see Willis 1977) is to miss the point about fractions within class groupings. Jenkins identifies three different pupil lifestyles: the 'lads', who are likely to come from a single-parent household, have a criminal record, gain few qualifications and enter unskilled work; 'ordinary kids' who do better at school and who are less likely to be unemployed; and 'citizens' who achieve success measured in terms of their entering skilled manual, white-collar jobs or going on to college. Similarly, Brown's study (1987) identifies three groups of pupil, 'Rems', 'ordinary kids' and 'swots', which conform in various ways to the types described by Jenkins. Both Brown and Jenkins point out that the distinctive orientation of the pupils they studied cannot be explained simply in relation to the selection processes in school or by a blanket reference to working-class culture (Parsons 1990). The message here, which has important implications for the study of truancy, is that there are significant variations within working-class pupil culture that complicate simplistic generalizations about working-class youth (as truants, rebels etc.) or the ways in which education reproduces certain pre-conditions of society. Wallace (1987), for example, goes on to argue that contemporary explanations of social and cultural reproduction also need to account for neglected variables relating to young people's experiences and relationships in the family, with parents, partners, peers, social workers and others. Allied to this, Wallace points to various other influences within the community, associated with illness, poverty, family breakdown, homelessness and other factors, which have been largely ignored in understanding the relationship between social class and schooling. This view is also supported by critics of the prevailing 'male model of reproduction' in education; McRobbie (1978), Deem (1980) and Griffin (1985) have demonstrated that female anti-school culture is less focused on over-generalized class or macho forms of internalization, and is more closely linked with the categories referred to by Wallace – issues which are taken up in more detail in Chapter 3 of this book.

The relevance of such analysis to this study is that truancy as a form of *social exclusion* (whether inflicted or self-inflicted) cannot be separated off from wider forms of race, class and gender stratification experienced by young people, particularly in economically depressed areas where pockets of persistent and intermittent (post-registration) forms of school non-attendance remain historically high (Rutter *et al.* 1979; Reid 1985; Reynolds 1985; Gray and Jesson 1990). Various longitudinal studies, for example, of young people in such areas indicate that they experience a combination of inequalities, poverty, poor housing, debt, unemployment, welfare and police scrutiny, which approximates to *civic exclusion* (Lockwood 1985; Coffield *et al.* 1986; Lee *et al.* 1990). Such factors, compounded by inadequate training opportunities, removal of the right to social security provision and rundown local health and recreational facilities, have, perhaps not surprisingly, had a depressing psychological and material influence on young people and their families (Coffield *et al.* 1986). According to Lee *et al.* (1990), this combination of experience has a marginalizing effect on certain residential neighbourhoods, estates and zones, which become ghettoized, further confirming the self-fulfilling prophecy of 'failure' among the citizens within, whose status renders them more liable to the forms of surveillance and supervision referred to earlier in this chapter. If, perhaps not surprisingly, evidence indicates above-average levels of school non-attendance in these areas (Gray and Jesson 1990) it should not be assumed that such school absenteeism necessarily constitutes truancy, or is causally connected with poor parenting, phobia or, indeed, progressive schooling. Neither should other forms of working-class resistance to schooling, as defined by Willis (1977), Corrigan (1979) and others, be confused with some consciously worked out pupil rejection of schooling.

It is important to understand the way young people's expectations of schooling are interlinked with social divisions generated in the 1980s, by *laissez-faire* policies towards unemployment, welfare, health, housing and education, which have undermined labour commitment, 'creating a disaffected, disadvantaged, divided and above all under-educated and under-trained working class' (Lee *et al.* 1990). According to Lockwood (1985), such policies have left already economically struggling families further isolated in contexts where schooling represents an even weaker mechanism of opportunity or control than before. In such circumstances, the more deregulated market forces become, the more unregulated the balance in local areas becomes, between school, employment, training, law and order, health and welfare provision – 'nor will market forces do much to eradicate the costly social insecurities in young workers' home lives which decrease their ability and willingness to learn and be taught' (Lee *et al.* 1990). In the circumstances, it would seem paradoxical that a government committed to reviving business enterprise, education and the family should pursue a deregulation policy which effectively atomizes all three areas, thereby reinforcing the contradictions it apparently seeks to address.

Viewed from this angle, headline interpretations placed on the Sheffield

University study (Gray and Jesson 1990), which indicates that one in four pupils persistently truant, with 25 per cent selectively missing lessons, provide a misleading picture of school non-attendance, particularly in relation to the dramatic 'discovery' of post-registration truancy, interpreted as pupil rejection of the curriculum by Stoll and O'Keeffe (1989). The picture invites comparison between, on the one hand, bloody-minded pupils, and, on the other, lax and disorganized schools; the solution being to stiffen penalties and punishments for school non-attendance by tightening up school regimes. Although it is tempting to explain school non-attendance in these terms, the evidence indicates that most pupils face problems that may or may not be directly linked or associated with schools (Wright 1977; White and Brockington 1983; Lockwood 1985; Lee *et al.* 1990). Moreover, as Wright argues, if it were true that post-registration truancy was increasing, one would also expect some increase in the number of pupils who were brazen enough to skip registration as well. 'And it is certainly not true that it is only in the last few years that pupils have "discovered" that they can register and then skip lessons; pupils have known that trick since schools were invented' (Wright 1977). Elsewhere, White (1980) questions the assumption that truancy is an easier option than attending school. In one of the few carefully documented studies of non-attenders and their families, White concludes that whatever the reasons for young people's rejection of schooling, 'they must be pretty deep rooted to sustain the youngster through the barrage of official interference (official visits, monitoring, assessment, supervision, court appearance, care, separation and so forth) which is the inevitable consequence of persistent truancy' (White 1980). And this conclusion receives support from the ethnographic analyses presented in Chapters 3 and 4 of this book.

Conclusion

What we have sought to demonstrate in this chapter is that truancy is not the easy option that it is sometimes supposed to be. School non-attendance is more complex than the term 'truancy' implies, and is mediated by historical, legal, sociological, political and economic relations that circumscribe schooling and the child's experience of it. While it may be expedient to blame schools, families or individuals for causing imbalances in such relations, this largely ignores ways in which issues of biography, history and social structure intersect with one another (Mills 1959). Equally, explanations of truancy as a form of individual pathology or anti-school culture are over-simplistic since they ignore the ways in which issues of attendance and non-attendance constitute two faces of the same coin. It has also been argued that research and policy premised on a 'discovery' of declining standards of attendance, behaviour and discipline is questionable precisely because the level of analysis from which it began is inadequate. Hence, the contention of this chapter is that issues relating to attendance, discipline and behaviour in schools should be viewed as part of a historically recurring debate (Reeder 1981; Wiener 1981; McCulloch 1991), which has perhaps more to say about the nature of British society itself (in particular state regulation of family–education–work relations), than about the individuals, families or schools caught up in the margins of market forces (Coffield *et al.* 1986).

Here it would seem important to remind ourselves of two principal points. The first is that universal secondary education 'for all' is a relatively recent concept and represents a 'new' experience for the majority of the population; popular support for it was not fully secured until the 1944 Education Act and the subsequent reform process generated late in the 1950s and 1960s. The second is that patterns of school attendance have remained remarkably consistent over time, if anything showing distinct signs of improvement in the latter part of the twentieth century as compared with the period 1850–1945. Moreover, there would seem to be no strong evidence that compulsion or legal threats have significantly influenced school attendance one way or the other. More pertinent perhaps is the way pupils, parents and families experience schooling, particularly in its changing relation with the economy, labour market and job opportunities (P. Brown 1991). In this respect it is important to recognize that families are not passive recipients of educational norms and that there is interaction with, rather than passive acceptance of, policy initiatives. Here, one is reminded of Johnson's (1976) observation that schools have never acquired the autonomous power that has been expected of them: they represent but one feature of cultural reproduction, and at the same time bear all the characteristic antagonisms of the social formation as a whole. 'Schools in other words reproduce *forms of resistance too*, however limited or "corporate" or unselfconscious these may be' (Johnson 1976).

Away from all the media and political hype about truancy and indiscipline in education the everyday reality is that most pupils go to school on a regular basis and are supported in this by a two-way link between family and education, notably on matters which relate to learning, behaviour and attendance (DES 1989a). It is when that link is seen to break down that 'trouble' arises and this, for our purposes, provides important clues about the problematic relationship between family, education and society. In particular, it is what such 'break-down' points tell us about the chain of relations and reactions, involving parents, children and schools, that signifies wider principles of legality, order, power and control in society, over and beyond simply being absent from school. Much of this has to do with historical and cultural prescription, 'with being in the right place at the right time' (Paterson 1989) and, perhaps more importantly, with the way 'truancy' touches on a sensitive and deeply rooted social nerve, which has its root in the very history and ethos of compulsory state education and its worth. Before addressing the empirical manifestations of this process (in the form of the empirical focus of the study; see Chapters 3 and 4) in Chapter 2 we describe the Norwest Project.

Notes

1 Other workers had 'wakes weeks' etc.
2 The term 'truant' derives from the Gaelic 'truaghan' (wretch), and was probably first used to describe poor Victorian pupils who absconded from school (Green 1980).

2

RESEARCHING SCHOOL ATTENDANCE

Introduction

When the Norwest school non-attendance project was first planned in 1986, two fundamental aims were identified, together with two related policy objectives and a number of theoretical concerns.

The fundamental aims were
1 To describe and explain the historical and contemporary conditions that have produced the 'problem' of non-attendance at school.
2 To describe and assess, by means of an in-depth case study conducted in Norwest, how provision for non-attenders at school operates both within the individual organizations and at the interface between courts, schools, social services and other welfare and regulatory agencies.

The policy-related objectives were
1 To assess the degree of congruity between the aims and methods of the different agencies (education, social services, police, probation, education welfare, courts) variously involved with delinquent or deviant school students aged eleven to eighteen.
2 To assess the extent to which different modes of inter-agency cooperation and intervention have differential effects, particularly in relation to:
   (a) returning school-age pupils to full-time or at least part-time education;
   (b) the entry of eleven to eighteen year olds into the criminal justice and/or penal system.

The theoretical concerns with which we were most concerned at the outset of the research were

1 *Jurisprudential* Particularly about the justification and practicality of applying a theory of general deterrence to the enforcement of school attendance.
2 *Sociology of law and education-related* About the relative importance of economy, law and education in achieving (or not) universal school attendance.
3 *Criminological* About the relationship between the criminal justice system and other regulatory modes for controlling the passage from infancy to adulthood.

This chapter describes the legal, social, ideological and organizational context within which the investigation was undertaken. It begins with a discussion of the possible careers of school non-attenders together with an exposition of the labyrinthine routes (legal, education and welfare) open to them as they proceed: at best, from school non-attendance to a resumption of regular attendance; or, at worst, from school non-attendance, through residential care – and absconding from it – to penal custody.

Enforcing school attendance: the intended and unintended consequences

The agents of the legal, welfare and education systems are required by law to enforce attendance at school. Attempts to enforce school attendance, however, have unintended (as well as intended) consequences.

Figure 2.1 sets out the course of school non-attendance careers, charting the routes that non-attenders take through the legal, education and welfare systems. After the initial act of not attending school a pupil embarks on a career which may be measured along two axes: continued school non-attendance, and the resumption of regular school attendance. At any particular point, regular attendance may be resumed, although there may also be a later return to non-attendance; so the process may as easily be circular as linear. If there is fairly consistent non-attendance, the pupil is likely to follow the route traced by the vertical axis in Figure 2.1 (the figure is slightly simplified, tracing only the major landmarks in the non-attender's career, leaving out the various possible permutations). This axis moves non-attenders from being absentees through the status offence act of truancy, to the position of being permanently out of school and in care. Along the way, they are subjected to a variety of interventions, either welfare or punishment-oriented, which have a number of intended and unintended consequences.

The first agency response to non-attendance generally comes from the school, which, defining non-attendance as wilful misbehaviour, responds with a series of punishments, escalating from putting the pupil 'on report' (requiring a system of lesson registration for a specified period of time) to at first

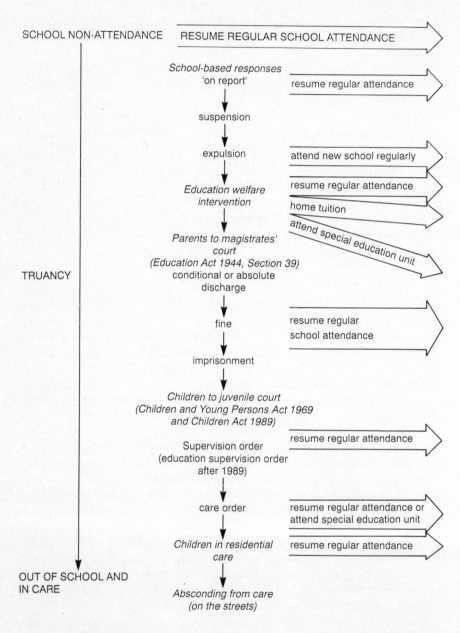

Figure 2.1 School non-attendance careers: routes through the legal, education and welfare systems.

temporary, and finally permanent, exclusion from school. The report system may or may not be successful in policing non-attenders (several interviewees described ways of getting around the system) but it is a first step in separating out a group of non-attenders from the main body of the school. Exclusions, whether temporary or permanent, operate best as a deterrent to persistent non-attendance: once implemented they have the intended consequence of short-term absence from school, and sometimes the unintended consequence of prolonged absences.

At the point when school-based measures are no longer seen to be effective, the education welfare service is usually called in. This service is intended to provide support to the child and family and thus to encourage the resumption of regular school attendance. An unintended, or perhaps hidden, consequence of educational welfare intervention is that the negative process of labelling families as deviant is begun in earnest, with education welfare officers employing a range of categories to facilitate their work (Galloway 1985; Wardhaugh 1990). By this stage, the construction of the deviant identity of truant is well under way.

At the third stage, parental appearance in the magistrates' court, the emphasis shifts again from welfare back to punishment: family circumstances may be taken into account to a certain extent, but generally magistrates deal with parents of truants as they would with any other offenders. Legal intervention takes place for the first time at this stage, and the concept of parental responsibility for non-attendance is brought to the fore. The intention is to bring pressure to bear on parents to ensure their offspring's regular school attendance, and this may well be successful. There may also be unintended consequences; the involvement of parents in the legal process includes them in the categorization process carried out by both education welfare officers and by magistrates. Dealing with cases in magistrates' courts also effectively criminalizes the status offence of school non-attendance (in Scotland cases are more frequently dealt with in family court settings), adding a further dimension to the negative labelling process.

Should the children still refuse to attend school, the parents may return to the magistrates' court, or the case may be directed to the juvenile court. The latter course signals a new stage in the development of the non-attenders' deviant career, in that they are by now deemed to be 'beyond the care and control' of their parents and thus responsible for their own actions. Non-attendance is *not* a criminal act for young people and therefore not punishable in law, so there is a shift in emphasis yet again from punishment to welfare. The remit of the juvenile court is to take full account of the children's circum-stances – physical, emotional, moral and intellectual – rather than to base intervention on their levels of attendance at school. The unintended con-sequence is that court action at this fourth stage may have far more serious ramifications for children than court appearances would for parents. While imprisonment of adults under the Education Act 1944 has been rare, the taking into care of young people under the Children and Young Persons Act 1969 has been all too common. At this stage social work involvement is added to the series of legal, education and education welfare interventions detailed above.

If care orders are made and implemented, non-attenders are faced with the possibility of removal from home, and possibly from current school, with the consequent disruption which that entails. If they persistently absent themselves at this stage they may be met with sanctions from the school and/or the children's home. Notwithstanding the fact that they have been subjected to the (fairly drastic) welfare measure of being taken into care, they may also meet with punishments at school and/or in care.

While some residential units make little or no attempt to enforce regular school attendance, others employ fairly severe penalties, including loss of privileges and periods of time spent in isolation. Some interviewees reported that these penalties were a contributory factor to their running away from care, an action which necessarily involved periods of absence from school. Having reached the 'end of the line' they are in effect back where they started from, that is, 'out of place' and on the streets (Paterson 1989). Having been subjected to a wide range of interventions – educational, welfare and legal – they are truants not only in the sense of those who are absent from school, but in the second sense of the word: those who wander. Ultimately, this wandering may lead to homelessness, charges under the vagrancy acts, court appearances for survival offences committed while 'on the run', and finally penal custody.

Legal context

The research upon which this book is based was conducted during one of the most intense and radical periods of legislative reform in relation to education and child welfare since the war. Two Acts of Parliament, both impinging directly on a study of school non-attendance, need to be discussed here. The Education Reform Act 1988, with its widespread 'reforms' affecting all areas of education, was the most important piece of education legislation since the Education Act 1944; the Children Act 1989 was the most significant reform in child care legislation since the Children and Young Persons Act 1969. In terms of policy and practice concerning school non-attendance there are close connections between the two. Indeed, the close relationship between welfare and education legislation has persisted since the Children and Young Person Act 1969 supplemented the school attendance provisions of the 1944 Education Act. The overlapping provisions of the Education Reform Act 1988 and the Children Act 1989 continued the dual approach.

Legislation governing compulsory school attendance dates back to the Education Acts 1870, 1876 and 1918, and has met with considerable opposition from both parents and children at each of these stages. However, education cannot really be said to have been universally available until the introduction of free education with the 1944 Act. Before 1944, poverty had always been a compelling reason for non-attendance at school (Humphries 1981). The 1944 legislation was enacted within the context of the post-war welfare state and established the guidelines for the provision of education for the next forty years.

The Education Act 1944 (as amended by the Raising of the School-leaving Age Order 1972) requires the parents of children aged five to sixteen to ensure that they 'receive efficient full-time education suitable to his or her age, ability and aptitude, either by attendance at school or otherwise' (Section 39, quoted in Reid 1987: 25). The penalties are fines for the first two offences, and a fine and/or imprisonment for third and subsequent offences. In practice, imprisonment has seldom been used as an option and, in any case, the power to imprison has been repealed by the 1989 Children Act, Sch. 15 (White *et al.* 1990).

An alternative legal measure to enforce attendance was provided by the Children and Young Persons Act 1969, which allowed for care proceedings to be sought within the juvenile court, under Section 1 (2)(e) of the Act, on the grounds that a child was not receiving 'efficient full-time education'. While, overwhelmingly, local authorities proceed to juvenile court under the direction of magistrates in the adult court, under the provisions of the Education Act 1944 and the Children and Young Persons Act 1969, technically they are also entitled to proceed directly to the juvenile court under Section 11 of the Education Act 1953. Within the literature there has been some confusion over the interpretation of these grounds. Reid (1987), for example, argues that care proceedings may be taken only if there is a failure to attend school *plus* evidence that the child is in need of care and control. Berg *et al.* (1988), however, assert that failure to attend school has been in itself sufficient evidence of the need for care and control, at least since a court of appeal judgment by Lord Denning in 1977, and this interpretation is supported by White *et al.*'s (1990) commentary on how the Children Act 1989 affects the provisions of both the Children and Young Persons Act 1969 and the Education Act 1944.

In practice, the view that failure to attend school is in itself sufficient evidence of need for care and control has been shared by many local authorities who choose to pursue cases through the courts on the grounds of non-attendance alone: in effect, the absence of a full-time education is seen as evidence of a lack of care, while failure by the parents to enforce their child's regular school attendance is seen to signify their inability to exert control.

Examination of the implementation of the legislation indicates a significant variation in the number of prosecutions, a variation not matched by fluctuations in attendance rates. In 1954, for example, there were 750 juvenile cases for non-attendance (Anon 1955), compared with 2,230 in 1980 (Reid 1987) of which 972 resulted in a care order being made (Pratt 1983). This overall increase occurred despite (or perhaps because of?) the Children and Young Persons Act 1969. The philosophy underpinning this Act was that children should not be divided into categories of deserving and undeserving but that all children in trouble should be seen as being in need of care, that the 'delinquent' and 'non-delinquent' should be treated alike. The 1969 CYPA, while apparently liberal in its philosophy, may have had the effect of 'widening the net', that is, of drawing into the formal systems of care and custody those truants who would previously have been seen simply as miscreants. And insofar as this net widening did occur it would have been at the same time that the move towards de-institutionalization was resulting in many care institutions being closed. Consequently, children placed in care were more frequently fostered (Frost and Stein 1989) or allowed to remain at home under social work supervision.

The result of both these trends has been that many young people have appeared in juvenile court merely on the grounds of school non-attendance, and have become subject to supervision orders or care orders (though often while being allowed to remain at home). In terms of gender, it is interesting to note that while the proportion of girls and young women appearing in juvenile court on *criminal* charges remains low, there are roughly equal proportions of females and males appearing in juvenile court on the grounds of truancy. Of those aged thirteen to fifteen years, for example, approximately equal numbers appear in court for truancy, while those prosecuted for offences show a proportion of boys to girls of about ten to one (Berg 1980). Thus, a purportedly 'welfare' measure has often been implemented in such a way that it was experienced as punitive; truants removed from home under a care order could be institutionalized for a longer period than if they had committed an offence (Pratt 1983). Furthermore, some areas of the country, for example Leeds during part of the 1980s, adopted a system of adjournments of juvenile attendance cases, a procedure justified by Berg *et al.* (1988) as being provided for by Section 20 of the Magistrates' Courts Rules 1970, but the legality of which is questioned by Pratt (1983). Many commentators (e.g. Pratt 1983; Grenville 1988; Harris 1989) interpret this adjournment system as being deliberately coercive and Galloway, for example, condemns 'this consciously primitive use [of legislation, which] was neither intended nor anticipated by the authors of the 1969 Children and Young Person's Act' (Galloway 1985: 110).

While such coercive legal procedures were called into question by critics, the researchers and practitioners involved in promoting the policy (Berg 1980; Berg *et al.* 1987, 1988) justified their coercive usage of the legislation by referring to two social ideologies dominant within the truancy literature. The first was the perceived link between truancy and delinquency, which they used as the basis of their argument that any measures to prevent truancy can be justified because of the consequent reduction in delinquency rates (Berg *et al.* 1983). The second was the perception of compulsory education as a necessary preparation for adult work habits, which provided further justification for their support of contentious legal practices: 'It is obviously highly desirable for children to acquire habits of regular attendance and to learn to conform with the routines of school life, so as to prepare them for work when they grow up' (Berg 1980: 145).

In 1983 John Pratt questioned both arguments, claiming first that care orders for truancy may increase rather than decrease involvement in delinquency, and secondly that, in the 1980s, far from education being the prerequisite for employment, it was too often the prelude to unemployment or, at best, government training schemes with no guarantee of employment at the end of them (Pratt 1983). In fact, in 1988 the most well-known adjournment scheme of all – that in Leeds – was abandoned, and juvenile court cases for school non-attendance are now rarely brought in Leeds (*Times Educational Supplement* 10 February 1989).

As stated earlier, the Children Act 1989 represents a landmark in child-care legislation, and makes several important provisions in respect of school attendance. Firstly, and most importantly, the Act marks a definite shift away from care proceedings on educational grounds alone. The government's own interpretation is that, 'Unlike the position under the 1969 Act, failure to educate a child properly is not in itself sufficient to enable the court to make a care order' (Department of Health 1989). The intention is that education supervision orders largely replace care orders, and that the emphasis should be on the welfare of the child (Berg *et al.* 1990). Education supervision orders (ESOs) will last for one year in the first instance and can be renewed for further periods of up to three years each, or until a child has passed the age of compulsory education. Persistent failure to comply with directions under an ESO will represent an offence on the part of the parent (Department of Health 1989). This change was prompted by the feeling that care orders were inappropriate under certain circumstances, such as in the situation which White *et al.* (1990) cite, of parents ensuring a child's physical presence in school and the child's subsequent refusal to remain on school premises. Under the new legislation such a situation is likely to be met with an education supervision order.

In Norwest, it became evident during fieldwork that education welfare officers believed both that in future care orders could no longer be made on education grounds and that education supervision orders would be the responsibility of social workers rather than education welfare officers. A careful reading of the Act suggests that both assumptions are wrong. Education supervision orders are *not* the only options open to the courts. A court may still make a care order if it deems that a child's intellectual development has been impaired because of a lack of reasonable parental care and control. In addition, parents may still be prosecuted under the Education Act 1944, and fined, but not imprisoned (Bridge *et al.* 1990). Secondly, the Act states that the local education department must *consult* with social services before taking any legal action, but not that social services rather than the education department should be responsible for the education supervision order so obtained. Thus, and as in the 1969 Act, there is an emphasis on welfare rather than punishment; but, also as in the 1969 Act, there persists the *option* of punishment. For although the emphasis of the Children Act 1989 is on a less punitive approach to school non-attendance, punishment is not ruled out as an option, it is simply 'hoped that the local education authority will in future take the more conciliatory course of applying for an education supervision order' (Bridge *et al.* 1990: 80).

In the field of education, the 1988 Education Reform Act shares with the 1944 Education Act the distinction of being a major piece of legislation, one likely to determine the form and content of the education system for decades to come. There, however, the similarity ends. The Education Reform Act sets out not only to reverse many of the fundamental principles of the 1944 Act, but also to remove the education system from its welfare state context and return it to its pre-war privatized and semi-independent status (Simon 1988). However, although the 1988 Act does not relate specifically to school non-attendance, attempts to include in the Education Bill measures to ensure that schools monitor pupils' attendance throughout the day were defeated in the House of Lords in May 1988, and this defeat helped to establish a political climate within which local initiatives on truancy began to flourish. In 1989 Westminster Council, for example, introduced a merit bonus scheme payable to head-teachers who were successful in reducing the levels of truancy (*Observer* 1 October 1989). National schemes soon followed, and the Department of Education initiated a programme to improve school attendance, encouraging local education authorities to bid for grants totalling around £2.5 million over three years (*Times Educational Supplement* 3 November 1989; *The Times* 16 April 1990).

Although the minister responsible repeatedly emphasized the concept of 'parental choice' in presenting the open enrolment provision within his Bill, some commentators have uncharitably interpreted this new 'freedom of choice' as being simply a mask for the government's intention to close down a significant number of schools, in the light of demographic change (Simon 1988). Maclure (1990) argues, moreover, that such closing of schools would inevitably lead to less, rather than more, parental choice. And, certainly, the emphasis on 'choice' bears an uncanny resemblance to Victorian governments' emphasis on parental rights, itself a precursor to the introduction of compulsory education, beginning in 1870 (Shaw 1981).

New arrangements for the financing of schools are closely related to the policy of open enrolment in that they ensure that funding follows each individual pupil, and allow for each school to manage its own budget (Maclure 1990). The consequences of open enrolment and LMS are likely to be that pupils will be seen to have 'a price-tag on their heads' (senior education welfare officer, Norwest 1988) and that schools will have to compete to attract them. Indeed, senior education welfare officers and education officers in Norwest commented that schools are likely to be less concerned with regular attendance and will just 'take the £1,300 or £1,400 or whatever they get for each child and...won't care what happens to him [*sic*] after that' (team leader, education welfare, Norwest 1989).

Finally, one major disadvantage of allowing schools to opt out of the state system is that they will have to forfeit local authority support services, such as education welfare and home tuition (Simon 1988). For those who do not 'opt out' but who, nevertheless, are responsible for managing their own budgets, there is a strong possibility that such ancillary and support services (including statemented pupils and special units as well as the education welfare and home tuition services mentioned above) will have to compete with other items of expenditure within the school budget, such as salary costs and building maintenance (Maclure 1990).

In 1989 Norwest education welfare officers were uncertain as to what their position would be under the new legislation. One speculated on forthcoming changes, stating her belief that in future education welfare officers might well be employed by individual schools rather than by the local authority: 'I think it will come down to that, so I'm taking a long-term view. I'm trying to make myself indispensable to the school, in the hope that they will keep me once all the changes come through.' By late 1989 no one had made clear how the education welfare service would be affected by the Act, nor considered the details of the service to be offered (for example, whether privatized or semi-privatized education welfare officers would still be empowered to take legal action against children and parents, or whether these powers would be devolved to other services). Clearly, the legislative changes are likely to have serious implications for non-attenders. Similarly, other (special) services, such as special units, hospital units and peripatetic teachers, which currently provide a service to school non-attenders, may also be affected (see Chapter 3).

Many of the provisions of the Education Reform Act 1988 rest on one major assumption: that an increase of parental choice, along with increased autonomy for schools, will improve the delivery of education services to the 'consumer'. While this assumption makes at least a superficial appeal to the 'common sense' of the market place, each element within it may be criticized in terms of the deeper processes it obscures (Simon 1988). First, the 'consumer' within this 'market' is generally assumed to be the parent, not the child. There is little or no mention of children's rights to be set alongside the repeated emphasis on parental choice (though see Stoll and O'Keeffe (1989), who in their research for the Institute of Economic Affairs Education Unit do make reference to the schoolchild as a consumer of education services). Second, the concept of 'parental choice' conceals the fact that parents are still legally responsible for the regular school attendance of their children (unless they can satisfy the education authority that they are being educated satisfactorily at home). Parents may still be fined for failure in this regard, and their children may still be taken into care on educational grounds, if they are deemed to be beyond parental 'care and control'. This element of compulsion is difficult to reconcile with the government's putative freely choosing consumer. Thirdly, increased independence and self-regulation on the part of schools must be offset against the likely increased cost of services within a liberalized market and the loss of specialist knowledge and services accumulated over many decades by local education authorities. Freedom must evidently be bought at a price!

Research area

Research took place in one of the English shire counties, with a population of around one million (Census 1981). The county, Midshire, incorporates a range of urban and rural areas, and is dominated in size and population terms by the conurbation of Norwest, which has over one-third of the county's population and is the centre of the area's main industries. Norwest, like Midshire, is a pseudonym and indicates an area comprising a major industrial city (population 250,000) and its neighbouring market town (population 117,000) (Census 1981). To the south and east of Norwest are several prosperous and expanding market towns, interspersed with small industrial boroughs. To the south-east lies a cathedral city (population 88,000) and a new town with its population of 64,000, representing an increase of 60 per cent over the previous decade. To the north lies a more sparsely populated moorlands area, with former textile towns and dairy and sheep farms.

In terms of distribution of the population, while the population of Midshire showed an increase of over 5 per cent between the years 1971 and 1981, the proportion of young people showed a significant decline (Census 1981). Thus the figure of 184,500 school pupils in 1975 contrasts with 157,900 in 1987–88. In Norwest the decline in numbers of young people was even greater than for the county as a whole, with 21.5 per cent of the population aged under sixteen contrasting with a county average of 23.3 per cent. A budget of £374 million was allocated to educate the county's children in 1988–89.

Figures on national trends of children in the care of local authorities show a decline in absolute numbers, and also in the rate per thousand of the population aged under eighteen years: thus, the reduction in numbers may be explained in terms of policy as well as demographic changes. The figures for England show a steady decline over a decade: 95,800 in 1978, 82,200 in 1983, 69,000 in 1985, and 64,700 in 1988 (Department of Health 1990). The rate per thousand young people has declined from 7.8 to 5.9 over the same period. The rate in Midshire, at 4.75 per thousand, was slightly lower than the national average (Department of Health 1988).

Of the total numbers of young people in care, research interest lay particularly with those taken into care under Section 1(2)(e) of the Children and Young Persons Act 1969, that is, on the grounds that they were not receiving efficient full-time education. Statistics for 1985 reveal that of the total of 69,000 young people in care in 1985, 2,300 (or one in thirty) had been taken into care on education grounds. However, of those admitted into care during 1985, 500 of a total 28,500 (or one in fifty-seven) were there on these grounds (Department of Health 1988). This clearly shows a significant reduction in the number of care proceedings brought on education grounds (under Section 1(2)(e) of the 1969 Act). Children taken into care under other categories of this Act, such as being in moral danger or being beyond parental control, also showed equally significant reductions at around this time (Department of Health 1988).

In 1975 in Midshire, 1,500 young people were in the care of the local authority, with around 750 of these accommodated in residential homes, the remainder being boarded out or remaining at home. In 1981, the numbers in residential accommodation had declined from 750 to around 440 (Census 1981). The most recent figures available give a total of 1,010 children in care in Midshire in 1989–90, but do not indicate how many of these were in care institutions (CIPFA 1989). For Norwest, the numbers in care in 1981 were 159, with eighty females and seventy-nine males (Census 1981). This equal distribution according to gender contrasts with national trends for the 1980s, which reveal around five young women in care to every six or seven young men (Department of Health 1987). Local authority residential care institutions in Norwest will be discussed in more detail later in the chapter, along with an overview of the juvenile justice and education systems in the area.

The literature on truancy

Definitions

In the literature on truancy, a wide range of terms has been used to cover school absenteeism, including 'school refusal', 'school phobia' and 'truancy'. Some studies exclude parentally condoned absences from their definition of truancy (Tyerman 1968), while others (along with some government reports) include this form of absence within the category of truancy (Pack 1977; Galloway 1985). Berg *et al.* (1978a), for example, draw heavily on a psychological model in defining the various categories of truancy, that is, truancy serious enough to result in a court appearance. They outline three major categories: 'clinical truancy', involving personal and educational problems; 'school withdrawal', characterized by social problems and condoning parents; and 'school refusal', which may be identified by a significant degree of social isolation.

In Berg's (and others') usage of the category, 'school refusal' is closely linked to 'school phobia' and indeed the two categories are used almost interchangeably by the same authors (Berg 1980; Waller and Eisenberg 1980; Yule *et al.* 1980). According to them 'school phobia' is characterized by emotional, behavioural or psychological problems in connection with school attendance, and is usually dealt with medically, by a range of behavioural, psychiatric and psychotherapeutic interventions. In the same literature, a major characteristic distinguishing between 'school phobia' and 'truancy' is that truancy is associated with 'antisocial behaviour such as stealing, lying, destructiveness and excessive fighting' (Hersov and Berg 1980: 2). A second major feature is that the truant, as opposed to the school phobic, is culpable and may be defined as anti-social (Farrington 1980). Tyerman (1968) accepts the distinction between the two, but argues that the treatment of the two categories should not be very different: he observes that the 'school phobic' is likely to be perceived more sympathetically but argues that children absent from school for whatever reason should be dealt with in a similar fashion.

Both of the foregoing usages of 'school phobia' and 'truancy' are based on a pathological model, that non-attenders are either 'mad' ('phobic' and therefore psychologically disturbed) or 'bad' ('truant-delinquent' and therefore socially and morally disturbed). A third, more recent, category, the 'sad' or 'truant-as-victim' category, owes its existence to the 'discovery' of physical and sexual abuse and neglect, beginning in the 1960s and continuing into the 1990s.

In this book we will be using conceptions of non-attendance at school that relate not to the type of *person* the non-attending school student is seen to be but to the way in which the *non-attendance* is perceived by the different people involved in its production as a social phenomenon (rather than a behavioural category). Thus we have created a conceptual space in which the phenomenon can be discussed without the definitional closure that accompanies definitions like 'school phobia' or 'school refusal'; for such behavioural categories imply that we always already know what an absence from school really means. By contrast, the definitional categories that we have developed to inform the analyses of Chapters 3 and 4, which we list below, relate school absences to the myriad sets of relationships wherein they are variously defined (or not), legitimated (or not) or responded to (or not). By use of such processual and relational definitions, we hope to avoid reducing non-attendance at school to a unicausal and teleological pathology (the symptom 'school refusal' is seen as a cause whereby school refusal causes school refusal!) and, instead, retain the phenomenon's processual and relational features. This strategy has *not* been employed so that we can claim that our analyses of non-attendance at school give a truer or fuller picture than do those of previous theorists. (We certainly have not wished to replace one mode of positivistic reductionism with another.) Rather, our aim has been analytically to construct, deconstruct and reconstruct some of the phenomenon's contradictions, continuities and downright puzzling features.

Processual and relational categories of absence from school

1 *Officially induced* Absences forced upon pupils by what are in effect 'lock-outs' precipitated by: shortage of teachers; teachers' industrial action; failure of school buildings to meet legal requirements in relation to, say, heating or safety; and disciplinary action towards pupils, for example, temporary or permanent exclusions from school.

2 *Officially approved* Absences officially recognized as being attributable to

personal or family reasons, such as illness, pregnancy, bereavement or parents' holiday periods.

3 *Officially illicit but unofficially condoned* Absences that are not officially recognized as being attributable to a legitimate cause but that are none the less not processed or recognized as illegitimate by schoolteachers and/or EWOs who, being the gatekeepers of 'truancy', are able to prevent the absence from being constructed as a problem ripe for further intervention. The likely candidates for such non-processing might on the one hand be difficult or disruptive pupils, or, on the other, middle-class or otherwise 'deserving' youngsters. (It should by now be obvious that the school absence of one and the same individual may variously be seen to be eligible for inclusion in a range (or all) of these processual and relational categories as more and differently constituted agencies enter the definitional fray.) It was frequently mentioned to us that increases in the amount of GCSE assessed work meant that increasingly pupils stayed away from school in order to finish their assignments at home. Although not exactly condoned, such absences were not targeted for educational welfare intervention.

4 *Officially illicit but parentally approved* Absences instigated by the parents (or carers) to enable a child either to assist domestically or to engage in paid work.

5 *Officially illicit but parentally condoned* Absences recognized and disapproved as being illicit by both school and parents but where parents (or carers) feel unable or unwilling to enforce attendance. Non-attending pupils in residential care often claim that one of the ironies of their situation is that although their poor attendance at school was given in court as a reason for their being taken into local authority care in the first place, social workers in children's homes had subsequently been as unsuccessful as their parents had been in attempts to return them to regular school attendance (see Carlen 1987, 1988).

6 *Officially illicit and parentally disapproved* Absences where at least some officials and the parents construe the absence as illegitimate and undesirable (though they may differ about the form official and/or parental interventions should take).

7 *Internal and illicit* Absence from lessons – even though the pupil may be officially recorded as 'present' at school.

Truants and targeted truants

For ease of expression we do use the term 'truants' in the text and when we use it without qualification we merely intend to denote the common-sense meaning of someone suspected of being illicitly absent from school. The term 'targeted truants' is used with more specific meaning and refers to non-attenders at school who do not merely receive one or two EWO home visits but who become recipients of regular EWO surveillance and threats and, in many cases, judicial intervention.

Incidence of 'truancy' (as specifically and variously defined by the studies cited)

Given the variation in definitions of truancy used in a range of research studies, it is difficult to cite 'truancy rates' that give much indication of the nature of the school absence recorded. Further, most truancy research findings are based on school attendance records, which simply record overall attendance levels, revealing little about individual attendance patterns or, indeed, about the reason for absence (Tyerman 1972; Galloway 1976a). Furthermore, they do not record 'internal' or 'lesson' truancy (Williams 1974). In research where other sources are utilized, rates of truancy may vary according to who is responsible for reporting the absence – for example, schools, parents, children, or education welfare officers (Fogelman and Richardson 1974; ISTD 1974; Belson 1975; Fogelman 1976; BMBEC 1977). Worse, in official surveys of absence from school, the period of the survey may vary from a day or a week to a term or a school year (DES 1975; NACEWO 1975; Galloway 1976a; ILEA 1981). Attendance rates vary considerably over each of these periods, though showing a general deterioration over time (Reid 1985). Reported attendance rates thus vary between 85 and 92 per cent, while the largest official survey, the National Child Development Study, gives national attendance rates of 89.4 per cent (autumn 1972) and 87.5 per cent (autumn 1973). For an individual city there are the figures of 6.9 per cent (seven year olds) and 13.9 per cent (fifteen year olds) 'unacceptably absent' during the spring term 1977 in Bolton (BMBEC 1977). Attendance rates in 1974 in secondary schools in Edinburgh averaged 86 per cent and in Glasgow 83 per cent (Pack 1977). The National Child Development Study recorded unauthorized absence rates ranging from 1.2 per cent for eleven year olds, to between 8 and 12 per cent for sixteen year olds (Fogelman and Richardson 1974; Fogelman 1976; Galloway 1985). Galloway goes on to note that other studies estimate the proportion of unauthorized absences as varying between 3 and 75 per cent.

The most frequently quoted figure for unauthorized absences derives from a one-day survey of all secondary schools in England and Wales (DES 1975). This survey reported that 9.9 per cent of all pupils were absent on that day, and that 2.2 per cent of all pupils were absent without good cause. Thus 2 per cent has subsequently been regarded as the national truancy rate (Carroll 1977), although some consider it to be an under estimate (for example, the National Association of Chief Education Welfare Officers' own survey in October 1973 revealed a truancy rate of between 3.5 and 7 per cent (NACEWO 1975)). More recently, figures have supported the NACEWO estimate, with a three-year study by Her Majesty's Inspectors suggesting that 7.5 per cent of pupils are missing from class each day (*Sunday Times* 20 November 1988). However, the absentee and truancy rates were misleadingly conflated by John Butcher, the then education minister, when he expressed his concern over 'an average truancy rate of 7.5 per cent', without considering what proportion of total absences may be attributed to causes other than truancy (*Sunday Times* 20 November 1988). The Prime Minister, John Major, added further fuel to this debate with his claim that one in four schoolchildren are truants (speech to Conservative Women's Association national conference, June 1991). This contrasts with evidence emerging from the Youth Cohort Study at Sheffield University, which supports the studies cited above in finding that 6 per cent of fifth-form pupils were serious truants (i.e. absent for days or weeks at a time), and that a further 10 per cent were selective truants (i.e. absent for particular days or lessons) (Gray and Jesson 1989).

In terms of the age of the absentee, Galloway (1985) reports an increase in absenteeism from age twelve, peaking in the school-leaving year. In terms of gender, Reid and Kendall (1982) note that, at both primary and secondary levels, girls are more frequently absent than boys although 'illegitimate' absence rates are virtually the same for both. These higher 'legitimate' absences for girls (if accurate) may be explained in terms of differential gender roles, especially the expectation that young women will fulfil domestic commitments, along with the lower social value placed on the education of females (Belotti 1975; Deem 1978, 1980).

Explanations of school non-attendance

It is in the context of the economic and legal discourses discussed in Chapter 1 and the paramedical discourses outlined above that non-attendance at school has come to be defined as a problem, and that the overwhelming concern within the literature on the 'causes', and consequent 'treatment', of non-attendance has emerged. Reid and Kendall (1982) identify the late 1950s as the starting point for research into the causes of non-attendance, work at this time looking mainly at the social and personality backgrounds of non-attenders; only in the 1970s did attention begin to turn to the school itself. This 'explanatory' literature locates four major *effective* 'causes' of illicit absences from school: personality, the family, the community and the school; and one major *formal* cause of truancy, the introduction of compulsory education.

Personality
Stott (1966) refers to his 'Bristol Social Adjustment Guide' to substantiate his claim that truants are three times more maladjusted than non-truants. This theme is taken up by Tyerman (1968), who correlates truancy with 'unhappiness' and 'unsociability'. (For other works on this theme see Croft and Crygier (1956), Hersov (1973) and Seabrook (1974). See also Carroll (1977) and Galloway (1980), who argue that there is no significant correlation between 'truancy' and 'maladjustment'.)

The family
Many studies point to the importance of the 'family' in creating truancy. A

range of factors has been identified but almost without exception each of these factors conforms to the 'deprived-neglectful family' scenario. They include poverty (Hodge 1968; May 1975); un- or semi-skilled employment (Mitchell 1972; May 1975); un- or under-employment (Blytheman 1975; Pirie 1975); council housing (Tibbenham 1977); overcrowding (Fogelman *et al.* 1980); disrupted home lives (Reid 1982); and criminal parents or delinquent siblings (Farrington 1980). Dissenting voices are few, but include Eaton (1979) and Mitchell and Shepherd (1980), who argue that family background has little effect on attendance rates.

The community

A third school of thought explains truancy in terms of so-called anti-social attitudes prevalent in working-class communities (Willmott and Young 1959; Tyerman 1972; Galloway 1976b). This work emphasizes cultural rather than individual or family pathology (although of course the three types of explanation are not mutually exclusive) and thus draws heavily on the 'culture of poverty' thesis popular during the late 1960s and early 1970s (Lewis 1966; Roberts 1971; Rutter and Madge 1976). Such work, though often accused of assuming the superiority of middle-class culture and the intrinsic value of schooling, at least recognized the material effects that the dominance of middle-class culture can have on working-class people. Nevertheless, not until the mid-1970s did we see a systematic critique of the social control functions of the education system, along with an appraisal of such features of working-class life as youth subcultures of resistance to such regulation (Davies 1976; Corrigan 1979; Barton 1980).

The school

An explanation which became popular in the late 1970s and early 1980s focuses attention on the school itself, wherein are located most or many of the factors contributing to school non-attendance. Authors tend to emphasize specific aspects of schools, e.g. size of school, staffing patterns, administration (Fogelman *et al.* 1980), or else to point to wider processes, such as the educational ethos of the school (Rutter *et al.* 1979). Reynolds (1976; Reynolds *et al.* 1980) identifies strict discipline and control, especially corporal punishment, as contributing to high truancy rates, while Booth and Coulby (1987) emphasize the connection between the nature of the curriculum and disaffection among school students. While each of these four schools of thought focuses on different levels of explanation, they have in common the definition of 'truancy' as a problem. The first three concentrate on explaining truancy in terms of individual, family or community pathology. The fourth, while apparently more 'liberal' in its assessment of schools rather than individuals, and in its emphasis on the need for a 'caring' rather than 'controlling' school ethos, nevertheless continues to make (or indeed assume) a link between truancy and delinquency (Reynolds 1976; Reid and Kendall 1982).

Interestingly, New Right explanations of non-attendance signal a move away from defining truancy as a deviant act, although for very different reasons from those put forward by Paterson and Shaw below. Their explanations centre on the notion of the pupil as a consumer, a perspective expressed succinctly by Baroness Cox, who argues that truancy results 'from rational choice rather than social deviance' (*Times Educational Supplement* 3 November 1989). By this she means that the pupil as consumer exercises choices as to the quality and relevance of education provision: thus truancy is a rational, rather than deviant, response to an inadequate education system.

While much of this New Right theorizing is relatively new and thus largely confined to news reports (*Times Educational Supplement* 7 July 1989, 2 February 1990; *Guardian* 30 January 1990), the writing of some of its major apologists has been published by the right-wing Institute of Economic Affairs. Pre-eminently, Stoll and O'Keeffe (1989) argue that truancy, especially post-registration truancy, indicates that pupils are voting with their feet, and rejecting the education that has been offered to them. Specifically, they point to teaching styles, the liberal curriculum and non-essential subjects as central factors causing truancy. By way of remedy they propose that the introduction of the National Curriculum, the possible lowering of the school-leaving age and the replacement of the 'liberal curriculum' with more technical subjects for the 'non-academic type' would all improve consumer satisfaction with education and thus reduce the truancy rate. In providing the ideological basis for radical (right) reforms, writers such as Stoll and O'Keeffe are not only concerned about non-attendance at school, they are attempting to set a new agenda for education.

Four of the five types of explanation of illicit absence from school outlined above assume the intrinsic merit of school attendance, and few works have questioned why young people attend school in such large numbers. Only recently has more work begun to emerge concerning a 'pathology of presence'. Sayer (1987), for example, argues that non-attendance at school is a rational response to the education system, as it is imposed on young people. A more pertinent approach to the issue would be to question why anyone attends school at all! This perspective, posing as it does questions about conformity, is similar to that known in criminology as control theory.

Control theory assumes that people outwardly conform while they perceive it to be worth their while to do so, but that they fail (i.e. choose not) to conform either when the rewards of conformity are seen to be no longer forthcoming (as in times of high youth unemployment when a job can no longer be expected as the usual reward for completion of schooling), or when they calculate that the gains accruing from non-conformity are likely to outweigh the disabilities arising from either deviation or its ensuing punishment. Such a perspective can be useful to policy-makers attempting to locate points for intervention into socially undesirable states of affairs. We, therefore, will be using this perspective in Chapter 3 when analysing the rationality of young people's decisions to attend school (or not); and again in Chapter 5 when assessing, first, the effectiveness of schools in achieving pupils' attendance and delivering education, and, second, the inability of the polity in recent years to deliver the expected benefits of universal education.

Social and economic explanations of truancy as a political problem
While most explanations of truancy fall into one or other of the perspectives discussed above, during the past decade some writers have begun to put forward more radical analyses of the formal causes of school non-attendance. Paterson (1988, 1989), for example, locates truancy within the context of the social and economic underpinnings of the education system. Arguing that, since Victorian times, the state has identified compulsory education as being consistent with the training of an urban, industrial workforce, she traces contemporary ideas about universal education to the economic and social transformations of the nineteenth century. Similarly, Shaw (1981) considers the processes whereby the Victorian state began to intervene in formerly privatized areas of family life, particularly the education of children. Focusing on the newly emerging concept of parental rights to education for their children, she argues that this concept was introduced to provide government with the moral justification for the enforcement of compulsory education. In short, both Paterson and Shaw concentrate on the *formal* cause of truancy – the introduction of compulsory education. Prior to the legal requirement for parents to send their children to school the formal education of children was seen as a privilege of the rich rather than as the prime mechanism for the state regulation of childhood.

Policy interventions

Much research on non-attendance has been by concerned professionals, including child psychiatrists, social workers, teachers and educationalists, and the majority of it has been policy-oriented, usually including reviews of current agency responses, and/or recommendations for future changes in policy and practice. This research falls under the main policy areas of education, policing, legal intervention, education welfare and psychological/psychiatric services. Research in each of these areas is reviewed briefly here, with the exception of the legal context which was considered in some detail at the beginning of this chapter.

Education
As in many other services, education professionals are divided between 'care' and 'control' orientations, and respond to 'truancy' accordingly. 'Control' measures include the 'report' system (whereby *either* pupils report regularly throughout the day to a specific teacher *or* they have to obtain the signature of

the relevant teacher to attest to their attendance at every lesson which they should have attended that day) and exclusion from school. 'Care' measures include special units within schools, pastoral care and child guidance. While there is an overlap of 'care' and 'control' functions within most measures, a particularly grey area is the use within schools of behaviour modification techniques, such as contingency contracts. Brooks (1974) outlines the system whereby young people are 'rewarded' in a systematic and explicit way for behaviour deemed to be appropriate to the school setting. This and similar techniques call into question the usefulness of the most probably overworked and sociologically simplistic care/control distinction. Outside of mainstream education, special units may be set up to deal with non-attenders; Grunsell (1980) gives an account of a pioneering intermediate treatment centre in Islington, which attempted to provide a non-threatening environment for youngsters deemed to have been failed by mainstream schools. Other units take a less radical approach, adopting either an educational or a therapeutic perspective in dealing with non-attenders (Lloyd-Smith 1984).

Policing

Historically, the police have always been concerned with the policing of adults and children not seen to be in their 'proper' place (see Chamblis 1964, on vagrancy laws). Thus while unemployed adults have perennially come under police scrutiny, since the late nineteenth century all children not at school during the day have, if seen by the police, been suspected of the status crime of truancy (see Humphries 1981).

Grimshaw and Pratt (1984) assess the police practice of 'truancy patrols' in some areas of Britain in the light of the extensive literature dealing with the supposed link between truancy and delinquency. They note in particular the link between positivist research on truancy and the formulation of official policy during the late 1970s and early 1980s (Tennent 1971; May 1975; Farrington 1980), and argue that the acceptance of a causal link between truancy and delinquency leads to the assumption that preventing truancy will also prevent delinquency, and therefore that enforcing school attendance is desirable as it brings about criminal justice as well as educational benefits (Berg *et al.* 1988). This assumption is clearly shared by policy-makers responsible for the implementation of police truancy patrols. Grimshaw and Pratt (1984) note that such truancy patrols are usually defined as crime prevention exercises, although they argue that the evidence to suggest that young people are in fact safeguarded from involvement in criminal activities or protected from moral danger is inconclusive at best. Despite such criticisms, police truancy patrols enjoyed renewed popularity during the late 1980s in several parts of the country and the case of Birmingham is discussed later in this chapter and also in Chapter 3.

Education welfare

The education welfare service (EWS) is one of the most under-researched of the welfare and educational services, reflecting perhaps its marginal position, located fully within neither the education nor the social services (MacMillan 1977; Robinson 1978). Even within the fairly extensive truancy literature, many authors make only passing reference to the service, despite the central role it plays in dealing with school non-attenders (Tyerman 1968; Hersov and Berg 1980; Reid 1985). This situation has begun to change only during the past decade, with authors such as Green (1980) and Galloway (1985) devoting fuller attention to the service.

Although it has been in existence for over a century, and despite the Ralphs Report's (1973) call for systematic development of the service, the EWS has always developed in piecemeal fashion, and its workers remain notably lacking in professional training, status and rewards. Yet, despite their lack of high professional status, individual officers have had considerable power in dealing with non-attenders, most notably in bringing cases before the courts under the legal procedures described earlier in this chapter.

Historically, the main task of the EWS has been to ensure regular school attendance, although from its earliest days there has also been a welfare function of providing aid to poor families (MacMillan 1977). Emphasis on this welfare role has increased steadily throughout the twentieth century, to the point where some services refer to themselves as 'education social workers' (see, for example, Grimshaw and Pratt (1987) on the case of Sheffield). However, this was not the case in Norwest, where a more traditional EWS was retained with officers carrying out both social work and policing functions (Wardhaugh 1990). The potential for contradictions between these two roles leads into the 'care versus control' debate familiar to commentators on legal and social policy, especially in relation to juveniles (Pearson 1975; Harris and Webb 1987; Hudson 1987; Morris and Giller 1987).

Child psychological and psychiatric services

These services are concerned more with youngsters defined as 'school phobics' than those categorized as 'truants'. They developed from the 1930s onwards, with a significant growth period during the 1960s and 1970s (Broadwin 1932; Johnson *et al*. 1941; Coolidge *et al*. 1957; Blagg 1987). While they have developed under the separate umbrellas of the education and health services respectively, and while they hold significantly different perspectives in some respects, the child psychological and psychiatric services do share certain assumptions and techniques. Both assume the unvarying appropriateness of the education system to all pupils, ascribing any reluctance to attend school to some personal or family trauma or dysfunction; and each relies on a variety of interventions, based on behavioural or psycho-dynamic models, including treatments such as 'desensitization' (gradual exposure to the feared object, in this case school) and 'flooding' (over-exposure to the same feared object) (Blagg 1987).

The interactions between the psychological and psychiatric services and other agencies concerned with school non-attendance will be explored in Chapters 3 and 4.

Truancy–delinquency link

Grimshaw and Pratt (1984) note that much research on truancy has had an institutional setting, often judicial or custodial, and that this has contributed to the establishment of a relationship (either causal or statistical) between truancy and delinquency. They question the evidence of a causal relationship, and point to the importance of definitions and selections. However, the reality of the truancy–delinquency relationship has been widely accepted, and has been influential particularly in policing practices – for example in the establishment of special patrols, and in inter-agency cooperation – the assumption being that the prevention of truancy is also a prevention of delinquency (on the link between truancy and delinquency/deviant adulthood see Tennent 1971; Tyrer and Tyrer 1974; Rutter and Madge 1976; Farrington 1980). Grimshaw and Pratt (1984) argue that even if there is an association between truancy and delinquency, there is not necessarily a causal link: instead, both 'truancy' and 'delinquency' may equally well be functions of some external factor, such as socio-economic background. Rather than adopt individual or cultural pathology models they look for more structural explanations, located in the social, political and education systems.

Much of the 'truancy' literature is descriptive and policy-oriented, and is largely unconnected to a wider sociological analysis. Writers are concerned overwhelmingly with the 'causes' of, and appropriate 'solutions' to, truancy, locating their debate within these narrow confines and largely ignoring the wider social, economic and political context. Pratt (1983) argues that much of this writing is based on 'professional gossip', common-sense assumptions about the nature of truancy, rather than on any sound empirical research (Tennent 1971; Farrington 1980).

The bulk of the literature on non-attendance at school belongs to the tradition which assumes that regular school attendance is evidence of a healthy adjustment, and hence that non-attendance is pathological. According to the perceptions of the specific author, this pathology may take the form of delinquency and/or neurosis (Tyrer and Tyrer 1974; Rutter and Madge 1976; Berg 1980; Waller and Eisenberg 1980; Blagg 1987). Some writers within this tradition point to the failings of the school, rather than those of the individual child or the home in producing truancy (Galloway 1976b; Reid 1982, 1987). In addition, a minority of writers take into account subcultural theories (Hargreaves 1967; Reynolds 1976). But overwhelmingly, writers on truancy ignore sociological and criminological analyses of deviance. The few significant exceptions are: Pratt (1983), who provides a detailed critique of the work of

Berg *et al.* (1977, 1978a, b) and Berg (1980); and Grimshaw and Pratt (1984, 1987), who provide a sociological critique of truancy, emphasizing in particular the role of official agencies in defining and constructing deviance. Refreshingly, they challenge the assumed link between truancy and delinquency, and argue that policy-making should be based on a more thorough knowledge of truancy as a social phenomenon.

Paterson (1988, 1989) and Shaw (1981) write from a perspective that is closest to that of the authors of this book. Paterson (1988, 1989) locates truancy within an economic and historical perspective, identifying the factors which led to its definition as a deviant act, and tracing the ways in which the identity of the truant is constructed. Shaw (1981) analyses the need of the modern industrial state for universal, compulsory school attendance, tracing in this the origin of the concept of 'parental rights' to free education for their children. Shaw also debates the intervention of state agencies into the privatized family sphere, examining the checks and controls they are empowered to exert over children while acting in *loco parentis*.

Researching school attendance in Norwest

Research into school attendance in Norwest took place at a time when major changes were being instigated within each of the main services dealing with young people of school age: education, education welfare, social services and juvenile justice. Within the *education system* demographic changes (i.e. falling numbers of young people of school age) led to the amalgamation and closure of many schools throughout Britain during the 1980s, and Norwest was no exception to this pattern. Two of the schools in the research – Wilton High and Blue Mount High – had each amalgamated with one other school, while the third – Hareton High – incorporated four secondary schools. Teachers, parents and education welfare officers all blamed non-attendance rates on the disruption caused by such re-organization within the education system. At the same time, the education welfare service faced an uncertain future nationally. Some areas reduced the extent of the service provided and then integrated the EWS with social services departments, or even abolished it altogether (*The Times* 16 April 1990). In Norwest at the time of the research none of these changes had yet been made, although in the light of the provisions of the Education Reform Act 1988 and Children Act 1989 the service still faced the prospect of radical change. In particular, EWOs expected to be affected by the new local management of schools (which would significantly alter the nature of liaison with the education system) and the 'decriminalization' of truancy (which would have important ramifications for dealings with the juvenile justice system).

In 1989–90, the management meetings governing the policy and practice of the service were re-organized in Norwest. The new chairperson expressed a three-fold commitment: to inter-agency liaison; to the more systematic collection of statistics relating to attendance; and to a reduction in stigma attached to non-attending pupils. While clearly occupying a powerful position, the new chair was nevertheless opposed by conservative officers who resisted the impetus for change; furthermore, he was also hindered by the traditional organization of a service which allows wide scope for individual discretion and thus for varying interpretations of official policies.

Before the research period, social services provision for school non-attenders was three-fold, and comprised residential family centres, intermediate treatment (IT) programmes and a community home with education (CHE). However, soon after the beginning of the research, all three elements of this provision underwent major re-organization, beginning in January 1989. The CHE was closed down, while the family centres and the IT programme became part of an integrated juvenile justice programme. Each of the three family centres joining the juvenile justice programme underwent significant local, and in one case national, controversy during this transition period. Two of the centres faced considerable local opposition to the accommodation of young offenders within the community, and one eventually transferred its residents to the other, and became instead a general family centre (*Evening Sentinel* 28 January 1989, 11 February 1989). The third centre attracted national attention as a result of its psychological and economic abuse of the young people in its care, and closed down as a residential unit pending a public enquiry (Levy and Kahan 1991). Some of the young people from the CHE were moved to the new 'community' and 'community support' units, while several of the teachers became part of the new juvenile justice education unit. These teachers established a small teaching unit for young people who had been excluded from school or who were persistent non-attenders; they also provided a peripatetic teaching service for the residential centres within the programme.

The transition described above took place within the context of a change in social services and educational philosophy away from residential establishments and the special units or 'sin bins', popular in the 1970s, and towards provision within the community. The move away from the making of full care orders resulted in the reduction and re-organization of residential provision. It also meant that the emphasis was put less on non-attenders and more on offenders: social services philosophy was moving towards the view that school non-attenders should not be taken into care, although it must be noted that Norwest adopted this position more slowly than other areas of Britain. There is also evidence that some workers in the education and education welfare systems did not share this philosophy and persisted in seeking full care orders on the grounds of non-attendance, an issue which will be taken up more fully in Chapter 3.

The difference of perspectives of education and welfare services is simply one example of many such differences between services: each has its own organizational philosophy, perception of the value of other services and typology of non-attenders. In Norwest there exists an inter-agency forum for discussion of appropriate intervention with offenders, but not with school non-attenders, an absence commented upon by the headteacher of Hareton High, who noted that 'We're very behind the times here, we had an inter-agency committee in Walsall twenty years ago, but no one wants to know round here.' This is not to say, however, that widespread *informal* liaison did not take place (as Chapter 3 documents in detail)!

Agencies visited and interviews conducted

Research contact was made with a wide range of agencies in Norwest, the main criterion for inclusion being that an agency had some dealings with non-attenders. The agencies contacted were diverse, but may be divided into three main types: education and education welfare; juvenile justice and social services, psychological and psychiatric services (see Table 2.1).

Within the Norwest education system four schools were selected, three of them (Hareton, Blue Mount and Wilton High schools) representing a major research involvement in terms of interviews with teaching staff (16) and with school students (15); the fourth (St Thomas More RC(A) High) served as a comparison. Two education welfare departments provided contact with nine officers. Interviews were conducted with each officer, and a total of twelve days was spent with officers on their 'rounds'. These days were spent observing the range of an education welfare officer's activities, including liaison with schools, home visits, discussions with parents and children on school premises, and

Table 2.1 Number of people interviewed: school non-attenders, parents and agency representatives

Category of interview	No. of interviews
School non-attenders	40
Teachers	12
Parents	10
Residential social workers	10
Education welfare officers	9
Juvenile justice workers	6
Areas for comparison (Birmingham, Leeds, Glasgow)	6
Residential care staff	6
Police officers	2
Education psychologist	1
Child psychiatrist	1
Psychiatric social worker	1
Voluntary sector worker	1
Total	105

court cases. Home visits with the EWOs were an important means of gaining access to parents for interviews and ten parents were interviewed. Further contact with the education welfare service took the form of attendance at four management meetings.

Three juvenile justice residential units were contacted which, along with three family centres and three children's homes, provided around half of the forty interviews with non-attenders, as well as interviews with social workers, team leaders and residential care staff. Access to young people in these centres was not denied by social services management, but was delayed on the grounds of the disruption caused by the re-organization detailed above. It was explained that 'Staff are under a lot of pressure at the moment, it would be best if you could delay your contact with them for a while. It's a very sensitive time' (Social services manager, 1989). Not only the time-scale but the order in which the centres might be contacted was specified. Such restrictions were accepted as otherwise access might have been denied altogether. But they were accepted with regret and in the knowledge that transitional periods like this can be of most interest to researchers.

Other areas of the juvenile justice system were less sensitive to investigation and therefore the changes in the intermediate treatment programme and the development of the education unit could be documented. A few interviews with non-attending students (3) and IT staff (3) were conducted before the re-organization meant that juvenile justice (formerly IT) programmes no longer dealt with non-attenders.

Despite the changes to the juvenile justice programme, and despite the change in social services philosophy, cases of non-attendance still appeared before the juvenile courts. The number of cases heard varied between one or two each week in a market town within the conurbation, to several each day in the inner city. Observation of two cases took place in each court and six interviews were conducted with magistrates.

Contact with agencies within the education/education welfare and juvenile justice/social services systems formed the basis of most of the fieldwork, while contact with the psychological/psychiatric services was less intensive. It was not a major focus of the research to document the careers of students generally called 'school phobics', nor to analyse the range of agency responses to them. However, while the focus was on 'truancy' rather than 'school phobia' (see pages 62–3 for our definitions) there is considerable overlap between commonly held conceptions of the two conditions, both within the literature and within educational and welfare provision. For that reason, interviews were conducted with staff within a child psychiatric clinic, a psychiatric residential and teaching unit, and the school psychological service in Norwest.

Observations made

While a great deal of detailed, qualitative material was obtained during the research contact outlined above, important themes of more general interest also emerged. In several different contexts is became clear that there was a significant gap between national policies and their local applications. For example, the national policy over recent years to reduce the numbers of young people in care has filtered down only very slowly to Norwest agencies, although the Midshire county as a whole has been more in line with national trends (Department of Health 1984, 1987). In Norwest there are still relatively high numbers of young people in care, any reductions that have been made being attributable more to lack of available funding than to a radical change in philosophy. Similarly, there may be an equally significant gap between local policies and individual interpretations of these policies. Within the education welfare service, for example, management expressed their frustration at the continued over-reliance on legal processes of some officers, and emphasized the importance of more conciliatory measures. However, the structure of the service was such that it was very much up to individual officers whether they favoured a social work or policing stance.

As well as variations within agencies there were also fundamental differences of philosophy between agencies. Each agency had its own agenda, which included the ways in which truancy was defined, perceptions of truants and their families, and approaches to dealing with non-attendance. While certain features were held in common (in particular a shared perception of the 'pathology of truancy'), differences of emphasis and approach were significant. This held true even for services within the same general field; for example, while education psychologists shared the medical model and some of the therapeutic techniques of psychiatric staff, the senior education psychologist for Norwest emphasized the differences rather than the similarities between the services. He opposed the hospital setting of the area's unit for school phobics (among others), favouring integration rather than separation from the community.

A second issue raised about the hospital unit is the question of the position of special units for non-attenders. Such units were popular during the 1960s and 1970s when the practice was to remove deviating pupils from the mainstream education system (Grunsell 1980). While these units fell largely into disuse during the late 1970s and early 1980s, during the late 1980s and early 1990s there was some trend back to the use of such units but no coherent national policy. Locally, this has brought about a situation where such units are used for non-attenders, but where the statutory services are unclear as to their rationale. Thus, teachers in the hospital unit were employed by the local health authority, and complained that the local education authority refused to recognize them as a school. Similarly, the juvenile justice teaching staff commented that, as teachers employed by the social services, they were neither welcomed nor fully recognized by either the education or social services departments.

The implications of such a situation for inter-agency liaison will be discussed more fully in Chapter 4; only one general point will be made here. Without exception, each agency participating in the research referred to at least one other agency as being largely or partly responsible for an ineffective approach to dealing with school non-attendance. The reasons most frequently given within this 'circle of blame' were that there was a lack of communication between agencies and that other agencies were either too lenient or too punitive in their approach. Yet it may be argued that it is perhaps not so much a lack of communication between agencies that leads to such frustration and blaming, but rather the fact that each sets its own individual goals. Recognition of such conflict should not obscure the fact that agencies systematically liaised over cases of non-attendance, regularly overcoming or accommodating their differences to ensure that at least 'something' was done to bring troublesome kids (and their families) into line. 'Blame the family' was the shared ideology which allowed *agencies* to cooperate, despite their simultaneous involvement in a circle of inter-agency blame; and despite too the oft-repeated assertions of *individuals* within agencies that given the incalcitrance of some truants the authorities could do nothing more effective than engage in a 'game of bluff' in the hope that persistent truants might be frightened into attending school more regularly.

Areas for comparison

Inter-agency liaison within Norwest may be placed in a nationwide context by means of a selective comparison with policies and practices in other areas of Britain. (See Appendix 2 for a full account of research contact with each of these areas for purposes of comparison with Norwest.) For example, the education welfare service in a nearby market town differed markedly from that of Norwest, one team leader explaining:

> We're very much more child-centred, really, Norwest EWOs belong to the old school, they believe in going to court whereas we'd only do that as a very last resort . . . they're mostly ex-services and the Territorial Army is very big with them. We did have some like that here, but they've been gradually squeezed out.

Her comments suggest that a change in philosophy from 'old-school' to 'child-centred' had been deliberately brought about as a result of majority support. In Norwest only a minority of officers were 'child-centred'.

At the same time, it is of note that Norwest education welfare service was not involved in more overtly punitive measures such as the police 'truancy patrols' operating in Bedfordshire and Birmingham during the late 1980s (*Times Educational Supplement* 10 March 1989, 21 April 1989). These patrols often took the form of police and education welfare officers stopping suspected non-attenders in the streets and returning them to school, although in Birmingham police officers alone were involved as the education welfare department refused to participate in the scheme. The patrols had the dual aim of 'preventing truancy and delinquency, and of protecting young people from danger' (Chief Inspector, Birmingham 1989). Critics have commented on the dubious legality of such schemes, and also on the questionable assumptions that truancy and delinquency are causally connected and that young people 'out of place' are necessarily in moral danger (Ekblom 1979; Grimshaw and Pratt 1984). Professionals are also divided over the issue of police truancy patrols with, for example, members of the National Association of Social Workers in Education likely to be opposed to the practice, and members of the education welfare service more likely to favour the policy (*Times Educational Supplement* 10 March 1989, 21 April 1989, 3 November 1989). In contrast, Norwest had no direct police involvement with non-attenders as such, the only relevant contact being in terms of education welfare officers' comments on the school attendance records of young offenders during juvenile liaison meetings.

Perhaps the best known truancy initiative in the country has been the 'Leeds experiment' of the 1980s, where juvenile magistrates and psychiatrists conducted a controlled experiment into the effects of various court disposals on the attendance patterns of truants. Again, questions have been raised about the ethics of controlled experiments within the juvenile justice system and the legality of the repeated adjournment system favoured by Ian Berg and his colleagues (Pratt 1983). In reply, Berg *et al.* (1988) argue that their procedures were justified by their success in reducing the truancy rate, and the concomitant reduction in the incidence of delinquency. Both of the juvenile courts in Norwest had heard of the Leeds system but commented that there was no intention of implementing a similar system locally. None the less, from observation of juvenile court attendance cases, it became apparent that in Norwest there were adjournments because of delays in obtaining school or social enquiry reports, or because of the absence of key participants in the case. In addition, there is some evidence that adjournments *were* used specifically to review school attendance, in a manner similar to that of the Leeds system. Analysis of juvenile court records in Norwest reveals that adjournments were made in half or more of all non-attendance cases, and that in a significant minority of cases (for example, 15 per cent of all cases in 1990) adjournments were made in order to monitor school attendance. (See Appendix 2 for further details.) Thus, there does seem to have been a *de facto* adoption of the adjournments system in Norwest, albeit less extensively and less deliberately than in Leeds.

At the other end of the coercion–persuasion spectrum lie voltunary projects which seek to provide support and advocacy for young people. In Glasgow, a Church-sponsored truancy project sought to bypass traditional procedures for dealing with truants and, by establishing direct and sympathetic links with young people, to return them to mainstream education. This project enjoyed good liaison with the statutory agencies, and dealt successfully with youngsters labelled as being among the most difficult and disruptive by the education and welfare systems. No such project existed in Norwest, a significant factor being perhaps that it did not share the long-established self-help traditions of Glasgow.

Norwest, then, shares many features with other areas, but also has its own individual interpretation of national policies. Geographically situated towards the middle of the country, it can also be located towards the middle of a spectrum of policies dealing with school non-attendance. However, as far as targeted truants are concerned, it has to be noted that topographically Norwest offered far fewer opportunities for determined non-attenders to evade targeting than, say, London, where shifting populations and multi-occupancy of houses make it much more difficult for EWOs to target persistent truants and their families.

Making sense of the data

Full transcripts were made of all interviews. These, running to nearly a thousand pages, were read and re-read innumerable times by Carlen and Wardhaugh in order that the reiterated themes, continuities and contradictions (in arguments; within and between agencies) could be taken up to structure and inform, first, the ethnographic analyses of the professional activities and discourses of those charged by law with regulating truancy in Norwest (Chapter 3); and, secondly, the modes of resistance to those activities employed by persistent and illicit absentees from school (Chapter 4). By claiming to have written an ethnographic analysis of the activities and ideologies of the truant-catchers we are not claiming merely to have described the substance of their professional activities and discourses. We are also claiming that by linking them to their structural enabling conditions in law, custom, and the prevailing ideologies of class, gender, education and schooling, we have attempted to understand why those activities and discourses take the form that they do take. (We had expected to link them also to racism but these connections were made only rarely and then tenuously.) Similarly, in writing of the targeted truants' modes of resistance to official regulation we attempt to understand how these strategies of resistance are in part shaped (and then later justified) by material histories of school re-organizations, school disciplinary regimes, poverty, youth unemployment and economic inequality.

We have not intended to be judgemental in any of our analyses. For instance, when in Chapter 3 we argue that the regulation of targeted female truants is structured by typifications of gender, class and race we do not wish to imply that most teachers, EWOs and social workers are any more sexist, racist or anti-working-class than the rest of us. Indeed, we assume that for most of the time most of them are not. None the less, what our analyses suggest is that when the chips are down, when the truant-catchers are at their wits' end about how best to deal with some youngsters, *then* it is that they invoke socially prevalent sexist, racist and anti-working-class ideologies to justify punitive and repressive modes of regulation. Not being peculiar to the truant-catchers, these archived ideologies are available to all of us and, if our analyses are correct, more likely than not to be constitutive of the actions and discourses of anyone who might be in a position similar to that of the truant-catchers. This is *not* to assume a determinism that allows for no social change and individual choice. It is to assume an ethnographic perspective that tries to make choices under-standable through delineation of the range of political, legal, ideological and material conditions within which decisions are made at a specific point in time and within a limited geographical area.

Finally, a few words are needed about empirical investigation and the case study method. In going out and talking to people, we worked on the assumption that empirical investigation and description of contemporary events is a desirable prerequisite to theoretical interrogation of political process and policy. Further, we worked on the assumption that what has usually been called the case study approach can, at its best, provoke questions which go beyond the particular case to a theoretical consideration of wider issues.

That is how we thought and what we did. Chapters 3 and 4 are what we made of it all.

3

MODES OF REGULATION

> Anyone who is absent for more than five minutes without warning
> will be marked down for half a day.
>
> (Foucault 1977: 178)

Introduction

Discourses on truancy and technologies for its regulation make one thing clear: non-attendance at school is a working class problem. Not in the sense that only children from the lower economic groups 'bunk-off' or 'wag', but in the sense that the brunt of the transcarceral regulation of school non-attendance is borne by a small fraction of working class parents. Their vulnerability to this specific (truancy-catching) nexus of control is determined first by their own economic marginalization and secondly by the discourses of pathological particularization within which the non-attendance at school of *their* offspring is represented as being both a major threat to social order and the *fundamental* cause of their children's poor job prospects.

As we have already seen in Chapters 1 and 2, compulsory schooling has never received the unambivalent support of all parents and children. From the time of its inception in 1870, the rule of universal school attendance has been more honoured in the breach than the observance, the relevant legislation having repeatedly to be enforced and re-enforced by a whole panoply of juvenile justice, education and welfare measures designed to secure compliance. These technologies of coercion have themselves given the lie to that official and middle-class common sense which perennially implies that 'schooling for all' is 'normal', 'natural' and always good both for individual and society. Yet the myth that 'schooling for all' is 'education for all' persists, and when, by voting with their feet, school students call into question the legitimacy of compulsory schooling, they also, implicitly, call into question the state's right to manage present relations of production and reproduction. Thus the regulatory agencies concerned with getting non-attenders back to school are engaged in a battle on two fronts: on one the physical task is to return the student to full-time schooling; on the other, the ideological prerequisite to the physical task is the normalization of schooling as a supposedly unquestioned good. To this end, the various agencies empowered to enforce school attendance pursue programmes of normalization which attempt to mould compliance to the myth of universal *education* by attempting strategies of exclusion from, and inclusion within, *schooling*.

The main arguments of this chapter are that:

● contradictions between and within agencies lead to alternating, discontinuous and dual policies of inclusion and exclusion from schooling, and to forms of tutelage and discipline which, at the extremes of regulation, also vary according to class, gender and race;
● the major conflicts between agencies centre on: disputes about appropriate models of truancy and the best methods for combating it, ownership of truants and costs of 'normalization';
● the inter-agency conflicts are manifested in circles of blame which result in the non-productive targeting of already-marginalized populations without achieving the resumption of effective school attendance by errant pupils;
● the surface contradictions between agencies are reduced by a general agreement and complicity about dividing non-attenders into two main groups for further targeting, i.e. (a) those who are seen to be amenable to the panoply of threats and coercive methods designed to return illicit absentees to school and (b) those whose non-attendance is seen as being symptomatic of an essential villainy qualifying for penal rather than welfare regulation.

The form that inter-agency responses to illicit absence from school took in Norwest can be represented diagrammatically as in Figure 3.1. In Chapter 4 the results of these contradictory strategies of inclusion, exclusion and selective targeting will be examined. This chapter begins with a description of the ways in which school student absenteeism was viewed in Norwest during the period of the research.

The chapter is in five main sections. The first part briefly outlines recent responses to truancy in Norwest. The second discusses the models of truancy causation held by the various agencies, together with their ensuing profusion of inclusionary and exclusionary strategies. The third part illustrates how truants and their families are targeted according to adverse typifications of class and race. The fourth part takes up from the second the theme of conflicts over ownership of truancy problems, and shows how these conflicts none the less result in definite forms of tutelage and coercion. We conclude the chapter by again looking at the differences between the truancy regulators, this time arguing that despite the plethora of their models of causation and strategies of control, the teachers, magistrates and EWOs we interviewed could find no

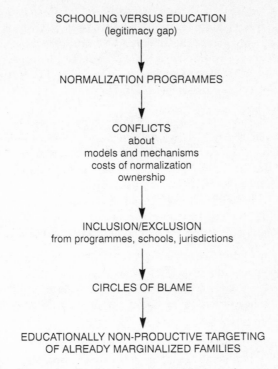

SCHOOLING VERSUS EDUCATION
(legitimacy gap)

NORMALIZATION PROGRAMMES

CONFLICTS
about
models and mechanisms
costs of normalization
ownership

INCLUSION/EXCLUSION
from programmes, schools, jurisdictions

CIRCLES OF BLAME

EDUCATIONALLY NON-PRODUCTIVE TARGETING
OF ALREADY MARGINALIZED FAMILIES

Figure 3.1 The form taken by inter-agency regulation of truancy in Norwest.

more fundamental justification for their regulation of truancy than that of the legal requirement of universal school attendance and the concomitant need to deter all who might be tempted not to comply with it.

Truancy in Norwest

The political concern over truancy which has existed since the introduction of compulsory education in 1870 has taken a variety of forms variously expressed according to changing economic, political, ideological and demographic trends. In the latter part of the nineteenth century, concern focused on the link between attendance levels and teachers' – especially head-teachers' – salaries (Reid and Kendall 1982). Psychological theories of the 1930s (such as systematic desensitization and flooding) found expression in a burgeoning literature on school phobia (Broadwin 1932; Johnson *et al.* 1941; Coolidge *et al.* 1957). In the 1960s, 1970s and 1980s the causes of non-attendance were in turn accredited to flaws to be found (variously) in individual personality, the family, the community and the school (Stott 1966; Hodge, 1968; Tyerman 1968; May 1975; Galloway 1976b; Reynolds 1976; Rutter *et al.* 1979). In the 1990s this cycle of concern is likely to come full circle with schools, once again, being managed on a local basis, and headteachers' salaries being linked, at least in part, to school attendance levels. Thus, at the end of the twentieth century, as in the last three decades of the nineteenth century, attendance problems will be both perceived and addressed at a local level, and national policy changes (Education Reform Act 1988) and demographic trends (decreasing numbers of young people of school age) will be seen as problems for local rather than national resolution.

In Norwest, during and immediately following the passing of the Education Reform Act, 1988, changes in national education policy were already beginning to affect the ways in which truancy was perceived and tackled. All local schools were faced with falling school rolls, and the education authority had responded with amalgamations. Nevertheless, some headteachers still felt the viability of their schools to be under threat. In addition, staff were faced with major changes resulting from the introduction of the national curriculum and local management of schools (LMS). The head of Hareton High complained:

> It all places an extra burden on the teachers, it leads to greater stress and higher levels of absenteeism. These changes are fine in theory, but they're often irrelevant to the needs of these children, especially when it's almost impossible to keep them in school in the first place. (May 1990).

To combat the threats to their schools posed by the new legislation local heads had adopted a variety of policies, in connection with which one of them commented, 'We are having to get to grips with the problem [truancy]. We are clamping down on them now.' The two key schools of the study – Hareton and Blue Mount High – had initiated major programmes designed to improve attendance levels.

At Hareton High, the new head had implemented many reforms to improve the general tone of the school and had also replaced an allegedly inefficient EWO with one more determined to tackle truancy. Indeed, the attendance incentive scheme, aimed particularly at first and second years and known derisively by them as 'the Mars Bar system', had been the brainchild of the new EWO (under it each pupil returning to school after a period of illicit absence received a Mars Bar as reward for a week's full attendance!).

At Blue Mount High School staff also worked closely with the EWO and there was coordination of teacher and educational welfare efforts with non-attenders. In addition, in 1988 the fifth form tutor had conducted an absence survey as part of the work of the school's attendance sub-committee. It found that 37 per cent of fifth-form pupils reported having truanted from school: 3 per cent once only; 26 per cent several times; and 8 per cent frequently. Attendance figures for the years 1985–88 were also collected, with significant variations being found according to the age of pupil and the time of year, with a yearly average of 80–84 per cent, including the extremes of 93 per cent attendance for first years in the first week of term and 65 per cent for fifth years in the last week of term. A general increase in attendance was shown in spring

1987, following the introduction of the 'attendance cup', a reward system for the form with the best attendance rates.

Whether or not Norwest schools admitted to a concern over attendance rates it was of course taken for granted that, as the ideal of universal schooling is enshrined in law and made manifest in state schools and in a myriad of agencies charged with enforcing attendance at them, 'something must be done' about those who failed to attend on a regular basis. But what? And it was over *what should be done* that there was inter-agency conflict. The different models of truancy held both between and within agencies were part-cause of the profusion of contradictory inclusionary and exclusionary strategies of coercion which, though they might in turn result in a small group of the targeted truants being catapulted into residential care or penal custody, allowed determined truants to 'play the system' and stay away with near-impunity until they were past official school leaving age. But we do not argue that because so many determined school students *were* able to be illicitly absent with near-impunity that the actions of the truancy catchers had no effect on them. As we shall see in Chapter 4, the alternating and confused strategies of inclusion in or exclusion from this or that programme, school or agency-jurisdiction that were directed at some families had at least two observable results: first, the engagement of truants' families in a number of resistance measures, some successful, some unsuccessful, which did not increase their willingness to accept schooling; secondly, the further alienation of children and parents who, already aware of their economically oppressed situation, could most have benefited from an economically liberating education – even though they were cynical about the promises of a normalizing school. It is our argument that for these families schools came to be seen as being *solely* places of schooling (rather than being at least in part places of education) and that the actions of the truant-catchers were largely responsible for the hardening of these perceptions. The contra-dictory nature of the policies and strategies pursued by the different agencies immediately stemmed: first, from their *differing legal remits* as outlined in Chapter 2; secondly, from the *differing models of truancy causation* that they held; and thirdly, from the *differing justifications for truancy regulation* adhered to (but very unsystematically and sporadically) between and within agencies. (The more fundamental conditions shaping truancy control in Norwest are discussed at the end of the chapter.) The differing models of truancy causation will now be discussed, together with their accompanying strategies of inclusion and exclusion and circles of blame.

Models of truancy causation

Chapter 2's 'literature on truancy' section isolated four major perspectives on truancy causation. Each perspective focused on a prime cause:

1 *Personality* Theories relating to variously caused and variously identified personality attributes of the child.

2 *Family* Theories relating to variously caused and variously identified features of truants' families.
3 *Community* Theories relating to variously caused and variously identified features of communities from which known truants were supposed to come.
4 *School* Both liberal and right-wing critiques explain truancy as a national response to an inadequate education system.

An additional perspective portrayed the formal cause of truancy as a political problem located in the nineteenth-century social and economic transformations that resulted in the introduction of compulsory education.

In Norwest all the agencies used all the models interchangeably. An educational psychologist's remarks on the range of causes were typical of the response we received when we asked what caused truancy. Referring specifically to 'school phobia' he explained:

> I don't say there is any typical case and I don't want to stereotype, but it usually starts with the kids who are used to hoodwinking their parents. I don't know if you have noticed but these kids are the absolute centre of things in the family and then it can either be an acute stress such as exams, or getting into trouble with the teachers and they won't go again. Or else it's a stress accumulator, a long fuse, a whole range of events . . . then again I could point to much wider causes, especially the curriculum. Schools just have to be made more attractive to young people. (Education psychologist, 1989)

Heads could talk about truancy being 'in the genes' or 'the cradle' and at the same time tell of their hopes of attacking it by improving the 'ethos' of the school. EWOs would invoke whatever model they thought might get them a positive result – and consequently brought down upon themselves the wrath of the 'psy' professionals who claimed that EWOs were too lowly (profession-wise) to invoke any clinical models at all. Of course, certain professionals in all agencies were committed more to one explanation or perspective than another, but what seemed most to decide the model of truancy causation used was whether or not a particular school, agency or court actually wanted to do anything about a specific truant. The targeted truants thus found that the definitions and causes of their non-attendance were open to constant change as they themselves were shuttled in and out of the various programmes, schools, agencies and court hearings.

Inclusion and exclusion

Given the variety of models of truancy held within and between agencies it is not surprising that professionals were prepared to try a variety of techniques to encourage or coerce truants back to school. At a more fundamental level they were divided about the purpose of enforcing attendance. Psychiatrists, psychologists, doctors and some EWOs tended to see themselves as merely deploying their skills and powers in the service of the law and did not question the fundamental purpose of compulsory schooling. By contrast, teachers, EWOs and some magistrates questioned the assumption that compulsory schooling for all would deliver education to all. Others were aware that interventionary action taken to enforce school attendance (inclusion) could provoke further marginalization of already alienated pupils by their reception into residential care (exclusion).

> You make the problem worse by taking the kid out of the system. I favour integration myself. (Education psychologist, May 1989)

> My overriding aim is re-integration into school, because I believe education to be generally beneficial. Regular attendance is 0.3 correlated with a good education, and a good education is 0.59 correlated with successful adult life, so it follows that school attendance is to be encouraged. (Child psychiatrist, July 1989)

Sometimes attempts to reintegrate students into school life were thwarted by teachers' wishes for their exclusion:

> Social services policy is not to take young people into care for non-attendance but the Education Department seeks care orders in some cases.... A number of schools are prejudiced against children in care and respond to even the slightest misdemeanour by asking the care staff to remove them from school. Frequently they refuse to have them back. (Residential social worker, 1990)

> Schools don't tend to recognize learning difficulties or special needs. They just see the child as troublesome. They are often relieved when the child won't attend school. (Child psychiatrist, 1989)

> We could do without Lenny in school anyway. He's a little so-and-so, he's all mouth. All the kids flock around him. (Teacher to EWO, Hareton High, April 1989. Lenny was later permanently excluded from school for disruptive behaviour, and his parents taken to court for his (and his sister's) non-attendance.)

One headteacher complained that teachers' attitudes were often at odds with his own best attempts to get pupils back to school:

> Senior management spend a lot of time trying to get kids back to school and when we do there are always one or two teachers ready to kick them out as soon as they come back.

Other heads took more direct action to exclude further those who had already excluded themselves. This was particularly so when ownership of the absence might be devolved elsewhere.

I'm going to exclude her because she has been absent for seven weeks. Her children's home don't seem to be trying to enforce school attendance. (Headteacher, November 1988)

Most frequently, however, conflicting strategies of inclusion and exclusion were brought to bear simultaneously on one and the same youngster – to the confusion of all parties.

EWO: By putting her on home tuition they've accepted she has special educational needs, for the rest of her school career.
Deputy head: The head wants her back in. *He won't agree to a change of school*... he thinks she's just a naughty girl... he insists she comes in.
EWO: But she's just not fit.
Deputy head: I know, but *he just won't listen*... he's given the girl and her mother a week to come up with a programme for her gradual re-introduction into school. (Hareton High, 1989)

What does the vast expenditure of human and financial resources invested in truancy control achieve? The end of the line for most truants is a court appearance, and this is the ultimate sanction available to the regulatory authorities. Legal action usually takes place only after a long series of persuasive, threatening and coercive interventions by a range of agencies. EWOs perceived this process thus:

There are problems of communication. They are referred to [the school psychological service] but we do not usually find out what happens. Of course it is a long-term process. It can take two months before they are referred and then they only have an appointment once in a long while, *and of course, all that time they tend to be out of school.* (EWO 1989, emphasis added)

We engage in a long process, we try a change of school, EWO visits and so on. Then you get to the climax of a court appearance. You have impressed on the child the seriousness of this, and that they will have to give an account of themselves. Then you get a supervision order, *then that's it, nothing happens.* (EW management meeting, December 1988, emphasis added)

We do go for supervision orders. You have to do something sometimes, *but I am not sure what difference it makes.* (Social services court officer, May 1990, emphasis added)

We can order supervision *but there's often not much point* (Magistrate, May 1990, emphasis added)

The implication in saying that there is 'not much point' in making supervision orders and that 'nothing happens' is that it is assumed that the only effective remedy for truancy is the full care order, which will remove a truant from his or her family. It is unlikely, though, that such a move will result in the resumption of regular school attendance. On the contrary, 'I would say 98 per cent of children in care, their attendance becomes worse after they come into care' (Residential social worker, family centre, October 1989). Thus it is that even after the so-called ultimate sanction for non-attendance has been applied, children in care become subject to still further punishment, both at school (detentions, being 'put on report' or 'in isolation') and at 'home' (being 'grounded', punished physically, losing privileges or being put on 'pindown') (see p. 89). What a care order *does* achieve is a shift in the ownership of the absence. Continual shifts of ownership of the truant, the absentee or the 'problem', combined with the manifest failure of all agencies to enforce regular school attendance, provoke the circles of blame which both constitute much of what is otherwise known as 'inter-agency liaison' and further add to the profusion of exclusionary/inclusionary experiences of targeted truants.

Circles of blame

> Off the record, there's a lot of negatives being thrown around, everyone's blaming each other. They don't get together to do something constructive. (EWO, March 1989)

> I'm not sure why you've come to us. I can see much more reason to start with the IT centres. They are the obvious failures. You should start there and then trace the kids back to the schools and other agencies. (Senior EWO, November 1988)

The education welfare officer's insight that 'everyone's blaming each other' was a consistent and recurrent theme throughout the whole of the research period. Occasionally, agencies denied that they had a problem; more often, they acknowledged the existence of one but held another agency – any other – to be responsible. Rarely, if ever, did an agency claim ownership of the absence. Blaming the 'others' involved four areas of dispute: financial accountability, hierarchies of knowledge, professional ideologies and aims, and procedures.

Financial accountability, or 'who pays?'

Conflict over who pays centred on the recognition of special needs, in particular the 'statementing' process. A statement of special needs consists of an assessment of a child's needs along with details of the provision an LEA intends to make in order to meet those needs. 'Statementing' is made under the 1981 Education Act (Childright 1988) and is an *official* recognition that a problem exists. It thus marks an important stage in a young person's educational career. Economically, statementing may require a three-fold increase in expenditure, from £1,500 per child per annum in mainstream schooling to £4,500 per child in special schooling. In a climate of economic restraint and emphasis on 'efficiency' this would provide sufficient cause for conflict even without the added aggravation of 'gatekeeping' by professions such as psychiatry and bureaucracies such as the Education Department.

> It's like statementing. I've had one child statemented but I should have had at least twenty, but that's where we get the conflict with the education psychologists. They will just say there is nothing wrong with the kid. This year I've had only one child statemented, but I estimate I should have had around sixty. (Headteacher, Hareton High, 1990)

> I have a letter from the child psychiatrist saying that he is at the low end of below average ability, but that he doesn't need a health service placement. It's so predictable, I knew it would happen. (EW team leader, October 1989)

Conversely, another child psychiatrist blamed schools for failure to recognize the existence of 'special needs'.

> Schools don't tend to recognize learning difficulties or special needs, they will just see the child as troublesome. They are often relieved when the child won't attend school. (Child psychiatrist, 1989)

> The Education Department refuses to statement our young people. If they did, they would have to recognize special needs and so they would have to provide special facilities and, of course, that would mean extra resources. They just don't want to face this problem. (Teacher, juvenile justice education unit, June 1989)

Hierarchies of power/knowledge

Given the lack of an agreed definition of truancy – legal, statistical or social – there is considerable scope for conflict between professionals as to entitlement to define truancy and to name the truants. The question of 'who knows?' is frequently linked to that of 'who pays?'

That there exists an easily identifiable hierarchy of power between professions was either implicitly or explicitly acknowledged by each agency. At the top of the hierarchy lies the court system, followed by the psychological services, juvenile justice, social services, schools and education welfare. An educational psychologist expressed his awareness of this hierarchy, and the conflicts it creates:

> They use us really. We have a history where when we worked in a child guidance setting with a psychiatrist, EP, and social workers, they just expected us to do all the running around. But really we have a different role to play than psychiatrists. The trouble is you have these hierarchies. (Educational psychologist, 1989)

At the same time even psychiatry could have its professional autonomy curtailed by the bureaucratic power of a local authority department. In such border disputes there was often the hint that decisions on state education were ultimately being made according to economic criteria rather than in the children's interest.

> The Education Department refuse to recognize our unit as a school, and they won't accept recommendations from Dr —, nor will they allow statementing to continue while they're with us. The child psychiatrist thinks it's because they would have to allocate more resources. And they just don't think social workers and medical staff are suitable as educators. (Psychiatric social worker, residential hospital unit for children, June, 1989)

Claim was met with counter-claim, the one that was always put forward as the clinching argument being that from the agency which thought that it had most knowledge of the student.

> The thing with schools is that they do not know the home background. They see two kids with the same ability and they wonder why one of them does their homework and the other doesn't. If they went into their homes they'd know why. (EWO, February 1989)

> Our EWO goes to these juvenile liaison meetings, but we feel we know the child better. (Teacher, November 1990)

Professional ideologies and aims

Closely linked to disputes over who pays and who knows are those concerning professional ideologies. Each agency, unsurprisingly, thought its own standard of professionalism to be the best and most appropriate. But, as we have already seen, there were differences as to the legitimacy of each of these claims, according to position within the hierarchy of professions. Thus, criticisms were sometimes made of those higher in status, such as psychiatrists:

> Well, they just have a hospital setting. You know if they took on board Blagg's [1987] work they could close down two wings of that place... he says that the medical model is just ineffective. (Education psychologist, referring to residential psychiatric provision for non-attenders, July 1989)

But it was much more common for the reverse to occur. Adverse criticism was mostly directed at the lowest status professionals, and education welfare officers were frequently accused of not knowing their place and thereby jeopardizing the work of the 'real' professionals.

> EWOs and social workers often attempt psychological work without really knowing what it involves. (Child psychologist, July 1989)

> Usually we work well together, but not always. Some officers want care to

mean [residential] care. I can only hope they retire soon. (Social services court officer, May 1990)

What you get is the professional job that we are doing being undermined by non-professionals. They can just assault kids, you know. They can go up to a lad in the street and grab him, and although they don't realize it, that's assault. (Psychiatric social worker, June 1989)

The internal politics of that department, you know what it's like up there, they are all involved in the Territorial Army so you just don't know who you are going to get, but I don't think that kind of approach is useful for this kind of job. You see, they are desperately trying to be social workers but they have still got this very low status. (Headteacher, Hareton High, May 1990)

Procedures

Inter-agency criticism was also widespread. It often contained within it fundamental disagreements about ideology and economic responsibility and, again, reflected relative positions within the professional hierarchy. For instance, on the aims, economics and procedures of social workers, two senior managers in schools had this to say:

The trouble with social services is that they are always changing. There is no real continuity and also you tend to find they just respond to a crisis. They are not interested in anything else but then, of course, they are seriously underfunded. (Deputy headteacher, Blue Mount High, May 1990)

It's not that I hate social workers, it's just that they get nothing done. I know they are under-resourced but there's not one of them man enough to tell the managers what needs to be done. (Headteacher, Hareton High, May 1990)

Similarly, social workers could complain about heads who were seen to be inflexible in dealing with individual pupils:

Colin did well with us for 15 months and attended school regularly. Then the new head at Hareton High introduced a new system of mixed ability classes and I felt this was the cause of his problems. He's of low ability and I think he felt inadequate in mixed ability groups. He started taking days off school and then one day a teacher found him curled up outside the classroom, apparently too scared to come in. So I asked the head to allow him to change classes but he said he was committed to the mixed ability system! (Residential social worker)

Other complaints about procedure provided a thin mask for deeper beliefs about hierarchies of professional competence:

EWOs are like an impermeable membrane. Once they get a case they never refer them on, and they should really, to other services who could deal with them better. (Education psychologist, July 1989)

But maybe some of the most scathing criticism was reserved for the contents of school reports to magistrates' courts, which, it was claimed, are 'awful, in that they tend to be extremely brief, make uniformly negative comments on pupils and don't offer any useful information on the context of each truancy case' (Magistrate, 1989; cf. Parker 1989; S. Brown 1991).

Finally, all agencies seemed puzzled as to how they should respond to the prolonged absences from school of some young women victims of sexual abuse. A social worker at one children's home explained that non-attenders with a history of sexual abuse tended to be treated differently by schools and social services to other non-attenders and, moreover, that this different approach frequently resulted in the schooling needs of sexual-abuse victims being given less priority than their other problems.

'Circles of blame' or 'inter-agency liaison'?

Blaming the 'others' was a consistent and dominant feature of inter-agency contacts. But although negative comments predominated, the overall effectiveness of working relationships was recognized. Furthermore, some problems of liaison were attributed as much to bureaucratic organization as to lack of communication or goodwill, it being admitted, for instance, that at least some of the difficulties between education welfare and social services stemmed from differential management-zoning of the same geographical areas. Ultimately, therefore, and operationally, the truant-catchers were able concomitantly to hold two opposing beliefs: that many truants are disadvantaged by inter-agency disputes between those charged with returning them to school; and that, despite its perennial operational difficulties, the inter-agency truant-catching machinery does grind on, day after day, to deliver targeted truants into the plethora of programmes designed for their regulation and normalization. To that end – of normalization via regulation – all of the truant-catchers were prepared to 'bend the rules' for the overall good of truancy management:

Our secretary insists it's all done right – by the book. But I know my families and I know what's right for them. (EWO, 1989)

I've made adjournments in about half the cases I've been involved with. I'm not sure it's quite correct technically, but it works, so that's all that matters. (Magistrate, November 1990)

Thus, an EWO might fear that:

The child gets lost in the system. The magistrates will give an order not necessarily based on the case but because of interaction with other professionals.

But a court officer could triumphantly state that:

> I have good liaison with education welfare. For example, the two cases that were heard this morning, we agreed our recommendations before the cases were heard. It's not collusion, it's more cooperation. (Social services court officer, 1990)

This last comment illustrates a crucial point: that, despite their mutual backbiting, the truancy regulating agencies *do* work together to catch and process truants. In so doing they also police, process and sometimes prosecute the families of targeted truants. These *targeted* truants are selected not primarily because it is believed that such intervention will be efficacious in returning them to school, but because their homes and families are seen to be especially pathological and in need of normalization. *In extremis*, agencies break the circles of blame by displacing culpability on to systematically selected families and putting *them* on trial.

Families on trial

The development of the personal social services has always had the policing of working-class families as one of its primary functions (Meyer 1977; Hall *et al.* 1978; Donzelot 1979). Operating at the interface between criminal justice, education and welfare, the truant-catchers have, like all others, engaged in the 'policing of families' (Donzelot 1979), developed a quasi-professional short-hand for distinguishing between 'good' and 'bad' families and 'good' and 'bad' homes.

Even those teachers and EWOs who did not exactly blame 'bad families' for their misfortunes could, none the less, recognize them with ease, knew in which geographical areas they were concentrated and, in some cases, saw the truancy of their children as being both culturally and biologically determined. Thus, between a magistrate's rather mild comment that 'very few truants come from normal homes' and a headteacher's wild assertion that 'truants are formed at birth, it's in their DNA or something', our informants provided a mass of evidence that, notwithstanding their inter-agency disagreements concerning what should be done about truancy, they themselves all knew 'bad families' when they saw them. And they knew too in which vicinities and social strata these might be found. (In fact, previous studies (Galloway 1985; Reid 1985) have suggested that students who are illicitly absent from school most probably come from all classes and backgrounds.) For in order to get to grips with the black hole of illicit non-attendance at school, the truant-catchers and other juvenile surveillance officers have developed a very fine web of operational definitions, which allow them to sift out the 'normal' from the 'pathological' family, and the 'salvageable' from the 'non-salvageable' truants. In constructing a geography of truancy and a morality (and pathology) of class and sexuality, they also systematically target certain marginalized groups (unemployed parents, gypsies, travellers, single parents, some victims of racist prejudice, and gender-deviant adolescents) as being always ripe for disciplinary surveillance and regulation – even before the reasons for non-attendance at school have been investigated. Once the non-attendance has been defined as illicit such definition in itself becomes justification for intervention into other suspect areas of the young persons' lives, especially into their sexual behaviour and general leisure activities. Thus, in Norwest we found that the manufacture of official truancy had been systematically facilitated by:

● the construction of a geography of truancy;
● the construction of a pathology of class and cultural difference;
● the construction of a gender/sexuality axis of normalization and control.

A geography of truancy

Education welfare officers in Norwest could, in describing their 'beats', give detailed explanations, diagnoses and prognoses of their clients' (and prospective clients') lives and behaviour. In some areas, truancy was unthinkable. As she approached the middle-class home of one non-attender, an EWO remarked:

> I don't think it can be truancy, not in a street like this. There must be something wrong, probably somebody's ill or there is a funeral or something – there must be some explanation. (EWO, 1989)

Yet whereas judgement was suspended for the middle-class resident, the denizens of council estates were more likely to be prejudged:

> You find a lot of parents are not committed to school ... they do not see the point of sending the kids.... You get that a lot on some council estates. With most truants you would be going into a working-class home and there won't be any books. Nobody in the house will read. (EWO, 1989)

> You find it is often a question of geography. Like in my patch I would say that 70 per cent of my truants come from just five streets. (EWO, 1989)

> People in [this particular area] do not generally acknowledge non-attendance as a problem. Local police say the problems are because of a high level of inter-marriage and this causes low IQ. I'm not sure about the IQ but they are very close-knit. You get negative attitudes to education going back three or four generations. (EWO, 1989)

Within the geographical area, a further sifting occurs. Not all non-attenders are targeted as truants. A blind eye may be turned towards the truancy of travellers' children (for a variety of reasons (see Worrall 1979); but see also Okely (1983) on the threatened prosecution of traveller children for school non-attendance); and some other non-attenders seen as being irremediably beyond 'saving' for schooling may be left unmolested by the truant-catchers so long as they keep a low profile and do not come to the attention of other juvenile justice agencies. (Children already in local authority residential care *because* of their truancy often fall into this latter category.) Two major groups *do* receive further attention and processing. They are: (a) those who are seen to be still amenable to the panoply of threats and coercive measures designed to return the illicit absentee to school; and (b) those whose non-attendance is seen as symptomatic of an essential villainy qualifying for penal rather than welfare regulation.

> All we can do is target the families and try to catch the younger siblings. Because you find it goes through families. If a kid stays away you'll find mother, aunties and brothers have all truanted in the past. (EWO, 1989)

> You have got some who will never get into school but there are others who are just sucked into truancy and really I do see much of our work as being to do with them, to try to get them into school. (Deputy headmaster, 1990)

> What I really want is to get back into school those who will benefit from education, and the rest, there's always some who will never come. I know you should never write off a child, but Christopher will just end up in prison. We should separate him and the other hard core cases from the rest. (Fourth-year tutor)

> I agree. Push them straight through the court system and take a more preventive approach with the others. With the good families a court case is enough – it scares them. With others, of course, they don't care. They're in court every week anyway. (EWO)

Thus in the war against truancy each professional battles for the middle ground, the joint effort being directed at a 'normalization' of the total population of young people of compulsory school age. Ideally, such a programme, if realized, would result in all eligible students being either in or out of school, with those definitely excluded being located in some alternative programme of disciplinary surveillance. However, because of the contradictory philosophies and objectives held by the competing agencies of welfare, education and juvenile justice, the sifting of the redeemable from the rest can take many months, during which time selected absentees from school will be exposed to the mix of the exclusionary and inclusionary disciplinary devices already mentioned and further discussed below. Foremost among those who bear the brunt of truant-catchers' contradictory disciplinary strategies are:

(a) those whose social structural position has been construed as infusing them with a morality which is pathologically antithetical both to schooling and to society; (b) those whose sexual activity or gender-deviant behaviour is seen as endowing them with a maturity which again is always antithetical to schooling and any of its programmes of normalization.

The pathologization of class and cultural difference

The claims of the Future are represented by suffering millions; and the Youth of a Nation are the trustees of Posterity.
(Benjamin Disraeli, *Sybil: or The Two Nations*, first published in 1845)

Sybil caused a sensation when it was first published in 1845. So vivid was its exposure of the gross inequalities of Victorian society – from the desperate poverty of the industrial workers to the gross and irresponsible excesses of the wealthy – that its subtitle *The Two Nations* has passed into the language.
(Anon: back cover of Penguin edition of *Sybil*, 1984)

That the phrase Two Nations is still as applicable to Britain in the 1990s as it was in the 1840s was made very evident to us as we listened to the characterization of truants and their families by the very mixed bunch of professionals involved in truancy regulation. One EWO graphically described the difference he saw between the world of his clients and the world of school:

I do not know if you remember Keith Joseph when he was in Social Services? He talked about the cycle of deprivation. I think that is very much what we have got here. It is just passed on from one generation to the next. I do not know how you break that. You see a lot of children are caught between the different worlds of home and school and they are in some sort of no-man's land between them. They can be on the way to school and just decide to take off. They cannot handle it. Like I had one case, the boy was going into school in clothes which they thought were unsuitable and he was sent home with a note. But I knew he just didn't have any other clothes. Some schools – say if they are known to be a good school – they feel they have got standards to keep up and the kids can fall foul of that. (EWO, 1989)

A headteacher also emphasized the very poor economic resources available both to the families themselves and to the schools which were supposed to provide them with the education that (see magistrate on p. 99) would lift them out of poverty.

The pupils we have here come from some of the most deprived areas in Norwest. The school faces problems of lack of resources, cuts in funding and this will soon lead to a reduction in staff numbers. (Headteacher, 1988)

Yet although several of the professionals acknowledged the economic inequality disadvantaging their clients, they none the less equated poorer
economic circumstances and different life styles with a culturally transmitted
social pathology which always already makes *them* forever different to *us*.

> Very few of them come from normal homes. The majority are single
> parents or they have a boyfriend living in and they are mostly on benefits.
> What can you do? (Magistrate, 1990)

> I would say half our kids are faced with some serious problem at home.
> Very often the parents don't care. In fact I would say that we don't have
> problem kids, we have problem adults and of course truancy is just a
> symptom of that wider division. In the typical home you will find the
> parents are incompetent. They stagger from crisis to crisis. Dad will come
> home drunk and mum will be pregnant again, or in many cases you will
> find there is a split home. You can go into some houses and there will be
> kids from three different marriages. For these kids school is just not
> central to their lives. There is so much going on for about half our kids
> that school has just not become a habit. They just don't take for granted
> they are coming to school. Every day they have got to make a decision
> about it; whether to come to school or take the washing to the
> launderette, or whatever else they do. (Deputy headteacher, 1990)

From interviews with the young people and the frank discussions held with
several parents, we know that the descriptions of the deputy headteacher were
not wide of the mark for the targeted families who become officially
known – and responded to – as 'truants' families'. What is more noteworthy,
however, is the frequency with which poverty and different household
arrangements were assumed to lead to (or be symptomatic of) an inferior system
of moral and social values.

> For months we had problems with the market. Lots of our kids were up
> there working full-time. We knew that they were there but we could
> never find them as they were protected by adults – they kept them hidden.
> It took us ages to crack that one. A team of EWOs got together and
> decided to raid it but it didn't work. They didn't find anyone. In the end
> we did crack it, because we got to the head man of the market and
> threatened to report it to the authorities. So you see, in an area like this
> the whole subculture is against us. We have got our value system and they
> have got theirs and they are just opposites really. They don't come
> together at all. (Deputy headteacher, 1990)

> The Potters' Holiday is very disruptive educationally. I am surprised it
> has not been done away with. Some exams this year will clash with
> Potters. Will parents care enough to sacrifice their holiday? (School
> teacher, 1988)

Condoned truancy is the biggest problem. There is a class feature. Working-class parents do not value education as much. They are more likely to condone truancy. (Schoolteacher, 1988)

Given, then, the recognition of a disadvantaging poverty and the con-comitant attribution of an essential cultural difference, *why* insist that young people attend school against their will? Three major justifications were advanced. The first two, 'truancy leads to delinquency' and 'education is a channel for social mobility', were predictable. The third was less expected, and although difficult to categorize might be most appropriately described as incorporating and subordinating the other two under a totalizing agenda for the normalization and diminution of social problems. Thus the magistrate who told us that truants were bound to get involved in offending, and advised a young man who had been brought to court that the advantages of education were always available ('I know, I went to night school myself. You just have to have a positive attitude and get out there and do it'), insisted in conversation with another magistrate that although truants and their parents were often economically disadvantaged they were none the less morally culpable.

Magistrate A: The trouble is, they are the people who are having babies, lots of them.

Magistrate B: The trouble is, they see no opportunities, they see no future work and they don't have very much in their lives. [To A] You see, that's the difference between what you are saying, which is the middle-class attitude, and those we see here, who by and large belong to the lower orders.

Magistrate A: But I come from a working-class background. We had very little money but plenty of everything else. My parents were something in the community. They had very high moral standards. It's what you make of yourself that counts. (Juvenile court magistrates, 1990)

If disadvantaged young people refuse to 'make something' of themselves then the normalization programme will aim to ensure that the new-generation bearers of socially constructed disadvantage are brought under a rule (universal education), the violation of which implicates the violators more visibly and damningly in the reproduction of their own oppressions. Certainly a sizeable number of the truant-catchers believed that their colleagues in the schools were not wholehearted in their pursuit of all illicit absentees, with one EWO seeing the label 'non-academic' as being class-related and yet another device for legitimating the delivery of a second-rate education to most working-class children.

We have to ask ourselves whether in fact schools want some pupils back. Truants are often disruptive when they are here. Teachers say 'Why did you bring him back?' (Deputy head)

I sometimes wonder why we bother. They should never have raised the school leaving age. Some should leave at fourteen or fifteen. What you have got is treating them all the same, trying to push non-academic children through the exam systems. (Fifth-year tutor)

I do not know what you think about the label 'non-academic'. You know everybody uses these euphemisms but we all know what it means and the kids feel they are unimportant. (EWO)

A couple of final quotations – from an EWO and a deputy head – provide summary illustration of the two major points we have made in this section:

1 The truant-catchers operate with one lore about the poor and another about the better-off.
2 The inconclusive, discontinuous and contradictory programmes of regulation brought to bear on youngsters suspected of illicit absence from school are directed more at the social control of an economic underclass than at provision of that equality of education only achievable as part of a programme for social justice in general. (Or, in other words, education alone cannot remedy structural inequality.)

At the grammar school, if children stayed off school, the headteacher didn't think of them as truants. Like if they went to Chester for shopping or something with their parents she would say, 'Oh well, they will be seeing all the architecture. They will be absorbing all that and getting something from it.' (EWO, 1989)

I would say that work on attendance is much more a social than an academic role. It's simply that I feel for kids when they are out of school, like up on the estate there is very often glue sniffing. No one tries to fight it anymore. And then there is the danger of drugs and alcohol. Really, when you've got all that it's safety I'm worried about, and academic achievement is by the by. There is one boy now just not coming into school and I'm afraid without that contact he is just going to get involved in petty crime. Basically, with the hardened cases we are social workers.

We do try to have positive policies on attendance. We give cups for good attendance to each form, and over the whole year the forms with the best attendance win a trip to somewhere of their own choice. The trouble is, that works against the bad attender when you get one or two in an otherwise good form. Like the travelling kids, they are very rarely in school ... the other kids go round saying 'those bloody gypsies are not in again'. And you see that goes against what we are working on in terms of equal opportunities and anti-racism and so on. (Deputy head, 1990)

It is, of course, ironical that the truant-catchers' programmes of normalization can result in an increase in the marginalization of, and prejudice against, those very minorities on whose behalf the various and so-called equal opportunities policies have purportedly been designed! But it is even less appropriate that, in the name of the amelioration of social deprivation, agents whose main task is the policing of truancy (and not the relief of poverty) should select for special disciplinary harassment those families already suffering from multiple disadvantages.

The construction of a gender/sexuality axis of normalization and control

In return for access to 'welfare', working-class women have been regularly called upon to open up their households to expert tuition and what Donzelot has called 'tutelage'. Much of that tutelage has focused on the regulation of sexuality. The deployment of sexuality as a mode of social structuration has been pinpointed and analysed by Michel Foucault in his *History of Sexuality Volume 1*, where he writes:

> The deployment of sexuality which first developed on the fringes of familial institutions ... gradually became focused on the family. ... In the family, parents and relatives became the chief agents of a deployment of sexuality which drew its outside support from doctors, educators and later psychiatrists. ... Then these new personages made their appearance: the nervous woman, the frigid wife, the indifferent mother ... the hysterical or neurasthenic girl, the precocious and already exhausted child .... And lo and behold, from the mid-nineteenth century onward, the family engaged in searching out the slightest traces of sexuality in its midst ... opening itself unreservedly to endless examination.
>
> (Foucault 1979: 110, 111)

> Mother is a prostitute, father is gay. No wonder the kid is in trouble.
> (EWO, 1989, talking of a five-year-old excluded from school for disruption)

Today, the sexuality of some young men and all young women taken into local authority care for a variety of reasons – often unconnected with any form of sexual activity – is still of overriding concern to their state guardians and assessors. The moral economy of welfare has, moreover, become more refined in its sifting and controlling of potentially deviant populations. Racist stereotypes relating to 'ideal' family patterns result in ethnic minority children being disproportionately represented in the care population (House of Commons 1984: CXIX). Indeed, the *Second Report from the Social Services Committee Children in Care Volume I* (House of Commons 1984) concluded that 'the unnecessary removal of black children from their families' was 'said to spring from "Eurocentric" views held by social workers about ideal family patterns and ideal family behaviour.' Idealizations of femininity are also operative in care proceedings.

A number of research studies (e.g. Casburn 1979; Hudson 1984; Webb 1984) support the view that:

> the majority of girls do not get drawn into the complex web of the personal social services because they have committed offences. It is more likely to be because of concerns about their perceived sexual behaviour and/or because they are seen to be 'at risk' of 'offending' against social codes of adolescent femininity.
>
> (Hudson 1990)

Working-class people claiming benefits and already in touch with social workers are much more likely than are their middle-class counterparts to feel called upon to show that they are 'good' parents by being censorious of their daughters' burgeoning sexuality. Already opened up to the social work gaze by virtue of their poverty, the familial relations of poorer people are also much more likely to be pathologized and subject to official intervention (usually by the children being taken into care) than are the more privatized family relationships of the better-off. Furthermore, the 'less-than-ideal' family arrangements of black people may be translated into racist stereotyping of 'black sexuality' once the young black woman is removed from her family (Lewis 1981; Lees 1986: 141; Chiqwada 1989).

Gender discipline is not imposed only on young women: normalization programmes for young men are also steeped in gender assumptions about masculinity. Thus although women defined as lacking 'femininity' are likely to be seen as a greater threat because of the way in which the patriarchal construction of the family is a necessary constituent of present capital–labour relations, young men construed as being less than 'masculine' are also likely to come under suspicion and surveillance. Staff in children's homes seemed particularly interested in the sexuality of their charges, both male and female:

> We think he is a homosexual. He certainly hangs around with other homosexual lads. He is very effeminate. (Social worker, about M. aged 15).

> He is not exactly gay but he is that way inclined. He is very lady-like. He is on the course where, if we are not careful he either goes towards being homosexual or on the verge of it. (Social worker, about P. aged 13)

But it was the actual or suspected sexual behaviour of young women that received most official attention, and given that there has been a history of females being disproportionately admitted to residential care on the grounds that they are in moral danger, this was not surprising.

For well over a century, the sexualization of all types of troublesome behaviour committed by young females has been a central constituent of the discursive technologies whereby a gender discipline has been systematically imposed on adolescent girls. The early attempts of criminologists to explain women's law-breaking in terms of their sexuality are well known (e.g. Thomas 1923; Pollak 1950). Yet the academics who appeared to assume that what goes on in women's reproductive or hormonal systems is more important than what goes on in their heads (or society) were not alone in their beliefs. Police, magistrates, judges, social workers, teachers and the administrators of the women's prisons have also formulated policies in relation to young women, which suggest that deviating females are at least doubly deviant – both as citizens and as women. As citizens who break the law or violate social conventions they deviate from socially acceptable standards of behaviour. In deviating thus they also deviate from their conventional socio-sexual destinies as women – unless they can be redefined as being mentally ill, a state which though always seen as pathological in men is too often adjudged as being *normal* for women (see Allen 1987).

The sexuality/gender/sexualization axis of social control, whereby deviations from *any* gender conventions are stigmatized as being evidence of a distorted sexuality (the girl is a 'slag' or 'butch'... or both!), is not only the site of a punitive regulation. It is also an all-pervasive mode of preventive regulation which can inhibit not only women's sexuality (see Griffin 1985; Lees 1986; Hudson 1990) but also their use of public space (Hagan *et al*. 1979), the successful presentation of self (Worrall 1989) and the acquisition of effective self and social knowledge (Cain 1989). While young women remain within the conventions of family, home, school, workplace or a male-related domesticity they are usually seen to be gender-controlled and are accordingly treated as being invisible. Once, however, they come to the attention of the authorities as a result of, say, aggressiveness, rowdiness, truancy or 'promiscuity', they are likely to be seen as being very gender-deviant indeed, and ripe for assessment and categorization as 'cases for care'. These assessments are constituted not only within conventional constructions of female sexuality and femininity, but also within individualized typifications drawn from class and racist stereotypes.

'By their class shall ye know them': official stereotypes of the sexuality of working-class girls in trouble

At the commencement of the research into school attendance we were already well-appraised of the fact that at least since the inception of state regulation of youth in the nineteenth century, sexualization of their conduct has been a constant feature of both the formal and informal control of adolescent girls. We were, none the less, surprised to find that in 1989 and 1990 so many female social work clients (both young women and their mothers) were still being defined most explicitly in relation to their (actual or suspected) sexual activities.

> Stephanie, for instance, is only thirteen and is known to be having sex with her boyfriend with her mother's knowledge. This means she is in moral danger and should be taken into care for her own protection. (EWO, 1989)

She will do all right, that one, do well on her back, because that is where she spends most of her time. (Social worker, about a young woman in a family centre, 1989)

I had a girl once – on her file it said 'This girl is inadequate, of low intelligence and has difficulty in keeping her legs together.' It was perfectly true, but it was on her file! (Probation officer, 1989)

We should not have been surprised. Parker and his associates conducting research on lay magistrates early in the 1980s had found that some of them also assessed young women according to their suspected potential for illicit sex.

That girl's had no intention of going to school. She had her story off pat – 'It's my nerves!' Then when she turned away and I saw her split skirt and high heels, I thought, 'You'll be on the game in a year or two.' (Magistrate in Parker *et al.* 1989: 102)

Implicitly, the young women were being defined in terms of what was to be expected of an unregulated 'underclass'. Indeed it was teachers' constant criticism of their personal style which had helped several of the young women decide that school was not for them. Susan had definitely had it drummed into her that good jobs were for a different class of person to herself.

I just don't bother with school now. Can't be bothered doing that stuff. You know, they don't like me hair, they don't like the way I dress, they don't like the earring in me nose – you know – jewellery and everything.... When I say I'm going to do clerical work they all laugh. They say 'You won't do that, not with that hair', and all this.

Kerry was also aware of, and had become apprehensive about, class barriers, which she thought would make it impossible for her ever to get on with certain types of foster parents:

Like these people who like going to restaurants for their tea and that. No, they got no hope of getting on with me, because I'm just not like that. I couldn't go out to a restaurant, I'd get all the forks and that mixed up. I'd prefer to go to the chippy. Can't do with it.

That the young women's self-esteem was low was not surprising, given the views of them held by some teachers. For instance, one teacher talking about a group of non-attenders explained:

They're a rat-bagging lot. The sooner they leave the better anyway. They are the sump class. They behave like the sump. (Teacher, 1989)

Derogatory remarks regarding the young women's class position were as frequent as – and usually linked to – remarks about their pathological sexuality:

The father works in the methane plant at the mine and that just about sums him up. He's got hands like shovels and a foul mouth. He'd land you one as soon as look at you.... I asked Mrs X why she had had nine children and she just said, 'He likes his drink and I like sex.' What can you expect of the daughter when the mother talks like that? (EWO, 1989)

In fact, social workers too often expect 'the worst' of young working-class women, whose interest in sexual pursuits is generally assumed to undermine their capacity for schooling and/or education. Talking of one young woman, a teacher explained:

She has now been excluded from school, school won't have her back. She has been taken into care. Her problem seemed to be her early physical maturity which led her into contact with boys to the neglect of her school work. This led to truancy and to other trouble, such as housebreaking. School seemed to be irrelevant – she prefers to spend her time with a friend, an unmarried mother, and will probably enter into early motherhood herself. (Teacher, 1988)

Moreover, and as Barbara Hudson (1984) has argued, whereas much behaviour seen to be peculiar to teenage boys is legitimated by discourses of adolescence that allow adolescent males a developmental space for behavioural experimentation prior to their emergence into adulthood, no such leeway is allowed to girls who engage in the same behaviours. In particular, young women are often faced with a choice between sex and schooling. Regular school attendance seems to be equated with the continuation of childhood status, while sexual activity (especially if it results in motherhood) is seen as being indicative of an adult womanhood, which is both threatening to the school system and essentially subversive of a young woman's desire to learn. Indeed, acquisition of sexual knowledge by young women is ofen equated with an undesirable and all-pervasive knowingness, which again is seen to undermine both their respectability and their femininity.

'With her being coloured you have to be careful or people will accuse you of being discriminatory'

While children from ethnic minority groups 'are disproportionately represented in the care population, the number of children of mixed parentage in care have been found to be *alarmingly* disproportionate' (House of Commons 1984, emphasis added). We only had one young woman of mixed parentage brought to our notice but certainly in that one case an EWO's comments suggested that she saw the sexuality of both mother and daughter as being of more relevance to the girl's absence from school than Leah's own contention that she had stayed away because of being bullied and called 'nigger'.

There are three children in the family who each have different fathers and Leah is a half caste. She has a lot of problems in the school. As for her relationships out of school, well, the rumours are that she's anybody's, though I don't know how true that is. The past few weeks she has been complaining of stomach pains and I wonder if she has got an infection – you know. But you have to be careful how you put it. It's a delicate issue and then with her being coloured you have to be careful or people will accuse you of being discriminatory. You know how it is.

Recognizing a 'hard-faced little bitch'

A constant complaint of young women in care is that, despite the state's supposed concern for their moral 'safety', they are seldom given informed and sensitive information or counselling about sexual matters or even the care and development of their own bodies. One reason for this may be that social workers and EWOs implicitly invoke the old Adam and Eve myth to conflate sexual activity with sexual and social knowledge. In our project we had innumerable references to 'hard-faced little bitches' whose sexual activity (or even experience of sexual abuse) was seen to be the source of all their delinquency. Indeed, even being a victim of sexual abuse was frequently taken as evidence that a young girl had been the sexually precocious instigator of the abuse in the first place! One EWO's references to Tracy and Melanie illustrate this process:

Tracy was raped by her uncle while she was still in primary school. Recently she's accused her friend's uncle of abusing her as well. She is sexually precocious, though…she's known as 'Miss Wet T Shirt'; I believe she won some competition.

Melanie was sexually abused by her father, though I'm not sure how far it went. He's of very low intelligence so I don't think he really knew what he was doing. Now if he tries to discipline her to make her attend school she will just say 'I will get the Social Services' or 'I will get the NSPCC on to you', so you see, really he is scared to do anything.

Refusing to take girls seriously

That young women's reports of sexual abuse are not taken seriously becomes less surprising when it is revealed how frequently the other problems of young women in care and out of school are trivialized. In fact, although the behaviour of both young men and young women can be viewed with cynicism by social workers and EWOs, it is the behaviour of young women which is more likely to be trivialized. The delinquent behaviour of adolescent girls is most frequently explained by reference either to a sexual 'maturity' that renders young women unamenable to 'reason' or to a presumption of a particular youngster's cunning, which renders her own definition of the situation worthless.

Oh yes, the girls are much more stroppy. They are more stubborn. You can talk to the boys and they will listen to you but once the girl has made up her mind there is no talking to her. They mature more quickly. They know what they want. (EWO, 1989, with two others present agreeing)

I told Kerry she is in danger of becoming a hypochondriac and will have to try to break the pattern. Last week she took Monday and Tuesday off, and on Wednesday she did a silly thing, she took a knife and cut her wrists. . . . She probably did that because she knew she had been off school and thought perhaps this would justify it in some way. (Social worker, 1989)

Shaming the 'slags'

I get on with lads mainly. Like I've been called a slag and everything because I get on with lads. (Kerry, 1989)

They call all the girls different names, on aspects of the body. (Sarah, 1989)

It has already been well documented by Griffin (1985) and Lees (1986) how young men control young women and young women similarly control each other through a process of name-calling related to sexual reputation. The girls were well appraised of this and mention was continually made of fights being triggered off by name-calling incidents. Even more disturbing was the way in which verbal abuse and shaming were incorporated into the discursive and disciplinary modes of EWOs and residential care staff. The following conversation between two female staff in a family centre illustrates the dubious logic which presently informs both the informal and formal control of adolescent female sexuality.

Social Worker A: They don't want her back at home, not at the moment. Her mum says that if her dad sees the love-bites on her neck he will go mad, so mum is just trying to prevent that. I mean that's fair enough.
Social Worker F: It's keeping them apart here, that's the trouble. I saw them out the window the other day, messing about. So I just called out 'Is it your turn on top then, Glenda?' I know I oughtn't to have said that but it worked, as it embarrassed them. Sometimes I sit on the landing outside her room because I saw David trying to get in there one night. I just sit there with my knitting. That annoys them.

Once families are brought under the surveillance of state officials they become subject to assessment and categorization procedures that usually result in their being subjected to a complex of informal and formal disciplinary programmes. Social workers, education welfare workers and teachers operate with cognitive maps that assist them first in placing absentees from school in the relevant structural and moral categories and then in deciding on the appropriate interventionary practices. These processes of categorization and normalization together form a disciplinary matrix, which, because it provokes even more resistance to schooling, fails to solve the problems of either those who would control (the truant-catchers) or those to be controlled (the truants).

In Chapter 4 we examine the modes of resistance adopted by families on trial for non-attendance at school. First, let us catalogue the techniques of tutelage and coercion whereby welfare, education and juvenile justice professionals attempt regulation of deviant school students by the contradictory and fragmented programmes of normalization that, via a concomitant push–pull of inclusion and exclusion from 'normal' schooling, signally fail to remedy (and may even aggravate) the problem of illicit absence from school.

Ownership, tutelage and coercion

> We have very few options. Our hands are tied. The EWOs do their best. They make all the visits and try to get them to school but there is a limit to what they can do. Even in care cases there are endless adjournments. (Magistrate, 1989)

Despite the many coercive devices available to the agencies responsible for the enforcement of school attendance, pursuit of non-attenders in Norwest was neither wholehearted nor systematic. In addition to the inter-agency conflicts there were inter-professional squabbles about the ownership of specific truancy problems. It was these disputes that enabled EWOs and schools repeatedly to postpone action on suspected or known truants until proprietorship of the illicit absence had been decided. This tendency to defer both the defining of the problem and decisions as to its ownership was also aggravated by the openly expressed beliefs of the truant-catchers, the teachers and the magistrates themselves that: (a) not much could be done about children determined to stay away from school; and (b) neither welfare nor schooling could in themselves compensate for the economic inequality suffered by the majority of 'targeted truants' families'. In such a context of disillusion concerning the ability of universal schooling to fulfil its promise of universal education, it is not surprising that even when intervention into a problem of illicit school absence had been decided upon, remedial strategies initially only involved a soft policing comprised of a tutelage of persuasion directed at the parents, and a series of in-school strategies aimed at the truant. The harder policing measures, involving the residential care packages supported by drugs, 'pindown' and corporal punishment, seemed to be reserved for those young people who had been targeted so early in their school careers that they had already been through the 'soft policing' machine several times before reaching their final year of compulsory schooling; or for those whose class and gender affiliations were seen to be so pathological that they had to be made an example of in order to deter the 'others'.

Ownership of the absence

Some heads take the attitude, 'Oh good! They're going into care, that takes the problem off our hands.' But that's changed. Now we say to them, 'Well, they're coming back to you tomorrow'. (Social worker, 1989, referring to local changes, involving the general reduction in the numbers of young people going into residential care, and in particular the end of the practice providing tuition on the premises of some care establishments.)

Something else we do that is not legal. We keep the child on the roll of the original school and persuade the new head to take them. Then if it does not work out they can just say it's not their problem. It's not legal but it's easier. It's common practice. (Senior EWO, 1989)

The usual inter-professional territorial disputes predicated upon both epistemological difference and conflicting material interest were, in the case of truancy in Norwest (as elsewhere), aggravated by the confused lines of professional demarcation laid down by the separate but overlapping bodies of juvenile justice, welfare and education legislation; as well as by a proliferation of the various major and ancillary bureaucracies charged with implementing the legislation, i.e. courts, police, social services and local education authority (Table 3.1 details the key agencies). Yet procedural rules that were cited as being barriers to what the relevant professionals saw as the required course of action were also gratefully invoked by teachers, EWOs and social workers who, in many cases, were pleased that the procedural rule allowed them informally to specify what should be done, secure in the knowledge that they themselves would not have to do it. Thus an EWO who thought that a truanting pupil would have been better off in school was none the less relieved that action taken by senior education officers had removed the responsibility from him.

Let me tell you about Joan Frazer. They sent her to the [psychiatric unit] but she ran away so they discharged her, won't have her back. She's meant to come back here [school] but no way is she fit for mainstream. I don't want to touch the case, unless I could get her statemented, back into the [psychiatric unit]. But they, the bureaucracy, decided what was best for her, though they didn't really know the case... they put her on home tuition which really wasn't suitable as she should be out of the house. But by putting her on home tuition they've accepted that she has special educational needs... for the rest of her school career. I try not to think about it, I don't want to touch it. (EWO, 1989)

At other times, the formal rule (1981 Education Act) requiring young people to be in school before they could be 'statemented' was invoked ('inclusion'!), resulting in their being hounded through the courts with threats that they would be taken into residential care if they failed to attend and then being immediately 'statemented' ('exclusion'!) or permanently excluded (1986 Education Act) once they did. Still others were put into residential care on the grounds that they were in need of control (Children and Young Persons Act,

Table 3.1 Nature of provision and powers of key agencies dealing with school non-attendance

Agency	Discipline	Therapy
Juvenile justice		
Church St centre (formerly IT)	Preventive work with offenders (and NA)	Attendance required by court order
Education team	Peripatetic service to YPAs. Tuition centre for NA and those excluded from school	Technically a legal requirement ('education otherwise') but rarely enforced
Young persons' accommodation (three centres)	Voluntary and statutory residential provision for NA and/or offenders	Centres have rights and powers of parents; police have a duty to return absconders; staff have right to enforce school attendance
Schools	Education and training for work facilities	Teachers assume parental rights and responsibilities during school hours; education authority (not schools) may take out school attendance order
Education welfare	Identify welfare needs of school attender and family; encourage regular school attendance	Provide basic education welfare resources; prosecutor in both adult and juvenile court cases
Family centres/children's homes	Residential accommodation for those on voluntary or statutory care orders; in latter case, including those on care orders on education grounds (CYPA 1969 S.1(2)(E))	Care staff act *in loco parentis:* like parents they have a duty to enforce regular school attendance

Table 3.1 Continued

Agency	Discipline	Therapy
Psychotherapeutic services		
Education psychology	Guidance and therapy with a range of school children including 'school phobics', and their families	With consent of parents can employ a range of psychodynamic and behaviourist techniques
Child psychiatrist	Psychiatric approach treating school-related problems as symptomatic of wider family disturbance; outpatient treatment	As above; can also prescribe drugs, including tranquilizers
Residential psychiatric placement (Whin Hill House)	Short-term placements in psychiatric hospital setting, plus education provision; individual group therapy	Voluntary placement requiring consent of child and parents
Courts		
Magistrates	Purpose is to remind parents of their legal responsibility to enforce regular school attendance	Fine, conditional discharge, imprisonment and/or direct to juvenile court
Juvenile	Ensure proper care and control of children, including the provision of education according to age, aptitude and abilities	Supervision order, care order or interim care order

NA: non-attenders.

1969), i.e. were failing to attend school, and then permanently excluded from school by the very headteachers who had supported their being taken into residential care in the first place. Sometimes action to get the child back into school would not even be considered until he or she had travelled round the full range of diagnostic services (psychologist, psychiatrist, hospital) and the file had come back to base laden with various diagnoses absolving their authors from any further responsibility. At this point the 'problem' might be handed back to the school and either the student would by this time be old enough to pass out of the system with no further supervision, or the whole process would begin over again with the truant now falling into the 'targeted truant' category and more likely to end up in court, residential care or perhaps (if he or she absconded) on the street. Even if placed in care, he or she would still be unlikely to arrive at school! The discussion between six EWOs of the cases of Sean Stuart, Basil Almoner and Carol James shows nicely how expediency, professional self-interest and the law itself can all be strategic in deciding who owns a particular truancy problem.

> Is Sean Stuart actually out of school now?
> No, so perhaps he shouldn't really be on the list.
> At some point we have to hand ownership of Sean Stuart back to the school.
> Yes, exactly . . . Basil Almoner is an Easter leaver, [shrugs] from my years of experience they just tend to slide.
> Yes, but the only problem is if he re-offends. He's been out of school for over a year now.
> That's what really worries me. We have to be seen to be doing something. Who in the end decides that it's gone on too long and something has to be done?
> I would just like to note that the law is that any child who has been out of school and is on home tuition . . . can leave on their sixteenth birthday and they don't have to wait until the Easter or May leaving dates.
> That doesn't apply if they are still on the school register.
> They also have to have been receiving tuition during that period, not throughout the period but at some point.
> Is it right, that Carol James's leaving date is 2001?
> Yes, she is not five yet. She was excluded from nursery school.
> So we can't just wait for her leaving date. We have to do something.
> [General laughter]

Before we move on to the professional tutelage employed to persuade parents to coerce their truanting children to attend school, it is worth noting that disputes over ownership of the absence (or truant) constitute another cause (in addition to the definitional issues discussed in Chapter 2) for statistics on illegal non-attendance at school being so hard to interpret. For sometimes no school and no agency will in effect claim ownership of particularly difficult absentees, even though, on paper, agency responsibility for the student may be satisfactorily accounted for according to the law. This is particularly the case with pupils permanently excluded from a previous school, traveller children, young people in care or newly released from a young offender institution and school-age mothers. Figure 3.2 shows the passing of ownership.

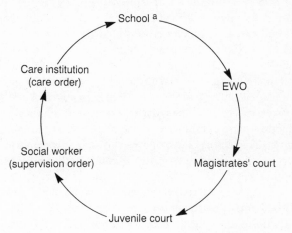

Truant–delinquent processing

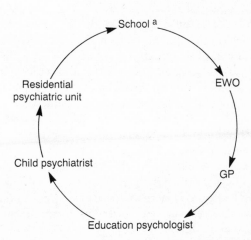

Truant–phobic processing

Figure 3.2 **Ownership of the problem of truancy by key agencies.**

Tutelage (the soft machine)

Although all of the truant-catchers could comment at length on the shared and disadvantaged class situation of their targeted illicit absentees from school, when it came to intervention in particular cases they individualized the problematic absence. For as we have already seen, not all illicit absentees were targeted for intervention, but only those who were selected, or constituted, as being particularly pathological specimens of their class or sex. Additionally, and as we have also seen, the mass of legislation under which the relevant interventions could be made is so contradictory, and its implementation so idiosyncratic to the various agencies empowered to activate it, that EWOs preferred initially to attempt a dual diversion – of parents from the criminal justice system and truants from residential care. Thus, EWOs visited homes, referred non-attenders to specialist agencies and threatened and cajoled for many months before deciding to take the parents to court. And in the short term they were often successful. The truants returned to school and the school played its part by providing combined carrots (Mars Bars at the end of the week for former truants maintaining improved weekly attendance; cups for whole classes with consistently good attendance records) and sticks (putting the students on report; see p. 84) to ensure continued compliance. However, whether pupils then ceased to truant for good depended on a multitude of factors beyond the control of the enforcement agencies (see Chapter 4).

If kids did start bobbing off again court action might still be avoided if the students played the system by not being absent long enough to constitute a case for action, or if the parents kept officialdom sweet, either by maintaining contact with the EWO or social services, or by playing the agencies off one against the other. (While there were no formal guidelines, and while this length of time varied between individual officers, many teachers reported the existence of a percentage rule of thumb, the consensus being that absences of 50 per cent or more of school time were likely to result in legal action.) If, however, absentees came to the attention of the police on criminal matters, or if they were stroppy with EWOs or at any of the assessment units to which they had been sent, the chances of their ending up in court were increased. Even then parents were often not fined immediately and endless adjournments both in the magistrates' and the juvenile courts aimed at (or at least had the effect of) preventing either the parents being fined or the youngsters taken into care. An EWO's comment on one case typified the general 'softly softly' approach taken by the truant-catchers, whose objectives in the lengthy initial stage of enforcement were: first, to assess the case; secondly, to remind the parents of their statutory duties; and thirdly to return the absentees to regular schooling.

I'm going to adult court with the case. I don't really want a fine, a conditional discharge would be great, to show them we can go back with them if we want. There's two kids and they've had good attendance since I served the papers. One of them I think I've scared enough so she'll never think of truanting again. (EWO, 1989)

Magistrates agreed.

> *Magistrate 1:*   Oh yes, I personally would be quite happy to go on making them [adjournments]. I'm not sure if its quite correct technically, but it works, so that's all that matters. If it secures 50 per cent attendance where there's been zero per cent well....
>
> *Magistrate 2:*   Of course, we always have in mind the impact on others. It is a game of bluff, it works if they *think* they might be fined £400, or that they might be taken into care.
>
> *Magistrate 1:*   Certainly, the whole justice system is a game of bluff – the same with schools, it's bluff. (November 1990)

With the good families a court case is enough. (EWO)

For the others, those who are already beyond the 'middle ground' where they can still be taught (and learn) their lesson, there is the hard machine. (Table 3.2 shows disciplines and therapies of the key agents.)

Table 3.2   Modes of regulation: the disciplines and therapies of key agencies in relation to school non-attendance

Agency	Discipline	Therapy
Education welfare	Monitor attendance; threaten and/or initiate legal action	Guidance and counselling
Schools	Punish irregular attendance	Reward regular attender; pastoral care
Social services	Regulation within residential care units	Supervision and guidance
Juvenile justice	Regulation with residential care units	Preventive approach to non-attendance; individual or small group tuition
Psychotherapeutic services	Behaviour modification, flooding, desensitization techniques	Counselling; group therapy; psychodynamic approaches; art therapy; play therapy
Courts	Punish parents (fines or imprisonment); take child into care	Guidance to child and/or parents; order supervision of child

Coercion (the hard machine)

Although the total of 66,000 young people in care in 1987 continued the past decade's downward trend in the numbers of children in care (Department of Health 1984, 1987) and although, too, the Children Act 1989 largely replaces care orders for truancy with education supervision orders, the option of a care order on education grounds is still available to the courts. Furthermore, recent research by S. Brown (1991), concerning the use to which magistrates routinely put the social (inquiry) information about youngsters, indicates that regularity (or not) of school attendance will continue to remain an important factor in magisterial decisions on whether or not to take offending youngsters into care. Certainly the magistrates we interviewed in Norwest were of that opinion, one of them commenting:

> New legislation won't necessarily change the way people think. You can bring in new laws but it will take a long while to filter through. It will be a long while before our practice changes. (Magistrate, 1990)

In fact, like all others involved with non-attendance at school, the magistrates believed that little could be done to make determined and persistent truants attend school regularly. Moreover, although they repeatedly complained that they had very few powers of coercion, when asked what powers they would ideally like, they could only refer to custodial or (with varying degrees of seriousness!) corporal measures.

> We should be able to send them somewhere they would have to go, like a boarding school. Just give them a short, sharp shock. (Magistrate, 1990)

> I would give them a good caning. That's what we used to do. (Magistrate, 1990).

In practice taking a child into residential care was the final sanction and, once there, previously truanting youngsters in Norwest might:

- not attend school again because social workers were prepared to turn a blind eye to their truancy providing they kept out of other kinds of trouble;
- not attend school because, although having a history of truancy, when they had attended school they had caused so much trouble they had been permanently excluded and no other school in the area would take them;
- not attend school because they had been 'statemented' as having special education needs which should be met outside 'mainstream' schooling;
- not attend school because of hospitalization (e.g. in the few cases of victims of physical or sexual abuse);
- not attend school because of absconding from care;
- attend school with the aid of drugs designed to modify behaviour or problems at school;

- be subject to various forms of 'negative incentive' involving the application of physical and psychological pressures designed to make them see school as a preferable alternative;
- be subjected to illicit corporal punishment for failing to attend school.

The main constituents of the 'hard machine' were therefore drugs, the programme known as 'pindown' and illegal corporal punishment.

Drugs

For several years there has been concern about the use of drugs to control the behaviour of children in care (see Taylor *et al.* 1979: 80; Freeman 1983: 172). During the non-attendance at school project, medically prescribed drugs were mentioned to us in connection with controlling young women's fertility and in helping youngsters come to terms with schooling. Fifteen-year-old Sarah's truancy had been part-cause of her admission to care, but, as is frequently the case with females, it was her sexual behaviour which had become a major concern of the social workers in the children's home.

> It was best she was put on a course of injections. We couldn't stop her sleeping with her boyfriend so we had to do something about it. She was another victim of abuse. She is very promiscuous, or at least she was. She probably still is, but does not make a lot of noise about it now. But we have put her on a course of injections anyway. (Worker in family centre, 1989)

Robert just could not 'take' school without pharmaceutical aid,

> Robert has a history of school refusal or school phobia but I don't think he has got a medical problem at all. Once he is in school he is happy enough but he has just got out of the habit of coming in. His mum is just incapable of getting him to school so the doctors put him on one valium a day just to get him to school to calm him down.

Although Robert was not in residential care at the time we were told of drugs being used to modify the behaviour of many children both in and not in care.

Pindown

For young people unwilling to enter into contracts 'negative incentives' were available to persuade them to attend schools. Church Street family centre (part of the juvenile justice programme), for example, had a policy of

> making the alternatives so unpleasant that they prefer to go to school. This ranges from a loss of privileges to going in the pindown room. In fact, we present going to school as a privilege, as moving on to an ordinary routine. It always works. Afterwards they're keen to have books, to return to school, and they're willing to enter into contracts. (Church Street team leader, March 1989)

'Pindown' they call it. You have to stay in your room with just your night clothes on, and you can't go out of your room. You have to be in bed at seven, all the lights out. It's dead depressing. Many people have put the windows through and all that.... The most I've been in there is two months. I run off once. I was on the run for a month and a half and when I came back they kept me under a pindown. That was bad, that was very bad. It doesn't really help because you just hate them, the people who've put you there. It makes you a lot worse and you're still not going to school. You know they'll give up in the end. (Susan, 1989)

On entering the Centre they go on pindown. For a week – no books, contact with other children, no going out. Only meals provided. It always works. Afterwards they're keen to have books, to return to school, and willing to enter into contracts. (Social worker)

Church Street is more controlling. They operate a 'pindown' room. It is totally illegal you know; the kids could complain if they wanted to. The procedures are very strict for juveniles in care. I think they are insane. If it got out! But presumably [a senior administrator] and all the rest know about it. (Juvenile justice worker, 7 March 1989)

The rationale for the use of pindown was that:

It's not punishment, more an opportunity for one-to-one contact with staff. They need a clear structure, and they want attention from staff, as they have lacked this at home. When they come here they're often upset or disoriented, and they need to calm down. It's easier for staff to communicate if they're away from peer group pressure. (Residential social worker, Church Street, March 1989)

Other family centres used contracts routinely but also used pindown as an 'ultimate sanction' if contracts failed to 'work'.

We hold family meetings and negotiate contracts to get the young person back to school. I see pindown as a fascist measure, really, and we try preventive measures first. But we have pindown as an ultimate sanction, and I think these combined measures work well. (Team leader, Hayfield family centre, March 1989)

These 'preventive measures' proceeded in four stages: a visit to the child's home or school; a visit by the young person to Church Street; inspection of the 'pindown' area; and a 'trial pindown' for an evening. The purpose of this last stage was to: 'induce the child to trust the social worker, who appears to rescue the child from pindown, then negotiates on their behalf with the care staff concerning their return to school' (Team leader, Hayfield family centre, March 1989).

This team leader did not go on to specify whether the therapeutic effects of the young person's 'trusting' the social worker, and subsequent return to school, outweighed the potential punitiveness of 'fascist' measures such as pindown. During the spring and summer of 1989 several social workers contacted us to say that they were disturbed about the use of pindown, especially as it seemed to provoke young people to abscond. And, although both males and females were subjected to this mode of control, concern was particularly expressed about the irony of taking young women into care on the grounds of their being in moral danger and then subjecting them to regimes which resulted in their absconding and thereby being at even greater risk. The fears of these social workers were vindicated. In October 1989 questions were raised in the Crown Court in relation to one young woman who had tried to escape from pindown. As a result the practice of pindown came to the attention of the media and in the autumn of 1990 an inquiry into it was opened (see Levy and Kahan 1991).

Corporal punishment

There's strict discipline in the home regarding school attendance, they all attend regularly now, even if they had problems in the past. I think that's up to the male members of staff to represent discipline, while the female members of staff provide a more caring role. (Team leader, Yew Tree House, November 1988)

'Discipline' took the form of corporal punishment in this home, and proved to be most effective in returning 'problem' attenders to school.

The staff can be moody sometimes. They punish us for the smallest thing and [the team leader] hits us all the time. I'm going to school now, because I'm here, but if I was still in Crossroads I would still be truanting. (Wesley, age 14, November 1988)

When I came here I found out that he was strict and he hits you and all that.... I don't like school, if I had the chance I'd still truant. (Paul, age 12, November 1988)

JW: Why do you go to school if you don't like it?
R: He hits us. (Robin, age 15, November 1988)

The use of corporal punishment in children's homes has now been prohibited, under The Children's Homes (Control and Discipline) Regulations 1990.

So, in attempting to divert truanting juveniles from court, care and custody the soft machine of tutelage sifts out the pathologically deviant from the 'normally' ('middle ground') deviant according to class and gender stereotypes of normality and then seeks professional cover by bringing the hard machine of coercion to bear on the recalcitrants. In Chapter 4 we will be assessing the extent of professional success in regulating truancy. Now we end this chapter by summarizing the legal, ideological and economic conditions and discourses that help to explain why the regulation of truancy in Norwest took the form that it did.

Why truancy regulation in Norwest took the form that it did

> Everything about us is unofficial at the moment. We have got no budget, no board of governors and no official remit of what we are supposed to be doing. We just work it out for ourselves as we go along. (Worker on one of Norwest's new projects for juveniles)

In describing their routine procedures, professionals working with juveniles in Norwest at the time of our research could indeed claim with some justification that 'everything is in the melting pot at the moment'. For although in 1989 and 1990 they could still only conjecture as to the changes in practice which the Education Reform Act 1988 and The Children Act 1989 would entail, the local Social Services Department had already embarked on a programmed re-organization of juvenile justice projects designed to reduce the number of young people in full residential care, while several schools were still finding their way as relatively new complexes constituted by the amalgamation of two, three or even four pre-existent schools. Yet, as the truant catchers ruminated on the justification for their push–pull policies towards illicit absentees from school, it became clear that although the philosophies, policies, procedures and practices of the various agencies might appear to be incoherent, the systematic confusion of truancy regulation was shaped by shared and fundamental legal, ideological and economic discourses, which endowed with a separate standpoint rationality the professional practices of the competing and contradictory agencies.

The legal conditions

> You are subject to the Education Act 1944 which states that you should be receiving full-time education appropriate to your age, needs and abilities. You are receiving insufficient education. You are in need of care and control which will come from the Children and Young Person's Act provisions. (Clerk of juvenile court, 1990)

It is a truism to state that the formal cause of truancy inheres in the body of education, welfare and criminal justice legislation, which requires young persons of a certain age to be in full-time schooling. Yet again and again magistrates, teachers and EWOs could not bring themselves to put forward any justification for enforcing attendance other than the statutory requirement. Some magistrates thought that the attempted regulation of persistent truants was a waste of time; others thought the project worthwhile but their own powers insufficient for the task. Many teachers were quite explicit about their reluctance to have unwilling and recalcitrant students in school. A majority of professionals from all agencies were of the opinion that the economic and social problems usually associated with targeted truants could not be addressed by enforced schooling. None the less, the law required the professionals involved to secure compliance. Hence there was a constant soft policing of the middle ground of occasional truancy, which could, by definition, be expected to show some positive results in the sense of getting children to attend school on a more regular basis; and a less frequent but harder policing of those truants whose pathological class or gender affiliations might result in offending, their sexual exploitation, or some other deviant behaviour which, if seen to occur during school hours, would reflect badly on all those responsible for enforcing school attendance. One deputy headteacher summarized the relationship between the legal and the social regulation, which intersects at the site of compulsory schooling:

> Essentially there are two levels in dealing with non-attendance. The first is to cover your own back, to make sure the documentation is okay. The second is the more caring role where basically we are dealing with incompetent parents or with social problems.

This brings into focus the ideological justifications for the policing of truants and their families.

Ideological justifications

Overall, three major justifications for enforcing school attendance were advanced. Two were explicit, and based on the ideologies of general deterrence (in relation to truancy) and diversion of offending or otherwise deviant juveniles from the criminal justice system to the community. These two explicit justifications, however, served a third – the taken-for-granted desirability of normalizing the behaviour of those whose class-based difference gives the lie to the ideology that schooling can in itself provide equality of opportunity for families already disadvantaged or torn apart by poverty (see Chapter 4). As far as the targeted truants were concerned, no one argued that enforced schooling was desirable on purely educational grounds, although some magistrates mentioned that employers are usually interested in the school attendance records of first-time applicants for jobs.

The strong belief in the ideology of general deterrence – that something 'must be seen to be done' about targeted truants – resulted in repeated court hearings, adjournments, fines, threats and short-term stays in residential units, which, although they seldom resulted in the students' regular attendance at school, often achieved negative effects, particularly if a student was taken into residential care (Carlen 1987). And, as in any war of attrition, once hostilities had opened, both the levels of resistance by the truants and the punitive attitudes of the truant-catchers quickly escalated. The non-attenders became hardened in their determination to stay away from school (see Chapter 4), while on the side of the enforcers references were made to the desirability of bringing back corporal punishment and imprisoning parents for fine default in relation to their children's truancy.

> If they went to prison it would be on the front page of the local newspaper. Everybody round here would know about it and it would have a deterrent effect. (EWO)

It was ironical that beliefs about the efficacy of *deterrence via punishment in custody* should have been so strongly held at a time when both nationally and locally the declared new policy was supposed to be *diversion from punishment in custody to punishment or care in the community*.

In 1988–90 the government was putting forward its proposals for less custody and more 'punishment in the community' (Home Office 1988a, b, 1990). At the same time, the Norwest Social Services Department was planning to move away from the use of full-time residential care for offending juveniles towards a 'shared care' system with young people in trouble retaining strong community ties even when removed into residential care for short periods. In such a political context, therefore, it was not surprising to find that the numbers of professionals holding strong beliefs about deterrence through custody (as described above) were well matched by those with a strong commitment to 'diversionary' programmes designed to keep young people out of the criminal courts and the young offender institutions. And these opposing ideologies also contributed to the push–pull of exclusionary and inclusionary techniques discussed earlier. However, it was in the disciplinary vacuum created by the ideological differences between those who would deter (via custody) and those who would divert (via the 'community') that the 'normalizing' 'caring packages' offered to the courts by social workers were able to develop. Invoking the sign of 'truancy' enabled magistrates to 'explain' juvenile delinquency in general and adolescent criminal behaviour in particular. In the cases of targeted delinquents, moreover, the formal juridical object-ives – of returning truants to school or, in cases involving criminal activities, deterring the offender from further delinquency – were alternately conflated and diffused, resulting in responses to truancy in Norwest being seen by all concerned as being juridically haphazard. Thus, under the signs of 'truancy' and 'care and control in the community', the machinery for the regulation of truancy in Norwest continued (and will most likely continue) to operate as it always has – not primarily to return illicit absentees to school, but rather to police families living at the margins of economic and sexual respectability. The justifications and techniques change but the targets remain the same. What was less clear to the competing 'care' and 'control' professionals in 1990 was the extent to which the practices of education authorities and schools would change in relation to truancy as a result of the Education Reform Act 1988. For under that Act the Thatcher government feigned abdication of its policy role in relation to the allocation of resources to state schools and in place of a social ethic for the governance of education invoked the myth of the market mechanism.

Economic conditions

The 1988 Education Reform Act's devolution of the financial management of schools to local level, combined with the funding of schools according to pupil numbers, may well result on the one hand in local authorities stepping up their policing of truancy, and on the other in headteachers turning a blind eye to the absence of pupils seen to be either intractable or giving the school bad publicity. Some EWOs thought that an era of new battles over ownership of the absence would commence, with the less popular schools being forced to take non-attenders rejected by other schools. They were, however, uncertain as to the role that EWOs would be required to play in the enforcement of attendance.

> *EWO 1:* With the Education Bill, you'll get the successful schools opting out and they'll just reject any non-attenders who'll end up in sink schools like Hareton.
>
> *JW:* Do you think Hareton would accept them?
>
> *EWO 1:* They'll have to, they need the numbers. There's over a thousand kids but with their being split site, they're still under their numbers. They could be faced with closure in two years. They'll have to take any they can get.
>
> *EWO 2:* This is a very cynical view of schools but under Section 19 when LMS comes in they are not going to want to take them on the roll. You know, they will register them, take the £1,300 or £1,400 and not care if they don't come in after that. I think that there should be financial penalties if schools exclude pupils. But I don't think Norwest are doing that.

The head of Hareton High believed that, given the economic poverty of so many of his pupils, there should be much more emphasis on putting extra resources into the school on the basis of *need* rather than numbers.

> Oh, we're winning and we're not winning. We can do so much, but we're still up against the culture here and that's endemic. Of our first year intake we've got 90 per cent below average in reading. . . . You have all the poverty and deprivation and so on. There's a limit to what we can do. But we do our best. Then we've had all the school closures and re-organization. It's more than that though. I think a lot has to do with the curriculum. After seeing the results of those tests [of first year pupils] I wonder if many of them truant simply because they can't understand the lessons.

[On LMS] It's OK. We are managing.... But their [LEA's/government's] attitude is just bums on seats. They want us to have higher numbers, but I think we're large enough.

Whatever calculations LEAs and heads make to further their schools' specific financial and educational interests, our research in Norwest suggests that under the new legislation the pupils most likely to lose out will still be those whose vulnerability to racist, sexist and anti-working-class stereotypes continues to make them prime targets for the normalization programmes of the 'human science' based professions.

4

MODES OF RESISTANCE

Shades of the prison house begin to close.
(Wordsworth, *Intimations of Immortality*
from Early Childhood)

Introduction

The aims of truancy research have primarily been two-fold: to assess the amount of illicit absence from school; and to uncover the causes of such absence. No one, to our knowledge, has asked, 'Why do the vast majority of children and young persons attend school?' Nor has the search for truancy causation gone much beyond either the effective (factoral) causes of truancy (e.g. personality, family, community and/or school) or its formal cause in statute. In particular, the contribution to the manufacture of truancy by the truant-catchers themselves has been largely ignored.

Chapter 3 analysed the inter-agency responses to truancy in Norwest and it was argued that in that area the truant-catchers' targeting of already marginalized populations failed to achieve the resumption of effective school attendance by errant pupils. In this chapter, the worlds of the non-attending pupils themselves are explored and the main arguments are:

- that the oft-reiterated opinion of teachers and EWOs that in certain working-class areas an anti-school ethic is passed on intergenerationally becomes a self-fulfilling prophecy when school non-attenders from such areas are routinely targeted for official exclusion from schooling and inclusion in a range of normalizing and disciplinary programmes, the main effect of which is alienatory;
- that despite their own adverse contribution to the task of combating illicit absence from school, the truant-catchers are correct in seeing material in-equality and class injustice as being two fundamental barriers to a universal

acceptance of the notion that schooling for all is equally advantageous for all;
● that the non-attenders and parents interviewed were in fact so cynical about the disjunction between the promises made about the benefits of schooling and the actual living and educational conditions on offer to them, that they were prepared either passively to ignore or actively to resist all attempts to compel effective school attendance – even when such resistance might result in penal sanctions.

This chapter is in five main sections. The first describes the truanting careers of some of the young men and women interviewed. The second part first examines the relationships between school, pupils and parents, particularly with reference to the official expectation that parents should be responsible for their children's attendance at school, and secondly reports the results of a small survey of non-truanting students' reasons for attending school. The next section discusses the many reasons truants gave for their illicit absences. The fourth part describes the 'truant worlds' – children's homes, high streets, stores and places of peace and quiet where illicit absentees from school spend so much of their time. Finally, we chart the modes of resistance employed by errant pupils determined to bunk off.

Truanting careers

Much of the literature on truancy distinguishes between types of truant – for example, the 'school phobic' and the 'delinquent' truant (Broadwin 1932; Johnson *et al.* 1941; Coolidge *et al.* 1957; Farrington 1980; Reid 1982). Such rigid typification was criticized in Chapter 2, and our intention here is not to engage in truant categorization. However, it is useful to refer to types of truanting *careers* as these can serve to illustrate the various ways in which truants may be regulated once they are perceived as being within one or other of the truant categories most commonly used by the truant-catchers. For, given that much of the literature on truancy has been produced by practitioners in the education, psychological, legal and allied services (Hersov and Berg 1980; Reid 1985, 1986), conventional typifications have at least contributed some knowledge of the ways in which absentees are perceived by the relevant agencies. In categorizing truanting careers, therefore, we have used four terms which encompass the major typifications employed by the truant-catchers: delinquent; morally endangered; abused; and phobic (Paterson 1989; Wardhaugh 1990). Yet as we recount the truanting careers of eight targeted and two non-targeted truants, it will become apparent that the truanting careers of some youngsters could as well be typified by one category as by another. For instance, both sexually abused young men and sexually abused young women are often seen as being not only abused but also morally endangered and this was made apparent by the usually implicit (but sometimes explicit) assumption that sexual abuse in childhood was a forerunner of either adolescent homosexuality in young men or heterosexual promiscuity in young women. Furthermore, Table 4.1, in summarizing the official responses to truanting careers variously involving delinquency, school phobia, sexual abuse and moral endangerment, suggests that the responses were not differentiated according to type of truanting career but that targeted truants were responded to by the whole range of coercive devices and programmes available to the authorities.

Targeted truants – types of truant careers

Tables 4.2 and 4.3 indicate the school years at which truanting began, and at which truancy was most prevalent among the forty non-attenders interviewed, and serve as a comparison for the following account of ten truanting careers (refer also to Figure 2.1).

Delinquent truanting careers: Lesley and Campbell

Lesley, aged fifteen, was one of the most persistent non-attenders, and her absences belonged to the 'officially illicit and parentally disapproved' category. Indeed, parental disapproval was a major factor concerning her entrance into a truanting career – in one of their altercations her mother had called the police. It had also been central to the escalation of her truant-delinquent career, involving a charge of assault arising from the physical conflict that took place between Lesley and her mother over the issue of school non-attendance.

Lesley had attracted a wide range of school-based responses to her non-attendance, including various punishments. None the less, she expressed the belief that the teachers had 'given up' on her, because although she continued to truant frequently the school was apparently taking no further action. She held similar views about education welfare and perceived herself as having 'called the bluff' of the EWO by refusing to take seriously his threats of legal action even though she and her parents had in fact been subjected to a wide range of court appearances and disposals. Following her parents' appearance in the magistrates' court Lesley herself had frequently been in the juvenile court for both her truanting and offending behaviour. At one stage she had appeared weekly in court as the hearings for truancy had been repeatedly adjourned.

The outcomes of these court appearances were complex. They included a supervision order for non-attendance, a voluntary care agreement because of family conflict, and an order that she be remanded into care as a result of offences. At the time of interview Lesley described herself as 'remanded into care, but I'd be here anyway on a voluntary care agreement'. Once in care, and still refusing to attend school regularly (indeed scarcely attending at all), Lesley had continued to be subjected to regulation. In particular, she was moved from Moorland Road (YPA) and placed on the 'pindown' regime in Church Street family centre, from which she absconded several times. By this stage, her truanting career was complete. Having progressed through the education, welfare and legal systems, and having experienced a wide variety of forms of

Table 4.1 Experience of regulation during progress of ten truant careers

Name (age)	School responses	Education welfare	Police	Magistrates court (parents for NA)	Juvenile court			Into care	During care	Residential psychiatric placement	GP	Psychiatrist	Psychiatric social worker
					Child for offences	For NA	Other						
Alicia (16)	Not in trouble as note provided for absences												
Annette (14)	Not specified		Contact in connection with truanting				Care order	In care (as a result of sexual abuse)	Loss of privileges, one-to-one counselling		Referral to general hospital (abuse and NA)		
Campbell (16)	Various punishments; contract; expelled	Frequent contact; threat of legal action	Contact in connection with suspected offences		Various including burglary, stealing car			Voluntary care; remanded into care; at home at time of interview					
Ian (15)	On report		Called in because of his behaviour at home							Whin Hill House (school attendance, own behaviour, family problems)		Yes	Yes
Kerry (15)	Various punishments; detention in 'isolation'		Contact due to participation in youth street activities and caution for shoplifting				Care order	In care (family breakdown)			Yes; care staff suspect faked illness		

Lesley (15)	Various punishments but 'gave up' in the end	Frequent contact; court cases brought	Contact due to family conflict, absconding from care and offences	Yes	Three charges of burglary and criminal damages	Frequent appearances and adjournments	Supervision NA; voluntary care agreement; remanded into care		'Pindown' for truancy and absconding			
Michael (16)	Some supervision but no punishment	Limited contact										
Robert (16)	Expelled for truancy	Contact	In connection with offences		Three appearances for burglaries		Care order	Several placements including family centres and CHE	Threatened he must leave current placement if NA continues			
Sarah (15)	In 'isolation'						Care order	In care (family conflict)	Contraceptive drugs; grounded (for truancy) School attendance monitored	Whin Hill House (family conflict)	Yes	Yes
Tom (13)	Expelled for behaviour in school						Care order	In care (CH) plus several earlier placements	Grounded for absconding	Whin Hill House (daily attendance)	Yes	

NA: non-attendance.

Table 4.2 School year at which truanting began among forty non-attenders

School year at which truanting began	No. of young people
Primary school	4
First year of secondary school	8
Second year of secondary school	11
Third year of secondary school	7
Fourth year of secondary school	4
Fifth year of secondary school	2
Not specified	4
Total	40

Table 4.3 School year at which truancy was most prevalent among forty non-attenders

School year at which truancy was most prevalent	No. of young people
Primary school	1
First year of secondary school	2
Second year of secondary school	8
Third year of secondary school	6
Fourth year of secondary school	12
Fifth year of secondary school	12
Not specified	8
Total	49

Nine young people mentioned more than one school year at which their truancy was most prevalent.

regulation, Lesley found herself in the position of being (more or less permanently out of school, and in (and out of) care.

In common with Lesley, Campbell (aged sixteen) may be categorized as an 'officially illicit and parentally disapproved' absentee. Another similarity between them was the extent to which family conflict had played a part in Campbell's entry into the care of the local authority ('me mum just couldn't handle me'). This had led to a voluntary care agreement, although Campbell was also remanded into care following court appearances for offences.

Campbell's truant-delinquent career had begun with regular truanting from school, along with disruptive behaviour while attending school. The teachers had responded with various punishments, and by placing Campbell 'on contract'. Commonly used by high schools in Norwest in an attempt to deal with difficult and disruptive students, contracts entailed written statements of agreed standards of behaviour. Differing perceptions as to the requirements of this contract between Campbell and his teachers had, however, led to further conflict, which escalated to the point where Campbell was permanently excluded from school.

Campbell had also had frequent contact with the education welfare service, and reported having been threatened several times with legal action. In the end, no court action had been taken for non-attendance and the escalation of Campbell's truanting career from education and welfare intervention to court appearances was a result more of delinquency than of truancy.

With his permanent exclusion from school, Campbell's absences had become 'officially induced', leading to his part-time schooling under the juvenile justice home tuition scheme. At the same time, family conflict, together with his continued delinquency, contributed to a situation in which he moved repeatedly into and out of care; voluntary care arrangements alternated with remands into care and with periods spent at home. Thus, towards the end of his truanting-delinquency career Campbell was receiving a part-time education, and was in and out of care.

Morally endangered truanting careers: Sarah and Robert

Sarah, aged fifteen, perceived the escalation of her truanting career to the point where she had entered care as having been a process largely initiated by herself. Although she attributed the initial truancy to having been bullied during her second year at high school, she also claimed that when she did not receive sufficient attention for truanting she 'had wanted to rebel more'. Thereafter, rebellion had taken the form of staying out late at night. This had led to family conflict, and to her being taken into care as being 'in moral danger' (Children and Young Persons Act 1969). Social services staff responded to her in terms of both her 'moral endangerment' and her truancy. (In the latter respect there was some conflict of definitions. Sarah defined herself as no longer having any significant unofficial absences from school; care staff continued to perceive her as being a persistent non-attender.) Labelled as a morally endangered truant, Sarah was next perceived as being sexually promiscuous and was put on a course of contraceptive injections. Social workers were concerned to 'protect' her as much from unwanted pregnancy as from the sexual act itself.

Having entered into a 'morally endangered' truanting career, Sarah found it difficult to change course. From the ages of twelve to fifteen, she had tried to change her perception of herself from that of 'rebel' to that of a 'good girl', although she believed that this effort had made little difference to the perceptions held of her by others. At the same time, and perhaps ironically, the bullying which had been the original cause of her truancy continued unabated, and was, according to her own account, somewhat exacerbated by the fact that she now bore the stigma of being in care.

Sarah experienced a range of agency interventions, including time spent in two family centres, and a short-term residential psychiatric placement. With more than a year of compulsory schooling still ahead of her, Sarah had little hope of leaving behind her morally endangered truanting career, or (because of continuing family conflict) of moving away from full-time institutional care. Sarah's truancy fell into the dual categories of 'officially illicit but officially condoned' and 'officially illicit but parentally condoned' yet she complained of not having received enough attention in relation to her truancy. Agencies had been far more concerned with family conflict and with her (perceived) sexual delinquency than with her school attendance.

Robert, aged sixteen, was similarly perceived to be a morally endangered truant, although his endangerment was defined differently. Moral danger for young men is seen by the regulatory agencies almost exclusively in terms of homosexuality, rather than in relation to the sexual promiscuity criterion more commonly invoked for young women. Care staff and teachers were actively engaged in preventing any possible homosexual contacts between Robert and other young men, and they were especially concerned that he might become involved in prostitution.

Robert's career had been a complicated one. Permanent exclusion from school for persistent truancy had been followed by re-admission to the same but amalgamated school along with a threatened second exclusion for continued non-attendance. Robert's absences thus alternated between the 'officially illicit' and the 'officially induced' categories. Extensive education welfare contact had led him to attend school more regularly for a time. However, conflict at school had then resulted in him running away several times from his family centre and for this he had been 'grounded' by the care staff. About the same time, he had embarked on a delinquent career, appearing in court several times on charges of burglary. These charges had led to a placement in Brooklands (CHE) prior to the current care placement. Thus, Robert's truanting career could have been seen as being that of a morally endangered (abused) truant, and that of a delinquent truant. Moral endangerment does not always take precedence over delinquency, and its attribution in individual cases in part reflects the contradictory perceptions and labelling processes of the different regulatory agents.

The truanting careers of abused truants: Annette

Just as a history of sexual abuse is often present in the background of those who are subsequently defined as being morally endangered truants, those defined as abused truants may also be suspected of being in moral danger. This connection has been made explicit elsewhere (see Wardhaugh 1990), and while it is very obvious in some cases, it was less so in that of Annette, aged fourteen. Nevertheless, it was a significant feature of a career that progressed from EWO supervision to a general hospital placement, through a residential care placement, to continued social services and police surveillance of her activities while she was truanting and out on the streets.

Both Annette and the care staff were unwilling to give specific information concerning the sexual abuse, but removal from her grandfather's care to hospital had signalled the start of her progression through the statutory care system. Although the social workers claimed that abused truants were treated more leniently than those who had not been abused, Annette experienced loss of privileges as a result of her continuing truancy. There was considerable intervention on the issue of her non-attendance at school, including one-to-one counselling and personal supervision carried out by social work trainees. Police intervention – relatively rare in cases of non-delinquent truants – involved intercepting Annette while she was wandering the streets during school hours, and removing her to the local police station to await collection by social services staff.

While it is thus clear that Annette had progressed through a wide range of agency interventions, the perceptions of the professionals were that her absences fell into the 'officially illicit but unofficially condoned' category. However, she was in fact subjected to regulation by education welfare officers, social workers, residential care staff and police. The official perception that action in her case had tended towards leniency may be attributable to the tendency of care workers to believe that they were acting to protect Annette as an abused truant and that, therefore, any intervention was simply 'for her own good'.

The truanting careers of truants seen to be school 'phobic': Kerry and Ian

Already in care in Priory Road because of family breakdown, Kerry (aged fifteen) had begun her truanting career during her first year at Hareton High. She had been subjected to a variety of school-based interventions, including detentions and periods spent in 'isolation'. Further forms of intervention, such as education welfare contact and legal action, did not take place for two major reasons. First, Kerry was already in care, and the relevant agencies (social services and education welfare) believed that in such cases there was little point in seeking further care or supervision orders. Secondly, Kerry's absences usually took the form of 'hidden' or 'internal' truancy. She was absent from lessons without leaving the school premises or else took great care to conceal her absence from the school premises from teaching staff. Nevertheless, although formal sanctions were limited, and her absences might be seen as being 'officially illicit but carer-condoned', Kerry was clearly defined by both children's home and school as being a truant. She acquired the label of phobic-truant, partly because of her own actions and partly because of the type of identity commonly ascribed to adolescent females (Lees 1986). She attributed many of her absences from school to illnesses, both real and faked: 'Yeah, I've conned me way out of school' and 'everyone knows me for going in the sick room, like.' Sometimes she was believed by care staff and teachers, and sometimes not. Either way, she was seen as a phobic-truant and, thus defined, was processed accordingly by referrals to a doctor to test the validity of her claims to illness. Her phobic-truant career did not progress further than this. Incidents involving self-injury did not result in referrals to a psychologist or a psychiatrist, the residential care staff dismissing them as resulting from Kerry's 'silliness'. So, again the key to this non-progression through the system may have been that as Kerry was already in the care of the local authority she was deemed to be already receiving sufficient care and supervision. In this respect, her career contrasts with that of Ian who, while remaining under the care and control of his parents, progressed through a range of psychiatric referrals.

Ian, aged fifteen, came to the attention of the authorities for a number of reasons, including his own persistent absences from school, noted by head-teachers and parents, and his stealing and aggressive behaviour at home, which had come to the attention of the police and the psychiatric social worker already working with the family. Furthermore, because Ian's absences were 'officially illicit and parentally disapproved', intervention was accelerated. Yet despite his stealing and some contact with the police, Ian was responded to as being a phobic rather than delinquent truant. As well as receiving ongoing supervision by the psychiatric social worker, he was referred to a child psychiatrist, and spent a two-month placement at Whin Hill House, under-going individual and group therapy programmes. At the time of interview, Ian appeared to be coming to the end of his phobic-truant career, as he was seen by both teachers and psychiatric staff as having largely overcome his problems.

Non-targeted truants

A few weeks short of leaving school, Alicia, aged sixteen, was planning to take several exams which she hoped would enable her to follow a career as an army nurse. Currently at her third high school (these school moves were a result of family changes of location rather than being indicative of a disrupted career more common to targeted truants), Alicia was used to taking fairly frequent days and half-days off from school. She spent the time sleeping or watching television; that is, engaging in the classic truant activity of 'dossing'. Despite her truancy, Alicia managed to make her way through the school system without attracting too much negative attention, and without coming into contact with the education welfare service. Her absences were relatively untroublesome to the regulatory authorities, in that they were neither so frequent nor so disruptive of her schoolwork as to attract much attention; in addition, there was an absence of other triggers for agency intervention, such as a history of abuse or an involvement in delinquency.

Michael, aged sixteen, was leaving school (Blue Mount High) a few days after interview, was hoping to take a business or management course at college, and expected that he would eventually follow his parents into public house management. He had liked school until the middle of his fifth year, when he had begun to 'get a bit restless'. He began to take occasional days off, either because he was tired, or to enable him to catch up with GCSE coursework. He had had some limited contact with the EWO, but had never been in any serious trouble.

Perhaps Michael was not targeted because his 'intelligent' use of his illicitly gained free time to complete coursework was condoned by his teachers, who expected him to pass his forthcoming examinations. Furthermore, while he presented himself as being a questioner of the system, he was not a rebel in terms of engaging in seriously disruptive behaviour or persistent truancy.

Home and school

The enforcement of compulsory schooling for children from late infancy to adolescence has, for the past century, been rooted in at least three beliefs about the relationships between schooling, 'ideal homes' and 'happy families'. They are that:

- schooling provides for the full development of children's innate abilities and adequately prepares them for making the best contribution they can to the common good via production (labour market) and reproduction (family);
- compulsory schooling keeps children out of trouble by providing a nexus of regulatory agencies, which controls the movement of (potentially troublesome) youth as they emerge from the private space of the home into the public domain of unemployment and employment, and also monitors the degree to which parents fulfil their state-imposed responsibilities;
- the normal school child can be supposed to come from a household where the parents have full control over the activities of their children.

Like all ideological beliefs, those about the relationships between home, family and school have only a partial truth. In many respects they are erroneous. Paul Corrigan, for instance, has shown how schools, far from bringing out the best in all young people, have tended repeatedly to school working-class children for working-class jobs (Corrigan 1979), while nowadays, with only 15 per cent of school-leavers in Norwest entering full-time employment, as compared with 47 per cent becoming unemployed or embarking on a youth training scheme, it is obvious that many young people cannot feel that this society has a use for them at all (figures are for 1989, the most recent available). Moreover, and as we contended in Chapter 3, the regulatory agencies empowered to enforce school attendance routinely manoeuvre some children into trouble rather than keeping them out of it. At the same time, and as will be argued later in this chapter, some of the truant-catchers' methods tend to alienate parents from, rather than enlist them in, the state's struggle to achieve near universal school attendance. However, in view of the continuing pressure on parents to take legal responsibility for their children's truancy, it is with the last belief listed above that we are primarily concerned here. The assumption that normal parents should have full control over their adolescent children, taken together with the widely expressed opinion that some marginalized parents live within a culture of poverty, one attribution of which is the low evaluation given to education, provoked us into posing the two following questions when we analysed the transcripts of interviews with parents and children.

- To what extent, and in what senses, is it appropriate to claim that certain working-class parents and children do not value education?
- How realistic is it to persist in the belief that the best way to reduce levels of absenteeism from school is to prosecute parents?

Views on education held by parents of targeted truants

> Those schools with the most developed links with parents and the community tend to regard these contacts as integral to the management of all activities.

So concluded an HMI Report in 1989 (DES 1989a). Although the same report argued for better home–school links it also pointed out that the quality of existing ones was variable. The teachers in the schools we visited in Norwest evidenced a close concern with the financial straits of many of their pupils' families while at the same time expressing frustration about the ensuing 'culture of poverty' in which parents were supposed to devalue education. Some of the derogatory assessments which teachers and EWOs made of truants' families have already been reproduced and commented on in Chapter 3. None the less, it is worth noting here how the truant-catchers tended to amplify a supposed cultural difference by using a technique which Jock Young long ago explicated in relation to the amplification of the deviance of drug takers. In speaking of truants' families, the professionals took an example of the atypical, presented it as stereotypical and contrasted it with a background of normality that was overtypical (Young 1971). The deputy head at Blue Mount High was well into this process when he stated:

> You can go into some houses and there will be kids from three different marriages and for these kids school is just not central to their lives. There is so much else going on for about half our kids that, I would say, school has not become a habit. They just don't take for granted that they are coming to school – or whether to take the washing to the launderette. Whereas I take for granted I'm coming to work. I just get washed and dressed and get in the car. (Deputy head, 1990)

Yet none of the ten parents we interviewed expressed an antipathy towards education or schooling *per se* and only four were antagonistic towards some of the schools and teachers with whom their children had come into contact. Furthermore, the majority volunteered the opinion that at least some of their children's troubles had been self-induced. Not surprisingly, however, all mentioned additional factors likely to have affected their children's non-attendance rates, the main ones being: the constant and confusing school amalgamations in Norwest, which had recently created schools lacking a sense of identity and community continuity; the amount of homework given to school students nowadays; and the guilty memory that they themselves had not enjoyed their own time at school. However, their main disagreement with the authorities was not about whether or not their own children should attend school. It was over the degree of their own culpability in relation to their children's truancy that the parents took issue with the state. For despite their general expressions of conventional goodwill towards education together with their acquiescence in the need for schooling, all the parents believed that the law was unrealistic in holding them responsible for their children's failure to attend school regularly.

Views of targeted truants' parents concerning their legal responsibility to ensure their teenage children's attendance at school

Of the parents we interviewed, only one set expressed any confidence in their capacity to act effectively in conjunction with the truant-catchers to return their truanting child to school. The others cited a multitude of social disabilities – the overburdening anxieties connected with unemployment, poverty, illness and other family responsibilities – to explain their inability to persuade their child to attend school regularly.

> I even took him up to the bus stop, watched him get on the bus, and he's got off. And I've told 'em that he's got on the bus, that he's coming. I've then not been in half an hour and the school board man's been here. Says 'He hasn't gone'. I said, 'Well, I can't take a big lad to school. I got little 'uns to see to.' (Mrs Smith)

> It seems as though they think its our responsibility to get the kids to school. I mean as far as we know these do go. Once they go out that gate they are going to school. I mean we don't know that they're bobbing. And yet the EWO think it is us making 'em bob. His attitude is all wrong. (Mrs Wexford)

> They told us to get her in school every day. I was sending her out for school. I mean, I can't live behind her. He expects me to hold her hand and take her to school while I got to see to this one. . . . He doesn't think as you've got other kids. (Mrs Elliott)

Tired and depressed parents could not face the daily morning battle to get the kids to school and then, later, the daily evening struggle to get them to do their homework.

> I've tried everything. I'll shout at her and shout at her. This morning I kept, 'Anita will you get up?' 'Will you shut up? I'm getting up.' And I keep thinking, 'Oh, don't do anything, it only gets you all wound up.' (Mrs Thompson)

> I give up. Because I'm tired when I come in from work. I don't want to sit there watching over him all evening, making sure he does something. (Ms Black)

> I just couldn't see me forcing 'em to stay in to do two or three hours homework. I just couldn't, er, haven't got that sort of, er, what do you call it... power... or whatever it is... over them. I haven't got that. (Ms Morris)

This sense of powerlessness characterized the parents' view of their relationship to their children's schooling. In the so-called partnership between home and school the parents felt that home was very much the junior partner. Mr Fraser was certainly the angriest parent interviewed but other parents indicated that they also felt that 'down the school you've got a no-win situation with them.' They felt powerless both in the relationship with the educational and welfare authorities and in that with their own children. Yet again and again they stressed that this lack of parental authority stemmed in part from material factors beyond their control rather than from any fecklessness on their own part. We shall, therefore, in ensuing sections of this chapter, discuss further how the economic situation of the families atrophied their ability to make the most of the meagre educational opportunities on offer to them. We conclude this section with a discussion of the policy implications of the parents' powerlessness to prevail against their sons' and daughters' determination not to go to school.

As we saw in Chapter 1, the early 1990s witnessed an upsurge of media and ministerial hype about illicit absence from school and the need for a more punitive approach both to the parents of truants and to schools 'with high levels of absenteeism'. Newspapers gave favourable reports of a Wisconsin, USA, strategy of tying welfare benefits to regular school attendance. The Criminal Justice Bill before Parliament in winter 1990–91 proposed raising the maximum fines for truants' parents from £400 to £1,000 – even though at that time only 3,000 cases a year were being taken to court, with one-third ending in conditional discharges (*Guardian* 16 April 1991). The Children Act 1989 enabled courts from October 1991 to make Education Supervision Orders, which were seen by at least one newspaper as a move towards 'forcing parents to improve their children's school attendance' (ibid.). On 15 April 1991 it was announced by the Education Minister that from 1992 schools would be required to publish their truancy rates and that the estimated £500,000 which such publication would cost schools would be 'taken into account by grant settlements' (ibid.). The extent to which the latter measure will push some schools into an ever quickening downward spiral is discussed in Chapter 5. What it is pertinent to note here is that although two of the parents we interviewed had already appeared in court and the eight others were aware of their vulnerability to court proceedings, none of them thought that they could coerce their children into effective attendance at school. (Of the forty children interviewed, eight had parents who had been summoned to answer for their non-attendance in a magistrates' court.) Certainly the parents of the non-attenders wished to avoid a court appearance or a fine, and, more importantly, they believed that education ought to be a good thing. None the less, they saw the enforcement of their own children's regular attendance at school as being quite beyond their power.

As we stated in Chapter 2, in this study we have chosen to examine truant careers and types of absence rather than types of truant. So, although it is apparent that the truant careers of most of our young people could have been put into one or more of the truant categories, such as 'phobic' or 'delinquent', we have also thought it instructive to categorize types of absence. In so doing we have come to the conclusion that most illicit absence is not parentally condoned in its initial stages. The majority of illicit absences in the Norwest study started off by being 'officially illicit but parentally disapproved', changed to being 'officially illicit but parentally condoned' once the parents (or carers) had come to believe that they had no effective means of getting the child to attend school regularly, and were also frequently put into the 'officially induced' category as schools excluded them from further attendance on grounds of either their bad behaviour or, in some cases, their truancy. Yet, despite their adamant refusals to attend school regularly, most of the youngsters we talked to expressed a desire for a 'good job' and the belief that schooling was a necessary prerequisite for getting one. In this they were in agreement with 63 per cent of the school students in our survey of 200 at Hareton High, whom we asked to write essays about why they went to school (see Table 4.4). For throughout the early stages of the research we were aware that whatever political capital can be made out of it by politicians with competing educational ideologies, truancy is in fact a minority occupation. The highest survey figure we could find for persistent absentees was of 13.9 per cent (fifteen-year-olds) 'unacceptably absent' during the spring term of 1977 in Bolton (BMBEC 1977) while estimates for the overall average percentage of illicit absence by all eligible children ranged from 2 to 9 per cent (see Chapter 2). However, references such as that made by Prime Minister John Major to 'one in four schoolchildren' being truants may draw on the figures for *selective* or *occasional* truancy (speech at Conservative Women's Association national conference, June 1991). Gray and Jesson (1990) give figures for 'selective' truants (absent for particular days or lessons) as 10 per cent of all fifth-year pupils, with a further 36 per cent absent 'for the odd day or lesson'. However,

Table 4.4 Reasons given by 200 school students for their regular school attendance (percentages in parentheses)

Reason given for school attendance	First year	Second year	Third year	Fourth year
Helps in getting job	50 (59)	19 (61)	57 (68)	126 (63)
Meet friends/socialize	45 (53)	21 (68)	31 (37)	97 (49)
Learn something useful	39 (46)	9 (29)	34 (40)	82 (41)
Enjoy lessons	51 (60)	15 (48)	13 (15)	79 (40)
Get qualifications	28 (33)	6 (19)	31 (37)	65 (33)
Like the teachers	21 (25)	2 (6)	9 (11)	32 (16)
Fear of court cases	2 (2)	9 (29)	19 (23)	30 (15)
Would be bored at home	15 (18)	1 (3)	11 (13)	27 (14)
'It's the law'	10 (12)	2 (6)	8 (10)	20 (10)
EWO would visit	4 (5)	0 (–)	10 (12)	14 (7)
Parents would enforce attendance	2 (2)	1 (3)	9 (11)	12 (6)
Go on school trips	7 (8)	2 (6)	2 (2)	11 (6)
Would be taken into care	0 (–)	0 (–)	10 (12)	10 (5)
Learn social skills	0 (–)	0 (–)	7 (8)	7 (4)
Would get into trouble for not attending				
General	1(1)	2(6)	1(1)	4(2)
From teachers	0(–)	0(–)	2(2)	2(1)
From police	0(–)	0(–)	1(1)	1(1)

Table 4.4 Continued

Reason given for school attendance	First year	Second year	Third year	Fourth year
'We have no choice'	7	0	0	7
	(8)	(–)	(–)	(4)
Safer at school than home	3	2	0	5
(while parents at work)	(4)	(6)	(–)	(3)
Provides free education	0	0	4	4
	(–)	(–)	(5)	(2)
Would become lazy if did not go	0	0	3	3
	(–)	(–)	(4)	(2)
Helps prevent involvement	0	0	2	2
in crime	(–)	(–)	(2)	(1)

only 6 per cent are classified as 'serious' truants, i.e. absent for several days or weeks at a time.

Table 4.5 indicates the different patterns of truanting behaviour of the forty Norwest non-attenders selected by us for interview. We concluded that while on the one hand explanations which locate the causes of truancy in personality traits tend to be circular and teleological, those which put all the blame on the schools fail to explain why it is that the majority of children, across all classes and located in a broad spectrum of privileged and less privileged educational establishments, *do* go to school and attend there regularly. We therefore decided at quite a late stage in the research to investigate children's reasons for attending school and the results are listed in Table 4.4. What was most instructive for us was to note that no more than 15 per cent gave fear of legal sanctions as a reason for attending and that when placed in rank order of frequency mentioned, the top six reasons given for school attendance included two that were instrumental ('helps in getting a job' 63 per cent, ranked 1; and 'get qualifications' 33 per cent, ranked 5) and four that listed aspects of school attendance seen as being pleasurable.

Once we had some indication as to why the majority of children in Norwest were attending school regularly, we asked why the positive attributes of schooling listed by the 200 regular attenders did not similarly motivate the illicit absentees. The majority of illicit absentees also held to a belief that a good educational record would help them to get the decently paid job that they, like their more conforming peers, wanted. That being so, it would obviously have been misleading to use control theory to explain illicit absenteeism from school by merely claiming that illicit absentees lack the motivation and/or inducements which help engender regular attendance in other students. Instead, therefore,

Table 4.5 Prevalence of different types of truanting among forty non-attenders

Frequency of truanting	No. of young people
Days	19
Weeks	14
Half-days	11
Lesson truancy	10
Months	5
Not specified	3
Total	62

The categories used in this table were derived from responses to the question 'How long have you stayed away from school?' Only three were unable to specify whether their non-attendance took place over days, weeks or months.

Twenty out of the forty interviewees reported more than one frequency of truanting; for example, during one stage of their school career truanting may have occurred over a period of several days and at another stage over a period of several weeks.

of explaining the illicit absences by an inversion which would have allowed us to claim that truants totally lack the motivations and inducements which attenders give as reasons for going to school, we decided to engage in an ethnographic analysis of our data in order to find out why it is that despite their commitment to education as a means to a job, the illicit absentees choose not to attend school regularly. In the rest of this chapter we will present data in support of our arguments that:

- most children attend school regularly because they see the 'schooling deal' (i.e. school attendance is rewarded by a decently paid job) as being relevant to their circumstances;
- persistent and targeted truants do not see the 'schooling deal' as being relevant to their material circumstances (see the next section), while the activities of the truant-catchers (as detailed in the previous chapter) alienate both truants and their parents even more.
- out of school, illicit absentees gradually develop individualistic alternatives to the 'schooling deal' and engage in modes of resistance to schooling, the official response to which makes it even less likely that they will resume regular attendance before they reach school-leaving age.

Shades of the prison house

When we asked the forty non-attenders why they did not attend school regularly, the factors they mentioned as contributing to their illicit absence could be placed in three main categories: school related; financial and labour market related; and home, family or residential care related. Analysis of the unstructured interviews in which these reasons were put forward also suggested that underlying the explicit reasons given for truancy, the young people and their families had a pervasive awareness of a powerlessness and economic deprivation which had already given rise to many of their problems and which, they believed, could not be remedied (and in fact were often aggravated) by regular school attendance.

School-related factors affecting school non-attendance

Bullying
Research on truancy has perennially provided evidence that bullying is a recurring factor in young persons' refusal to go to school regularly (Holmes 1989). The Norwest research was no exception. Ten (25 per cent) of the young people interviewed volunteered the information that they had experienced bullying at school, most of it restricted to verbal abuse about their physical attributes, their sexual reputations and their being in residential care.

> I hated school... because I used to be much fatter than I am now, so I used to get picked on for that. (Kerry)

> They kept on calling me gay. (Tom)

> They pick on me for being in here [residential care]. They say, 'At least I'm with me mum and dad, and you're in a home.' (Sarah)

The discipline of schooling
Asked why they truanted from school, the majority of our interviewees gave the not very illuminating explanations that they did not like school and/or they had quarrelled with particular teachers. Yet, as they talked, it became clear that schooling had become problematical for them not solely because of the specific features or teachers of the schools they had attended, but also because of the ways in which many features of schooling aggravated their already existing feelings of social and economic powerlessness.

It seems that since the inception of compulsory schooling there have always been some children who have violently objected to being herded together in classrooms with twenty to thirty others. Humphries (1981) recounts in some detail how nineteenth-century truants sought peace outside the discipline and hustle of schooling, and Chris Tchaikovsky gives a vivid account of her own resentment of compulsory schooling in the 1950s:

The frustration of losing all those precious happy days collecting snakes, feeding the beach ponies, swimming, running free! To me it was unbelievable that I was classroomed and expected to sit in small wooden stocks [and] not move (only it was not moving any more, it was 'fidgeting').... At school I was assailed with meaningless doodles that had wriggled their way from the sand to our blackboard and were called sums. At school I had to stand among friends in assembly, who, like me, were not convinced that any of this was 'New Every Morning' as the hymn book told us... I became aware of, and did unspeakably funny things, and was not able to laugh, even quietly.... It was those first removals from assembly to stand outside the head ogre's door that energised future rebellion, or more truly, future refusals to do what was required. Lines, bad reports, detention, no gold or silver stars and mean thumb-in-the-back teachers all combined to make sure that I was not going to take any of this schooling business.

(Tchaikovsky 1985: 14–15)

Although not as articulate as Tchaikovsky, several of Norwest's young truants put forward similar views:

I just sort of craved not to go to school. Like if it were a nice day, could be I'd just sit around and do nothing. So I wouldn't go to school. (Edward)

When there's loads of people in one room it gets a bit hot and stuffy and I don't like it, especially when it's nice weather like this outside. (Mike)

Certain people, like they are aggro-ing the lesson. And I can't put up with that. Does me 'ead in. (Ian)

With so many of the truants having troubles out of school (in residential care or in poverty-stricken or otherwise troubled homes (see Chapters 3 and 5) it is not surprising that they felt particularly aggrieved at those aspects of schooling which spilled over (illegitimately, they thought) to encroach upon dimensions of their lives that they believed should remain school-free. Thus homework (and particularly the increased amounts resulting from GCSE coursework) was seen as an encroachment upon their free time, while insistence by schools that their pupils wear uniforms was taken as an assault upon their private and personal space.

Homework

It has already been seen that many parents resented being expected to force their children to do homework. In homes already under stress as a result of illness, poverty and fraught personal relationships it was not surprising that homework was seen as a further irritant. Campbell had been suspended because of constant refusal to do homework. Rosemary's mother expressed views similar to those of at least eleven of the young people interviewed when she argued that: 'There's no need for them to have homework. They're in school long enough without having homework.'

School uniform

However much the young people disliked being set schoolwork to do at home, on no one aspect of schooling did they and their parents discourse so vehemently as upon school uniform. Comments from pupils and parents who objected to schools laying down the law about students' clothes and personal appearance ranged from those that were contemptuous of the pettiness of such rules to those concerned about the extra and unnecessary expense that school uniform requirements impose on poor families already overburdened with financial worries.

> It's ridiculous really, you got to wear your tie at all times. But I forgot to put mine on. (Mike)

> If I've got the wrong sort of clothes on they send me home. (Dawn)

> If you don't wear your tie at school they give you half an hour detention. (Rosemary)

> They told me not to have me hair cut around the sides and I did. They told me not to wear earring in me nose and earrings in me ears and I still did. For school I usually wear black leggings and a skirt over the top and no socks, just slip-on shoes. They don't like that. (Susan)

> Basically, they don't like the way I dress. When I first came to the school in the first year they said wear grey or black shirt and we've never had anything different since. So I came in this today. Teacher stops me and says, 'You're not supposed to be wearing that.' I says, 'I've been wearing a grey or black shirt since I came to school so I'm wearing a black shirt.' A year after he says 'White shirt'. Not that I take any notice anyway. It isn't the best organized of schools and I don't agree with the headmaster using controls like this. (Michael)

> Can't wear me own clothes like. Couldn't even wear cords.... I'd had enough by the time I was in the third year. (Campbell)

Leah's mother, a single parent, was outraged that her daughter had not been allowed to wear to school the denim coat bought for her by her father. The story, as told by Leah and her mother, epitomized the war of attrition that can escalate into suspension or even expulsion when on the one hand a school elevates the wearing of school uniform into a major disciplinary issue, and on the other the recalcitrant pupil converts it into a site of resistance.

> *Ms Morris:* There's a silly rule at Knighton that they couldn't wear denim jackets or coats. Even if it was the new style denim, not necessarily what the rockers wear.

> *Leah:* It was the only coat I had. He'd [father] paid forty-five quid for it.
> They said she'd [mother] got to buy a new coat. You can't go in trainers
> or anything like that. It's winter and it's freezing cold weather, can't go
> to school in trousers! At first they said you could have black trousers.
> Well, they stopped it. So I went out and bought some trousers.
>
> *Ms Morris:* She told me she could go in black trousers so I bought her a
> pair, about thirteen pounds. And then she went to school – and what
> happened? Were you suspended? In the end she had a skirt. The EWO
> came here with four skirts, old ones, you know.
>
> *Leah: She* wouldn't have worn them! They were puddled, horrible, I'd
> not wear them.
>
> *Ms Morris:* She wouldn't go in. 'I'm not wearing it, I'm not going in.' But
> there have been times when she hasn't been able to go because I've been
> short you know. It's difficult when you've got a low income. I've been on
> supplementary, on family credit since October. I mean, you can't just
> buy a uniform. She wants clothes, not just a uniform. She can't go out
> at night with her mates with a uniform on.

The school as 'other'

The schools' insistence upon the wearing of expensive uniforms was only one
factor that provoked many non-attenders and their parents to see the school as
'other', as catering for a class of pupils whose finances and style were very
different from their own. The expense of bus fares to school for pupils not
qualifying for a free pass, and money required for cookery classes and other
activities were seen as indicative of a schooling system unsympathetic to the
economic realities of single-parent, low-income or unemployed families.

> This'll make you laugh. He wouldn't go school. He was bobbing it like I
> said and I'd even put him on the bus. Now his dad wasn't working and we
> went about free dinners for him. They said we couldn't have 'em for Kirk
> and we said 'Why?' They said 'Because he's under a care order.' We said
> 'What's that got to do with it? We still got to feed him.' I said, 'They're
> on your back about him not being at school, and he's coming home for his
> dinner!' They might know he won't go back once he's home. (Kirk's
> mother)

> I mean that cooking, that's some'at else isn't it? Like a lot of people, we
> just can't afford it. They expect it every week, don't they? The last recipe
> would have cost £6. For two chocolate cakes. Well I mean... (Mrs.
> Wexford)

Given such financial pressures, it was not surprising that children and parents
alike indicated that they were very conscious of a class difference between
themselves and the teachers. Thus, while Susan manifested an acute awareness

of being in the 'care class', both Michael and Mr Fraser (Lenny's dad) portrayed the class difference between home and school in more conventional terms:

> Most of the kids who've been here [children's home] have gone to that school, and some of them haven't left very good records behind them. So when they say, 'Oh! She's from the hostel', they think, 'Oh, another one of them' and automatically, as soon as I went in the school, I don't think they bothered. (Susan)

> My parents always came down [to the school] to speak to him [headteacher]. My parents are, you know, dead impressed with the middle classes, businessmen, anyone in suits. (Michael)

> I just class them as pricks. That headmaster, deputy headmaster, in my eyes they're pricks. They're bred into money. It's not what they know or what their capabilities are. (Mr. Fraser)

But the schools to which the non-attenders should have gone were also seen as 'other' in a second sense. Pupils and parents were convinced that the local state schools were under-resourced and that several re-organizations involving the merging of previously separate schools had created split-site, second-rate institutions which were difficult to manage.

> As soon as you look at the building as you are going up the drive, everything is falling down. You ought to go in sometime and have a look at it, have a look at the green on top of the ceiling; 't isn't like mould, but big green patches. You go along some corridors and the paint's falling off and everything. (Campbell)

That the larger schools and split-sites were unattractive to children who were, in many cases, already caught in a revolving-door syndrome between parents, residential care and other relatives was made quite explicit. Furthermore, both pupils and parents saw the size of the amalgamated schools as being responsible for some illicit absences, while teachers and EWOs mentioned the split-sites as being particularly conducive to lesson truancy.

> Hareton, it's changed names a couple of times. It was Morley, then we joined up with the Laurels and it became Springdale House and now we've joined up with Meadowlands and we're called Hareton. (Kerry)

> When The Laurels first came up it was all messing about and we had to sit in one room all day so we were missing all the work anyway. Then Meadowlands came down and that was all messing about. (Jackie)

> It was ever so silly. They put the Broadlands' kids in with Cranley, all together in one big school, ever so big. It was over one thousand children and about ninety teachers. It was just too overcrowded then. And the teachers didn't know whether they were coming or going. You don't want to go to school. (Leah)

I think there's too many children there to kick off with, since they merged schools. (Mrs Fraser)

Most people you speak to say that it was a bad thing they shut Cranley High and put them all together. I think with that being such an overcrowded school they got to try and keep as many trouble whatsits out of it. (Leah's mother)

It's a right mess here. With all the amalgamations the staff just don't know the extended family networks. With us [Hareton] being split-site you don't even get the same person taking register in the morning – a child might get three different people in one week. So how are we supposed to identify problems? (EWO)

Financial and labour market factors affecting school non-attendance

All forty young people indicated that they wished to get a job when they left school and several of those not in residential care were already engaged in paid work at the time of interview. Parents living in poverty themselves were sympathetic to the youngsters' desire to leave school and earn money, even though the part-time jobs which their children had were of the 'cheap labour' kind.

I think most of the kids when they get to the fourth year do want to leave, don't they? They want a bit of money in their pockets. (Mrs Smith)

I wouldn't really mind anything so long as there is money in it. That's all that most people bother about. (John)

But although the young people paid lip-service to the idea that you needed 'qualifications' to get a good job they did not believe it was realistic of them to try for academic qualifications when they had already missed so much schooling. What most of them wanted was to get their own jobs independently of the YTS (Youth Training Scheme), which they saw as being exploitative. For those who had higher ambitions the army or the police force were seen as the only realistic avenue of upward mobility, the only means of escape from the poverty and unemployment of the areas in which they lived.

I got a job, so no worries now. Don't need qualifications on it. I'd rather have that than YTS. (Campbell)

I don't think I could stick that YTS thing. (Kathleen)

I work as a labourer. It's better than YTS. (Geoffrey)

YTS is not worth doing. (Kirk)

[His brother] was twelve months on YTS and they did the dirty on him.

They got rid of him. . . . There's been times when I haven't had nothing to buy any food but I've never gone shoplifting. But you can understand them what do. (Kirk's mother)

We have YTS down where I work. Believe me, they work for their money. (Anita's mother)

I think the best thing he can do is join the army because there's nothing around here for him. I mean, when I left school I could get a job, finish the same day and get a job to start the next day. . . . I was always employed. . . . Today you can't do that. I mean YTS is cheap labour at the end of the day, so I think he's better off joining the army. (Lenny's mother)

In the already marginalized worlds of the non-attenders there seemed to be but three economic certainties – poverty, unemployment and a need for money – with only four options on getting the latter: low-paid employment, YTS, crime or joining the army or the police. Seeing their futures thus, it is not surprising that the non-attenders also failed to believe that schooling could win any economic rewards high enough to outweigh the pains of compulsory attendance. Harassed by the contradictory and disciplinary targeting and interventions of the truant-catchers, and already troubled by a myriad of problems at home or in care, the young people we interviewed just did not believe that the schooling on offer to them was relevant to life as they had known it.

Home, family and residential care factors affecting non-attenders

According to the prevailing ideology that the majority of people live in 'happy (nuclear) families' it could be argued that (ideally) young people's lives are located within the twin domains of home and school, with much of their time spent in negotiating the often conflicting values and competing demands of the two. In this scenario the journey to school represents a transition from the private to the public domain and it is the failure to complete this journey which first enmeshes young persons in the deviant worlds of the truant and then subjects them to the range of contradictory agency interventions documented in Chapter 3. Public space is associated with the worlds of work and education; it is a communal, visible and predominantly male space. Private space is the world of the home, an individualized, domestic and female space. Within this scenario the classic formulation of the 'school phobic' is that she or he fears the public world of school and seeks out instead the comfort and security of the 'private' home (Blagg 1987).

For the forty non-attenders in our study the world was not like that. Twenty were (or had been) in residential care (only four for education-related reasons) and for most of them (as well as for several still living with their parents) home had not been a place of security or comfort. Rather it had been characterized by illness, unemployment, divorce and/or serial marriage or cohabiting, which latter had often left the children feeling excluded or unwanted. At least three of the young people had been taken into care as victims of sexual abuse and two as victims of parental (or step-parental) physical violence. Social workers mentioned several others of whom it was known or suspected that they had been victims of sexual abuse, even though it had not been as such that they had been taken into the care of the local authority.

> When I was little me dad's brother used to get funny, he'd touch me, like. That was between when I was four and seven. And I didn't understand what was going on, whether it was right or it was wrong, but I knew I didn't like it. (Susan)

The spectre, reality or, in some cases, desired option of residential care was so dominant in the discourse of the majority of non-attenders that we discuss the young people's actual experience of the various children's homes (and other residential placements) in the next section of this chapter. To end this one we document their views on the effects that either the threat of or actually being in care had had on their school attendance and illicit absences.

At the time when we were conducting the research Norwest social services were moving towards an increase in shared care programmes for young people, programmes which endeavour to keep young people in residential care in regular contact with their parents or other relatives *in loco parentis*, and to return them to their homes as soon as possible. Implicit in the thinking behind the concept of shared care is the assumption that young people should ideally live at home with their parents. It was a belief that several of the youngsters interviewed did not hold.

In reply to our question as to whether being in care had helped him with his school attendance, Geoffrey replied:

> In some ways. They've done things and they think they are helping me, but in my eyes it's making me worse, like us spending some weekends in care like.... When I was at home, in their [social workers'] eyes that was a good thing, in my eyes it wasn't. I had a chance to go back home. I had a talk to me mum and dad and me social worker, and I said, 'I want to start doing things on me own now,' so I came back here. My social worker didn't want me to come back here [children's home]. She wanted me to go home. But, it's like I said to her, I didn't want to go home.

Ironically, and sadly, the young people in care who had already excluded themselves, or been excluded, from school too often found that, once removed from home, they quickly became marginal not only to the worlds of home and school but also to the nexus of placements which constitute residential care. Having already been moved from school to school before entering care, once in care they had been moved from placement to placement. Finally, after still refusing to attend school regularly, they had suffered yet another exclusion.

Against their will they had been returned to their parents. Susan's experience of this school-age revolving-door syndrome was typical. Interviewed in a family centre, she told of the four schools and several local authority residential placements she had experienced, as well as of her troubled relationships with her divorced parents.

I liked it there [assessment centre] and I ended up telling me Mum I hated her and didn't want to go home. So they kicked me out, because they were frightened that I'd never want to go home. I moved back home and I went to see the psychiatrist. She said 'Go back to school and try your hardest.' So I went back to school and a couple of months later . . . when I'd been in [the assessment centre] I'd started sniffing gas . . . Me mum walked in one afternoon and I was sniffing gas and I was high like . . . with a can of gas in me mouth. So she kicked me out. That's when I went to live with me friend. I got expelled from school shortly before I went to live with me friend. They got me back in school and then I got expelled again, so I moved in with me Dad. I've been through quite a bit. (Susan)

Constantly on the move between homes, Homes and schools, young non-attenders in care were well-placed to play off home against Home, and home/Home against school. Likewise, wily headteachers could usually put off having to take back an undesirable pupil in the hope that the next care placement would remove the recalcitrant student from the school's catchment area altogether.

Last time I was down here [Moorland Road family centre] I was sleeping up me mum's and coming down here in the day and he [EWO] came and asked me where I was living. I said, 'Well, I'm sleeping here.' He goes, 'Well, that's no excuse for you not going to school.' I says, 'Yes'. He says 'Why?' I says, 'Well I got to be down home everyday.' He says, 'That's no excuse.' I says, 'Yes it is. Any excuse is good enough for me.' (Lesley)

They won't have me back. He [headteacher] said 'Sorry, we can't have you back.' The reason he said he can't have me back is I aren't in the catchment area now. (Patrick)

Marginalized thus, the targeted non-attenders oscillated between home, local authority care and school and, in the interstices between them, carved out alternative and less legitimate worlds.

Truant worlds

Home from home from school

Chapter 3 discussed the many and varied ways in which the Norwest authorities attempt to regulate the lives of truants by relocating them in their proper place at school.

In schools, the two major regulatory measures were isolation (from peers) and increased surveillance (by staff). Isolation and surveillance were used for relatively minor truanting episodes. Kathleen told how she had been both isolated and under closer supervision as a result of 'bobbing'.

> You know you get these boards where you have the art things on. Used to put me behind those so that nobody could see me. I used to hide. Then I had the teacher sitting beside me when I was working. That was horrible, that was. She would come to the toilet with me to make sure I didn't go home. I used to have me dinner outside the headmaster's office, that was dead embarrassing. I weren't even allowed out at break. I had to sit outside their office.

Exclusions from school, whether temporary or permanent, were used for more serious misdemeanours. Both persistent truancy and more widespread disruptive behaviour were deemed to warrant the removal from school premises. The irony of excluding from school those who already felt no strong motivation to be there was not lost on the young people themselves. Chris spoke for several others when he exulted about his exclusion from school: 'I was over the moon.' Others were more ambivalent:

> It didn't bother me suspended. It's expelled that's like the worst. It's sort of the end, there's no turning back. (Edward)

> I was kicked out of Hareton. . . . I wasn't bothered the first time, but then when they started saying it again, I thought, well *twice*. (Robert)

Exclusion from school changed the meaning of a pupil's non-attendance. An illicit and/or parentally condoned absence became transformed into a state-enforced school lock-out. The young people's presence in the home during school hours was legitimized but at the same time they were often subjected to even greater surveillance. In private homes this might involve regular home tuition and/or visits from welfare officers. In children's homes residents were commonly required to remain on the premises during school hours, engaged either in doing schoolwork or in completing tasks for staff. Their initial pleasure at being legitimately absent from school soon disappeared in the face of a more supervised and yet less structured existence.

A majority of the non-attenders had suggested that by truanting they had sought to avoid the hassle they had variously experienced during schooling. Furthermore, about 50 per cent of them claimed that when illicitly absent from school they stayed in their own homes or in their children's home or hostel. Yet neither in their own homes nor in local authority institutions did they find peace and/or security. Those few non-attenders whose parents were in full-time work did indeed stay in bed, watch television or 'just doss' for long periods. Others, however, had discovered that being at home all day either with their parents or under the supervision of residential social workers could be just as stressful as the school, the classroom or the playground. Parents certainly thought that their children's presence in the home during school hours contributed to family strife:

> Then they expelled him and he's been at home doing my head in ever since. He has me in tears, he does, with his mouth. . . . This is what he does all day, sits eating. Torture. (Mrs Fraser)

> This morning it was a struggle to get her to go [to school]. . . . It only gets you all wound up, so I try to keep out of her way. (Mrs Thompson)

> I just don't know what to do with him. Like this morning I just had to get out. It was either him or me. He just blows up, he's got a violent temper. You just have to mention the word school to him, and that's it. He hits me sometimes. Mind you, I hit him . . . like this morning I said to him about school and he just smashed the furniture. He does that all the time. (Mrs Brindley)

None of the youngsters who said they stayed at home all day actually claimed that they enjoyed themselves there; they said either that they were bored or that they quarrelled more frequently with other family members. Some young people in children's homes or other local authority centres seemed to experience even more troubles. Cindy pointed out that it was difficult to do homework because of the hostel's general noise and bustle, Tom remarked that he felt good if he managed to get through the day at the hostel without being involved in a fight, and generally the talk of children in residential care was studded with references to fights, petty rivalries, continuing quarrels with parents at home, drugs and absconding. Sadly, too, because of the turnover of social workers they had not found in care the security they had lacked outside. For example:

> Marie-Clare was my social worker before that; and before that April Jones; and before that Bill Raynor. I've had quite a lot, you know. At one time I refused to have a social worker at all because I was just talking to them and then after a couple of weeks, months, whatever, they'd move on. I've got used to that now. I don't really open up to [them]. (Susan)

Being in care did not seem to improve the school attendance record of those who had not already been officially excluded. All kinds of school-avoidance strategies were engaged in by the young people (see below) and, as we saw in Chapter 3, those social workers most determined to get children back to school tended to resort to illicit measures themselves – notably programmes like the (by now) notorious 'pindown' or corporal punishment:

> Bill [residential social worker] hits us all the time. If there is trouble here [hostel] I can always go and take it out at school. But if there is trouble at school you can't bring it back here. Bill says we should treat this place as

home. But I can't. My parents come to see me on Wednesdays but I can't talk to them when they come. You are never left on your own. (Wesley)

Given the disincentives to stay indoors while illicitly absent from school, it is not surprising that about 50 per cent of those interviewed said that while truanting they sought out open spaces and/or roamed the streets.

Beyond school and home

Despite the fact that the majority of the forty non-attenders said that they were bored in school and out of school only twelve had ever been charged with criminal offences. Moreover, the crimes of three of them had been committed while they had been absconding from care. Most of those who said they spent the majority of their time in public places while they were truanting also claimed that their main priority was to avoid attention. Either they went to places where they felt free of constraints or they wandered around the shops, where they believed they could merge with the crowd. Rosemary's favourite place had been 'down by the brook', Kerry went to the park, Ian 'used to go down the woods' and Susan frequented the park, the cemetery, the canal and, sometimes, the shopping centre.

Sometimes I go to the park because it's quiet there. Or me favourite place is the cemetery because it's really real peaceful and you could lie there all afternoon, take a nap. Then you got the canal. (Susan)

Notwithstanding the claims of some of them to the contrary, the targeted non-attenders who occupied public space during school hours *were* vulnerable to the surveillance activities of the truant-catchers, as well as to temptations to engage in drug-related and criminal activities.

We used to just walk round the streets up the town. Look at the shops and spend our dinner money on fags. If the police ever stopped us we would just say that we had been to the dentist and were on our way home. Another time my mate's social worker stopped her car and told us to get in. My mate said it would be alright, she would not tell on us. But she did. She took us back to the home. We were grounded [kept in] and had our pocket money stopped. (Wesley)

Most of the time, you know, we'd just sit around doing nothing. Or we'd go and hassle somebody. There used to be a Pakistani shop just across the road. We used to go across and give them some hassle – throw little pebbles at the door. One time the police came. I was on me bike so I went. . . . When we were older we used to skive school and go shoplifting. (John)

I know a lot of people who are on drugs and I don't want to be like that. Got drug addicts down that area. (Kerry)

There used to be a time at Broadlands I'd bob school and like me and a load of me mates would go into [the town] and if it was near Christmas or birthdays we'd pinch things from the shops. (Susan)

It was because of the persistent assumption in the literature (Tennent 1971; Tyrer and Tyrer 1974; Rutter and Madge 1976; Farrington 1980; Graham 1988) and by the courts (Parker *et al.* 1989; S. Brown 1991) that there is a causal link between illicit absence from school and law-breaking that we carefully questioned all forty non-attenders about their experiences of the criminal courts, and asked the twelve who had either admitted to or been convicted of offences about the time and place of their delinquent behaviours. Seven had committed offences while truanting; three had been involved in crime while 'on the run' from residential care; one had committed burglaries with two adults in the evenings; and one had been charged with assaulting her mother. Thus only 17 per cent (approximately) of the forty non-attenders had actually committed crimes when they should have been at school, with another 13 per cent (approximately) committing offences at times or in places when they should not have been at school in any case. This finding supports the conclusions of Grimshaw and Pratt (1984) who, after reviewing the literature on the relationship between truancy and delinquency, contended that 'the prevalence of delinquents among truants may be less than is sometimes assumed and... this rate may be accounted for by factors other than truancy.'

One weakness in our research may have been our failure to probe very deeply into the young people's experience of gambling (fruit machines) or illegal drugs. Although EWOs talked freely about their fears in relation to young women at risk of sexual exploitation and some young men's vulnerability to various kinds of delinquency, they did not make explicit any fears they might have had about gambling on fruit machines or illicit drug usage. One deputy head thought that some truants were likely to be drug takers and several of the young people interviewed knew *other* young people on heroin. But only two of the forty non-attenders even admitted to going into pubs while truanting, one admitted to having been 'on drugs' and one (Susan) admitted to sniffing glue. If addictions to either fruit machines or drugs are factors affecting non-attendance in Norwest a more specifically addiction-focused study than this one will be required to probe into it. At the same time, it can be noted that EWOs in Norwest did not appear to think that there was a simple causal link between crime and truancy, pointing out that most crime by school students was committed at the weekends and in the school holidays. Finally, a senior probation officer's view of the relationship between truancy and persistent offending ironically suggested that school attendance was as much related to crime as school non-attendance. He said: 'They tend to plan shoplifting expeditions while in school. And then leave school to commit the offence!'

Modes of resistance

Having talked at length with teachers, EWOs, social workers and school students (both regular attenders and truants), we have come to the conclusion that the majority of illicit absence from school in Norwest is either spasmodic or temporary and is dealt with effectively either by in-school sanctions, such as being on report and under increased surveillance, or by a visit from an EWO. The illicit absences of a second (and smaller) group of students are likely to be officially condoned either because no headteachers are prepared to enrol them if they have already been excluded from another school, or because they are not seen as being at risk of delinquency and/or are soon going to reach school-leaving age. The third group is comprised of the non-attenders targeted for all or some of the reasons described in Chapter 3. The non-attenders in this latter group had developed many modes of resistance to regulation by schools, EWOs, social workers and courts.

In-school strategies or 'tricks of the trade'

Pupils who truant have to employ several strategies to avoid detection and, initially, they are developed at school, and often in relation to 'lesson' or half-day truancy.

> What I did, I would go in for registration in the morning, like late when none of the other kids were there. So the teachers would think I was in school and then I'd go. So all the other kids think I'm not in school – see? (Because I came in late and weren't there then and they'd already gone to lesson.) And I'd do the same at dinner time. Tricks of the trade! (John)

> Teachers would say, 'Where are you going now?' I'd say, 'I'm going the toilet,' or, 'I'm running a message,' so I used to go about quite easily. (Kerry)

> Then other times I'd go, and when break comes you are allowed to go in the bogs. Teacher would be on one side, you'd run round the other and go home. (Campbell)

> You'd stay away when you wanted and the next day you'd grab hold of the register before the teacher comes in and mark yourself in. (Glenda)

> Sometimes I would play games with the teachers. I would go all week and then Friday afternoon they think, 'God! if we keep her here she will have done a full week.' What they don't realize is that they don't know about the lessons where I haven't been in the week. (Susan)

> We would just take the odd lesson or half-day. But we would still go for registration, and then go out. (Cynthia)

Once truanting students had been detected the first response of the schools was to put them on report. Determined truants could easily subvert the 'report' system.

> At the end of each lesson the teacher has to sign the yellow form. At the end of the day the headmistress has to sign the yellow form so she knows if you skive, like. But we worked out a system where I copied down all the names from the yellow form for her, and went in with it. (Cynthia)

> They tried to put me on report. But I got a note. One of me mates forged a note for me and I took it in. (Campbell)

As we saw earlier, parents who knew of their children's truancy generally felt powerless to do anything about it, knowing from bitter experience that even if they accompanied their children to school it would take force to keep them there.

> One time [the EWO] used to have to pick me up [from home] and bring me back. So I used to go in one gate and come out the other. (Kathleen)

And even though schools were strict about demanding notes from parents explaining a returning pupil's absence, determined non-attenders could cajole their parents into providing an exonerating note by saying that unless they were so provided they would not return to school at all.

Stopping, starting and stopping

Young people who had been threatened with care orders often took a conciliatory stance, returning to school for a few days or weeks and then absenting themselves again.

> I'd go back for about two days, then go back home. (Kathleen)

> They put a supervision order on me and said if I didn't start going to school, I'd be put in care. So I went back to school and then I stopped going. I never missed a day for a couple of months and I just started having days off again. So I was back to square one. (Lesley)

In the cases of children already caught up in the revolving-door syndrome of home, Home and school, a syndrome which itself is often further complicated by the contradictory devices of inclusion and exclusion from schooling practised by the authorities, it was difficult to pin ownership of the problem on to any one school or agency. Determined truants soon realized that if they held out long enough and did not get into any more serious trouble the authorities would give up the struggle to get them to school and they would be left in relative peace until, with the attainment of school-leaving age, they could be free from compulsory schooling forever. In the meantime, being determined not to go to school, they ignored all threats of further punishment, took evasive action to avoid the rigours of 'pindown' and once restricted by coercive regimes in children's homes or by the primitive (and illicit) 'pindown' itself were prepared to abscond rather than submit to forced schooling.

You will never get me to go, so don't threaten me. (Leah to her mother)

I used to hate school that much that they said, 'We'll put you in care.' But I'd rather be in care than be in school. (Kathleen)

They couldn't really do much about it because they would have to sort of lock me in a room to stop me. (Edward)

The boss [of the children's home] used to lay down rules. If you didn't go to school he would have pocket money taken off you, or nights knocked off. But now he's just given up. You know you can't keep me at school. Try your best, you still won't do it. (Susan)

It [pindown] didn't put you off running away. It just put you off staying away too long. So you wouldn't get sent up there. (Cynthia)

I've been on pindown. Got out of that one, though... I ran out in my 'jamas. I was on the run for a week. (Lesley)

Once young people abscond from care institutions they are at great risk of subsistence-related crime and sexual exploitation. If they subsequently come before the courts their poor school-attendance records will be used to justify stiffer penal sanctions (Parker *et al.* 1989; S. Brown 1991). Already excluded from home, school and even residential care, the persistent and targeted truants will then be likely to have their first experience of the state's ultimate exclusionary sanction – penal custody.

The evidence presented in this chapter suggests that, far from returning persistent and targeted truants to school, the increased regulation and sanctioning of them and their parents aggravates their already considerable and many-sided social disadvantage. Most truanting is effectively regulated by school sanctions and EWO supervisions. Once these 'soft machine' controls are exhausted and harder measures are invoked the battle to legitimate compulsory schooling has already been lost. In Chapter 5, therefore, although it will be argued that there *is* no alternative to compulsory schooling, it will also be argued that schools by themselves can never remedy the gross economic and educational inequalities which presently make schooling appear so irrelevant to a minority of young people.

5

SCHOOLING, TRUANCY AND THE NEW ERA

Truancy isn't just an educational issue... it's a political one.
(Education Officer, Norwest, 1991)

Introduction

In this book we have identified a number of recurring themes, characterizing various contradictions in the continuum between care and control, inclusion and exclusion, compulsion and entitlement, and education and schooling. One such contradiction is the unintended consequence of care and welfare provision in actually reinforcing patterns of school non-attendance; another is the ambivalence towards school-based education shared by otherwise committed professionals, such as EWOs, social workers, care officers, court officials and teachers, whose legal and professional mandate is to return non-attenders to mainstream education (Jackson 1987). Thus, as the data and ethnographic analysis of pupil and family experience in this study demonstrate, there is much pain, hurt and suffering around current educational arrangements. This suffering is, according to Johnson (1991), epitomized in the humiliations of exclusion and failure: 'the pain of being treated as a child, the screaming boredom of being talked at routinely at a complete tangent to a teacher at school.' Equally, however, Johnson argues that teachers, EWOs and social workers, who daily risk something of themselves in their work, also experience the pain of rejection or worse, and this is linked with the ambiguity surrounding their care and control functions (Levy and Kahan 1991).

The apparent inability of pupils, clients and professionals to deal with their common problems is, as we have demonstrated, historically located in a process where care can often turn into punishment; where, in their frustrations with the extreme difficulties of it all, the carers often turn on the cared and vice versa. This and other such conundrums to which we have referred, in which discretion becomes the rule of thumb in the policing and prosecution of certain categories of young people and their families, suggest that the criteria involved relate more to the socio-economic-sexual status of non-attenders than to the nature of their problems and ways of solving them. As the empirical data and analysis in Chapters 3 and 4 of this study suggest, the discretion of the system is far from impartial and serves ultimately to place blame on clients rather than on the complex range of factors (itself included) that constitute the problem in the first place. In other words the system not only obscures its own role in the marginalization of deviance but, perhaps more importantly, acts as a questionable measure of status and social respectability. Consequently, under the aegis of countering truancy by care and control in the community, the machinery for regulating school non-attendance in Norwest is less concerned with re-integrating young people into mainstream education than with controlling families living at the margins of respectability – a form of system abuse largely overlooked in the media hype currently surrounding parental abuse of children. For this reason our study has sought to question common-sense perceptions of assumed causal links between schooling and truancy. These perceptions, enshrined in policy, practice and research, paradoxically define schooling as being both the cause and the solution of the problem. Thus, if evidence in Chapters 3 and 4 suggests that schooling is a contributory factor in the process, it is also argued that school non-attendance is mediated by factors other than school alone, including family, economic and political relations, as well as those associated with the impact of localized, legal, welfare, housing, medical and other agencies including 'expert' professional activity.

This chapter draws together the main implications of the study and does so along three dimensions. First, in relation to the Education Reform Act 1988, some of the likely consequences of market forces on the determination of schooling and opportunity structures for young people are explored; secondly, aspects of broader ecological factors defining the relationship between family, education, economy and labour market in Norwest are analysed (Eggleston 1977); and, finally, possible strategies which might in the future radically re-form relations between education, citizenship and schooling are considered. To begin with, we turn our attention to the relationship between the Education Reform Act, market forces and school effectiveness.

School improvement and market forces

As we have noted, the passage of education reform from the launch of the Conservative government's New Training Initiative (NTI 1981) through to the Education Reform Act (ERA 1988) has been both rapid and dramatic. Ostensibly, such reform has centred on raising standards of education, in particular those associated with literacy, numeracy, vocational awareness, behaviour, discipline and attendance, as well as improving school effectiveness and teacher skill levels. According to HMI (DES 1987), school non-attendance at a time of rapid social and technological change threatens standards of education for both attenders and non-attenders alike in relation to levels of attainment, progression and access to further education and job opportunities. In recent years initiatives such as YTS, TVEI, LAPP, COMPACTS and similar work-related community-based projects have been specifically targeted to improve pupil motivation, and to accentuate the importance of attendance in the progression between school, college and work. Moreover, the impact of GCSE, involving course and project work, and the National Curriculum itself have also drawn attention to the significance of pupil attendance in completing key phases and stages of assessment, thereby placing issues such as school attendance at centre stage. Understandably, in anticipating the various ways in which disruption and truancy can adversely affect the reform process, both HMI (DES 1987) and the DES (1989a) have sought to provide guidelines for making schools more effective. Drawing on the work of Rutter *et al.* (1979), Mortimore *et al.* (1988) and Reynolds (1985), and on other evidence, the Elton Committee of Enquiry (1988) concluded that successful schools possess a distinct atmosphere characterized by, among other things, effective leadership, management, teamwork, communication and community support.

> This does not mean that schools can eliminate the effects of social differences between pupils. A child from a disadvantaged background is still likely on average to do less well than a child from an advantaged home when they attend the same school. But if the disadvantaged child attends an effective school he may well do better than a more advantaged child attending an ineffective school. ... The general conclusion which seems most relevant to our work is that some schools appear to have more punitive regimes than others, and that punitive regimes seem to be associated with worse rather than better standards of behaviour. This does not mean that punishments are not necessary. All the effective schools in the studies we referred to as well as those we saw in action, had punishments and used them. The message seems to be that, in order to create a positive atmosphere, schools need to establish a healthy balance between punishment and rewards.
>
> (Elton Report 1988)

If making schools more successful has been the battle cry of a decade or more of Conservative educational reform, culminating in the ERA, the quantitative and qualitative aspects of such reform are not easily reconciled. Although the ERA has significantly influenced the legal, administrative and financial underpinnings of schooling, this alone does not necessarily affect the quality or effectiveness of schooling. In this respect, a noticeable feature of the struggles underlying the Conservative educational reform process has been the attempt to reconcile two apparently contradictory principles: one, the policy and legislative battle to deregulate post-war educational provision (1944–79) in favour of market principles; secondly, the ideological battle to construct the new criteria of successful schooling, in order to legitimate the reform process itself. However, the gap between establishing the new legislative structures of schooling, National Curriculum guidelines, testing, LMS, opting out, open enrolment and so forth, and the qualitative and contextual response of schools to the reform process has been neither clear-cut nor straightforward. In reality, the emphasis placed in the National Curriculum on the universal delivery of core and foundation subjects, phased assessment and statutory testing at key stages and ages has not received universal acclaim among teachers, parents and pupils and remains a continuing and unresolved source of conflict. In these circumstances, and notwithstanding the importance of nailing the elusive concept of atmosphere or ethos, many of the characteristics of school effectiveness described by Rutter *et al.*, Elton and others read rather like a list of professional common-sense homilies (Robinson 1989): hard to disagree with in principle but more difficult to pin down in practice, particularly in the current climate of market-led educational reform. It is to this issue that we now turn.

If in the post-war period, from 1945 to the 1960s, schools were seen as important both to society and to the individuals who attended them, their importance lay mainly in their socialization and allocation functions (Durkheim 1956; Parsons 1959), preparing pupils for their future adult, social and occupational roles. Moreover, as we have already noted in Chapter 1, the momentum towards comprehensive education reform in the 1950s and 1960s also represented, in part, a belief in the relationship between schooling and social justice, in challenging rather than reproducing long-established educational, social and economic inequalities. In this period, access to educational opportunity was interpreted by government and LEAs as a right of citizenship rather than as a privilege conferred or constrained by accident of birth, geography, class, sex, race or gender. In contrast, education run on market principles breaks with the tradition of a publicly planned and provided for education service, which traditionally characterized education provision from the 1870 Act through to 1944, and ended with the passing of the 1988 Education Reform Act. What is significant about the ERA is the way in which it both introduces market forces into education, involving concepts such as competition, consumption, production, goods on offer and choice, and alters the policy context in which schools are adjudged effective. According to Robinson (1989):

> The 1988 Act is much more than the attempt of law-makers to keep the legislation up to date with an evolving educational system, removing anachronisms, resolving ambiguities as the existing legal framework is interpreted by the judiciary. The 1988 Act represents a change in the ideological underpinnings of the English and Welsh educational systems. In the 1960s the search was for a common school, a common form of educational provision which would enable all to have the same educational

opportunities. The 1988 Act espouses values of the free market and establishes a view of education in which opportunity is enhanced through diversity as in the provision for City Technology Colleges, the creation of Grant Maintained Schools and principles of local financial management for secondary and larger primary schools.

Thus, instead of relying on public intervention to guarantee standards, the ERA has decentralized the decision-making process, thereby neutralizing the influence of the 1944 Act and LEA control, ostensibly empowering parents with greater choice about which schools their children attend. The theory of placing schools in the market place is that their success will depend upon selling themselves to prospective clients, with weaker institutions eventually going out of business. Although, as we have seen, the education market is highly regulated and historically contentious, the ERA has sought to break with the historic idea of universal provision by creating a particular kind of education market embracing diversity, differentiation and choice, with the National Curriculum representing the minimum benchmark of basic curricular standards. Paradoxical as it may seem, the National Curriculum and assessment of children at key stages are not, according to Robinson (1989), intended as the centralization and nationalization of schools, but the guarantors of diversity. The thinking behind ERA is that schools' success will depend on them selling themselves to prospective clients, with choice acting as an essential mediator in what counts as effective schooling. One consequence of this is to view schools like businesses, the parent being the customer and the pupil being the product. This, linked with the requirement that schools make publicly available test and attainment scores, including information regarding attendance rates, exclusions and other disciplinary matters, has resulted in many schools becoming more protective of their public image as they face competition from neighbouring schools. Moreover, the signs are that open enrolment and provision for opting out provided by the ERA will increase competition, especially in situations of falling rolls and where LEA influence has significantly waned. Such competition between schools is accentuated by local financial management, which effectively links school funding to the number and type of pupils they can attract. Though the ERA does not include voucher provision it is, as Ball (1990) notes, effectively the same thing: 'each pupil who comes through the school gate will carry with him or her a cash bounty and the staffing, materials, facilities and equipment the school wants or requires will have to be paid out of the monies accumulated in this way.'

Consequently, by deregulating control over school funding, and with provision for schools to opt out, schools that attract greater pupil numbers will gain in terms of funding, resources and staffing, with the opposite situation holding true for those that do not. As others have commented (Ball 1990; Lee *et al.* 1990; Centre for Contemporary Cultural Studies 1991), this element of educational policy finds its expression in parallel areas of government, social and economic policy linked with de-regulation of industry, employment, health and welfare, and it accepts that those who cannot stand on their own feet go to the wall. Yet, if on the surface local financial management, open enrolment and provision for opting out look appealing in terms of increasing efficiency, diversity and choice in the system, the reality is that the relationships between family, education and society do not operate in quite such perfect competition; education, for example, does not constitute a consumption good in the conventional sense of the term and schools do not simply go out of business. Moreover, the lines between producer, consumer and product in education are not clear-cut, are mediated by social relations across family, community, school and work, as we have observed in Chapters 3 and 4, and are also overlaid by relations of class, race and gender. The point here is not simply that the market principle is neither a fair nor an efficient distributor of life chances, but that under the ERA the market principle is largely illusory in delivering greater diversity, choice and school effectiveness. According to Ball (1990), there is nothing neutral or inevitable about how the market operates in education; it simply represents a *disciplinary mechanism* to eliminate poor schools in response to changing movements of taste and fashion. Yet, paradoxically, little or no attention has been given to the consequences of such a policy for the 'losers', particularly in terms of its differential influence on pupil attainment, motivation, discipline and attendance, including its contradictory effect on what, elsewhere, the National Curriculum is seeking to achieve in raising educational standards across the board. This, again, brings into sharp relief ways in which the current educational reform process generates the very problems it ostensibly seeks to address, in particular accentuating differences between 'sink' and 'star' schools and the implications these have for truancy.

Power, choice and schooling

The way school and community have been caught up in the social divisions of the 1980s and 1990s is significant in this study, since both bear the imprint of sharp inequalities within and between occupational classes which have long characterized Britain's industrial decline. Thus, a feature of truancy as a form of social exclusion is that it is not linked only with school, but with the ecology of the area, catchment or neighbourhood, and involves an intricate balance between family, labour market, housing, health, recreational, leisure and other factors. Moreover, the effects of class stratification on school, community and labour market became acutely accentuated in the 1980s, drawing sharper distinctions between residential neighbourhoods and the people who live in them. If one effect is to generate segmented labour markets, another has been to reinforce segmented neighbourhoods, the most deprived of which often sit alongside the more affluent, but whose inhabitants remain excluded from the opportunity structures therein. This is noticeably true of the two principal neighbourhoods linked to the three schools mentioned so far in this study.

In the main the parents interviewed in Chapters 3 and 4 live in two sprawling council estates, Rose Hill and Buxton Manor, which traverse both inner-city and suburban areas of Norwest, including both rundown and owner-occupied areas of Victorian terraced housing. In many respects neither residential area is dissimilar from other such estates in modern Britain, built on community-proof architectural principles of the 1950s and 1960s. Typically, there are the occasional shop, community centre, local school and health clinic, with little or no access to and from by public transport. Although they are not 'high rise', and on first appearances are attractively laid out, with semi-detached houses verged with grass trim and ample garden space, closer inspection of the estates reveals another story. In addition to the absence of any central community services, including the lack of adequate and convenient shopping facilities, cinema, recreational, leisure and other services, Rose Hill and Buxton Manor are made up of a continuous series of similarly shaped houses, some of which are either in a serious state of dilapidation or are boarded up, with upstairs windows smashed, graffiti daubed on walls and rubbish left unattended in derelict gardens. Not only are both estates considered 'notorious' among education, social, welfare and legal agencies for their rates of crime, delinquency, alcohol and drug abuse, they also have high levels of unemployment, debt, sub-standard housing, truancy and industrial illness, the latter being associated with the proximity of two local industries, mining and ceramics. Most recently a major health survey of the Norwest region pointed to above national average figures for infant and adult mortality, particularly in Rose Hill and Buxton Manor, and showed increasing numbers of young people of school age suffering from bronchial conditions necessitating the use of inhalers. Perhaps un-surprisingly, the combined effect of such factors, including a high incidence of family breakdown, ensures that the population of Rose Hill and Buxton Manor is characterized by, on the one hand, a process of movement and rehousing and, on the other, a fixed and static population containing two or three generations of families, some of which are considered 'notorious' by the authorities for their 'inbreeding'. This, linked with a housing policy that relocates single parents, rent and rate defaulters, debtors, the mentally ill and the homeless to such neighbourhoods as a last resort, reinforces the stereo-typical sink status of the area. In reality, however, the population of Rose Hill and Buxton Manor remains a settled and stable community; its major problem being one of experiencing more than its fair share of unemployment, poverty, poor housing and inadequate health, welfare and educational provision.

Despite the apparently high-profile nature of such neighbourhoods, the families and children featured in this study sought desperately, though not always successfully, to make themselves invisible. For families experiencing the combined effects of poverty and unemployment *self-exclusion* had become the principal strategy for dealing with the day-to-day problems they faced. Perhaps the real hidden injury of class experienced by families living on the estates rests in the constant pressure felt by them to demonstrate that they care for their children, that they value education, are good mothers and can turn their children out clean and tidy. In these circumstances, it is perhaps not surprising that some families seek to evade the attention of official agencies when things go wrong, and where obvious signs of poverty and distress (often manifested in outward signs of inadequate clothing, poor personal hygiene, fatigue and behavioural symptoms among children) may further marginalize them among peers, teachers and officialdom in general. Being a free-dinner child, not being able to pay for the ingredients for domestic science lessons, skipping a school trip through lack of money, being unable to provide PE kit (or avoiding showers because of the state of one's underwear) are all factors that, no matter how sensitively handled by the school, affect self-perception and bear heavily on the children of the poor. Yet if making oneself invisible, ducking and diving, bunking and skiving represents a strategy for avoiding authority and surviving, it is precisely this privatization that is held in suspicion by education and welfare agencies who view such behaviour as at best indicative of social inadequacy and, at worst, confirming a predisposition towards crime. Clearly, families on the margins know this, recognizing that the threat of social investigation by the authorities may well reinforce the self-fulfilling prophecy. This, coupled with reduced training opportunities under YT and ET, and linked with cuts in benefit, reinforces the poverty trap and serves to marginalize both the residents and their neighbourhood in the eyes of the outside world. As others have argued (Coffield *et al.* 1986; Prout 1988), the culmination of such experiences both ghettoizes and confirms the 'notorious' stereotype in such areas, which in turn renders them more accessible to policing by various external agencies.

From the evidence considered in Chapters 3 and 4, it is clear that many families living in such circumstances experience a combination of inequalities, associated with unemployment, poor health, debt and inadequate housing, as well as high levels of police and welfare surveillance, which approximates to civic exclusion (Lockwood 1985). A further factor that separates off such communities from mainstream society is the workfare principle, which links citizenship, training and social security. Yet despite the absence of available employment and training opportunities in such areas as Rose Hill and Buxton Manor, the civil right to social security for many young people has been removed, even though they are already excluded from the labour market and have lost their right to work (Lee *et al.* 1990). Although some young people and adults did find permanent full-time employment in mining and ceramics, the vast majority of the population of Rose Hill and Buxton Manor were unemployed or worked part-time in service industries or in 'self-employment', where their loss of citizenship rights could be hidden from them by the right to work in low-skill, low-waged jobs (Lee *et al.* 1990) – a pattern of inequality mirrored in the destinations of school-leavers (Table 5.1). Noticeably, this pattern of school-leavers' destinations reveals two things: first, the way in

Table 5.1 Destinations of school-leavers

	Total	Percentage of fifth years
Job employment	41	20
YTS	86	42
Sixth-form	18	9
Jones Technical College	10	5
Unemployed	34	16
Not known	18	9

Total of 207 school-leavers' destinations, Hareton High School (1990).

which school closely mirrors the opportunity structures of the community; secondly, how low levels of participation in post-sixteen education and training further reinforce such inequalities. Thus, despite the resilience, pride and self-sufficiency of people living in Rose Hill and Buxton Manor, often supported by the best endeavours of heads and teachers to raise expectations and standards, market forces, contrary to theory, remain unresponsive to such endeavour. How is this to be explained?

Choice, opportunity and schooling in Norwest

Perhaps not surprisingly in the circumstances so far described, many parents interviewed in this study talked of leaving the area, of wanting a better future for themselves and their children, of feeling trapped by their experience of living on the estates. This view was aptly summarized by one pupil in his summation that 'employers won't even look at you when they see where you live and which school you went to.' Whether accurate or not, such an account not only displays something of the way some young people see their futures, but also provides comment on the increasingly 'sink' status of certain types of schooling under the ERA. Evidence in this study confirms Alder and Raab's (1988) conclusions that the Parents' Charter is leading to the emergence of a number of magnet or sink schools, and thus to increased inequalities of provision. This is particularly evident in relation to the three schools referred to in this study, which, in addition to suffering from falling rolls, express concern about losing their more able pupils to star schools and, in return, taking in pupils from such schools rejected on the basis of selection or exclusion or both. According to Ball (1990):

> Sink schools will take some pupils deflected from star schools and will have a captive population of pupils whose parents are unable or unwilling

to meet the demands and costs of arranging travel. They may even choose as a survival strategy in the education market to specialize, say, in responding to the needs of pupils with learning difficulties.

Although it was too early on in the implementation of the ERA to discern any massive outflows from the schools in this study there was growing anxiety among the heads and teachers that we interviewed, that dumping would occur once open enrolment, LMS and opting out provision began to bite. What concerned them most, however, was the arbitrary distinctions made between star and sink schools, which despite the ERA remained linked to class, status and residential catchment, with the most successful schools drawing on a full complement of mixed-ability pupils from within and beyond their own catchment, leaving schools in less prosperous areas to recruit from a long special needs tail. The danger here is that as successful schools become more successful, they have the facility under the ERA to accrue more resources and to become more selective, thereby discarding less able or disruptive pupils to local 'secondary modern' schools, which are then left to pick up the LMS tab.

Although, under LMS, schools with falling rolls may increase their numerical and financial establishment, they also risk inheriting a disproportionate number of pupils with special needs who require additional resources and help. As we have indicated, LMS and open enrolment have highlighted this issue in various ways, since under the present delegation scheme in Norwest, the funding for an excluded pupil remains in the school at which he or she was a registered pupil at the January count. Thus, a school that permanently excludes a pupil in May of any year continues to receive funding for that pupil up to 31 March of the following year: at current values in the budget formula of Norwest this means that the school saves £1,134. The corollary of this is that, if such a pupil is relocated to another school, that second school receives no additional funding until the next year's budget is calculated. One implication of this is that timing of exclusions and referrals will become strategic in the new processes by which 'reciprocity' will be negotiated between schools under LMS, with the increased risk of dumping from over-subscribed successful schools to under-subscribed sink schools. This is a process tailor-made to ensure institutional survival for some but likely to reinforce divisions between winners and losers, and manifesting little thought for the educational requirements of the young people involved, particularly those with special needs or those in care (Jackson 1987).

The regulations under the ERA relating to local financial management of schools require pupil numbers to be the main source for allocating funds. Currently in Norwest, 82 per cent of the aggregate school budget is allocated on age-weighted numbers, with proposals to reduce this to about 77 per cent in due course. What Norwest LEA proposes is a case for amending the LMS scheme so that a pupil taken off the roll of a school, whether admitted to an alternative school, to a unit or to home tuition, should 'carry' the unexpired portion of his or her resource to the new location. There would not, however, be a simultaneous deduction from the releasing school in mid-financial year. What the Norwest LEA working party (referred to in the LEA as the Elton Working Party) propose is for an adjustment in the subsequent year's budget, an example of which is, for a fourteen-year-old pupil permanently excluded in May 1990:

> The budget of the releasing school will have been credited.
> (a) four months as a fourteen-year-old (1.4 weighting) = 0.47 units
> (b) seven months as a fifteen-year-old (1.6 weighting) = 0.93 units
> The pupil value of a pupil unit is, say, £810
> Amount to be transferred is £810 × 1.4 = £1,134

This example is not only indicative of the financial complexities involved in placing a price on pupils' heads, it also illustrates the sensitive relationship between pupil numbers, school resources and institutional survival. Although the Norwest LEA working party report acknowledges that aspects of this proposed transfer of funding require more detailed study, its focus on disruptive and excluded pupils deals with only the tip of the LMS iceberg. It does not, for example, address wider aspects of open enrolment and parental choice in circumstances where parents may wish, for other reasons, to transfer their children to other schools in mid-financial year, where similarly no adjustment is made to the alternative school's budget share. Perhaps the most disturbing question posed by all this, and a matter to which we will return in due course, is where the educational needs of young people are to be met under the welter of new legislative and financial arrangements, especially among those in care, those with special needs and in circumstances where there is a significant delay in achieving an alternative school for an excluded pupil (Levy and Kahan 1991). Partly in response to this question but more particularly in relation to the various ways agencies tackle 'the tragic theme of children lost in a limbo between social and education services', a *Times Educational Supplement* editorial leader offered the following observation:

> Once a school has expelled a child as too hard to handle, the problem is passed to the LEA, which has a duty to provide education. That may in the end lead to home tuition. Social workers may not think education is as important as care, or even that school is part of the problem. And when responsibility is split between children's home and the nearest school, it is now plain that the temptation for teachers to assume when a child does not turn up that there is a safe pair of hands at the social services end is too easy an option. Of course, the most important moral for teachers is that achievement must not be neglected because of emotional difficulties. Although they cannot be blamed for what happens in children's homes they might, as with child abuse, consider whether – as outsiders with a pupil's confidence – they could do more to pick up warning signs. If

teachers and social workers cannot work together across the departmental turf, it becomes less easy to see the point of a local authority
responsibility for the services.

('Someone to speak for the children',
Times Educational Supplement 7 June 1991)

Clearly the matter of improved inter-agency liaison is an important one. Yet
perhaps the quality of the education and care provided to young people is
equally important. In this respect it would seem naive to blame key 'players',
social workers, teachers and local authorities, whose apparent failure to
respond to the issues is matched only by successive governments' indifference
to and failure to invest in the professional training and support necessary for
agencies and families working with troubled children. Ostensibly, the main
provisions of the Children Act, which came into effect in October 1991, focus
more pertinent attention on the welfare of the child in relation to all the inter-
agency matters to which we have so far referred, linking police, court, criminal
justice, family and education matters. Following on Warnock (1978), HMI
(1987), the Elton Committee of Enquiry (1988) and the ERA, the Children Act
emphasizes the requirement for closer mutual support roles of education
department and social services personnel, and is designed to speed up legal
proceedings involving children, rendering EWOs responsible for educational
supervision orders (see Section 26, Education Supervision Orders, Children
Act). Yet, if the intention of the ERA, Children Act 1989 is to define the
interest of the child as 'paramount', and to achieve more effective inter-agency
cooperation, a question mark remains about the likely consequences of
legislation whereby pupils accrue a cash value and schools are expected to
compete for them in the open market.

Inevitably, a market mechanism of this kind leaves schools such as Hareton
High in a difficult position, in terms of how they invest their resources and of
what kind of school they become, a position discussed in the following
interview with the Deputy head at Hareton High:

> *Deputy head:* This school, though newly designed in 1988, has gone
> through two amalgamations in 1985 and 1986 and in 1988. It changed
> its name at least three times and is effectively an amalgamation of
> four schools. So, it's a new school but with a history. Despite its
> capacity for over 1,000 pupils we are in a falling roll situation, down to
> 650 pupils. We lost ten staff last year and expect to lose six this year.
> With falling rolls you have the obvious problem of morale and staff
> motivation and this isn't helped by other factors over and above actual
> falling rolls. We are for instance the main school serving three quite
> widespread catchments, or what were catchments, so not surprisingly
> at the top and bottom ends or outer limits, call it what you will, there
> are schools nearer to a number of our pupils and some of them are going
> there. This isn't helped by the bus company putting up fares, which is

also a disincentive for some families with one or more children who can't afford to send them here. Also with open enrolment, parents now have more choice. Many parents are looking at schools more closely now in terms of exam result, in terms of discipline, behaviour, attendance and all those aspects.

DG: How do you respond to this? Is this something that worries you?

Deputy head: It's not so much that, but the present climate in which all this is happening does worry me. A good school should be continually reviewing these things. We are a good school and we've got great kids. As a new school we've invested heavily in our pastoral care system. We take great care in liaising with parents. Much of our recent school-based INSET has been given over to questions about making the school more effective, much time and effort has gone into reviewing behaviour, discipline and attendance, we have set up various working parties monitoring these things, staff have been on a number of residentials and we give a lot of thought about the physical environment of the school, and we are heavily involved in all the new curricular changes going on at the present time, in IT, TVEI, national curriculum, community projects, school/college liaison and much more. What worries me is that despite all we do we feel beaten back, we are being judged on performance criteria, you know, such as exams, attendance, behaviour and discipline, which takes no account of our pupil intake and the problems children and families face in this area. We have for example a disproportionate number of pupils coming to us with below average reading and mathematical ability scores – we have a long special needs tail – we also take a lot of pupils excluded from elsewhere. We also have many pupils from very poor homes, parents unemployed or split up or both, a large number of pupils on court orders. These are not excuses, they are facts. We have got more children on inhalers in this school than almost all the other schools in Norwest put together. The danger is that no matter what we do we get to be seen as a sink school which makes parents want to send their children elsewhere.

DG: So what do you do? How does the school respond?

Deputy head: We press on. We continue to work on being a good school, we are a good school, but this is not always recognized in the current climate. The main challenge we have is to raise the expectations of the children. They have low expectations of themselves, and even our more able pupils don't go on to sixth form or further education studies, but it's also a matter of raising the expectations of the staff to bring out the best in everyone, to build up esteem and morale all round. This is hard to do when there is so much unemployment about, and local employers don't seem to value what we are trying to do. One option may be for us to become recognized as a centre for excellence in special needs. I'm not necessarily advocating this or us opting out, but it is an area in which we have expertise. It may well be that with our intake and open enrolment this is all we are left with, unpalatable as it may sound. But the real message is that you just can't judge a school like this on a predefined yardstick. It doesn't work and does untold harm to what we are trying to do here. We feel as if our hands are tied behind our backs.

Our purpose in quoting this interview at length is to demonstrate something of the way schools such as Hareton High are already anticipating their fate under the ERA. If becoming the special needs school in the area is considered to be one option, ostensibly turning 'dumping' to creative advantage, this inevitably reinforces the segregation between sink and star schools further, and may increase the flight of more able pupils away from the school. Inevitably, such considerations are likely to have a significant effect on the ethos of schools such as Hareton High, not least in terms of their own institutional survival. The question remains however: how far are a fight for survival and the pursuit of school effectiveness compatible?

Successful schooling re-visited

In the circumstances described above, attempts at making a school successful, and creating the sort of atmosphere referred to in the Elton Committee Report, confront two major problems. The first concerns responding to the market orientation of the ERA and, in particular, the divisive influence of LMS, open enrolment, opting out, city technology colleges and the National Curriculum; and the second involves overcoming the deregulated effects of government social and economic policy, which find their expression in the most disadvantaged sectors of the population, such as Rose Hill and Buxton Manor, communities least able to compete on equal terms in the open market. If in the period to the late 1960s and early 1970s these communities received minimal protection from a welfare state committed to full employment, universal education and social security provision, including some elements of (EPA) priority funding, such support structures no longer exist. Although deprivation in Rose Hill and Buxton Manor is not a recent phenomenon, its nature has taken on an altogether different picture in the 1980s, when the plug of welfare-ism has been pulled in favour of *laissez-faire* policies, opening up such areas further to the unregulated effects of market forces. We have argued that such policies have undermined labour commitment in such areas as Rose Hill and Buxton Manor, creating a disadvantaged, divided and, above all, under-educated and under-trained working class (Lee *et al.* 1990).

The relevance of the foregoing discussion to our analysis of school non-attendance is that truancy as a form of social exclusion (imposed or self-inflicted) cannot be conceptualized separately from wider forms of class and social stratification experienced by young people and their families. This is particularly so in economically depressed areas where pockets of persistent school non-attendance have always been high. One interpretation of such inequalities can of course be in terms of a culture of poverty or cycle of deprivation, which assumes that ghettoization can be explained largely with reference to learned experiences, attitudes and beliefs passed on from one generation to another. In other words communities learn to become failures and, in a perverse way, collude in their own downfall, by reproducing their own inadequacies, bad habits and cultural traits. The bleak determinism of this view is not, however, supported by the evidence of this study, which suggests that far from being self-inflicted, the problems of poverty, illness and neglect experienced by the residents of Rose Hill and Buxton Manor are, in the main, politically and economically generated. It is now increasingly evident that the fascination with achieving efficiency and reform in education, training, welfare and employment via the unregulated actions of markets has had calamitous effects on the relationship between family, school and community as described in this study. Leaving education, training and welfare to market forces has resulted in under-provision, skill shortages, low morale and waste of young people. The danger is that the market orientation of the ERA reinforces rather than transcends such inequalities, confirming instead of challenging the relationship between sink schools and sink communities. In so doing the ERA fails to recognize that pupils' responses to schooling are interlinked with their occupational aspirations, which are in turn closely related to self-esteem, motivation, attendance, attainment and behaviour in and out of school. Thus, in reality, and for the majority of parents and pupils in Rose Hill and Buxton Manor, the ERA simply represents another variation of schooling, of which the central ingredients, 'choice', 'opting out' and 'entitlement', remain remote and illusory concepts. Despite the vocational principles underlying a decade of educational reforms, there is little sign of current educational and training initiatives being linked with corresponding changes in work. As a consequence, the lack of relationship between education, training and productive labour has led to initiatives based on the containment of youth, largely based on job substitution and vocational discipline, control and employer-led considerations above all else. Our argument here is that attempts to raise standards by placing education in the market place, alongside deregulated employment, health, housing and welfare provision, are unlikely to capture either the support or the imagination of families and schools that are marginalized by such divisive policies, and that, in a perverse way, are currently being blamed for their own lack of ambition. It is to some of the principles of and alternatives to this current scenario that we now wish to turn.

Principles and alternatives

In the period from the New Training Initiative (1981) to the Education Reform Act (1988) the speed at which educational innovation and change has taken place, with the plethora of new policy, legislation and programmes arriving in quick succession, has been immense. However, a feature of such change is that it has been initiative-led, with one scheme, course or acronym (YTS, GCSE, TVEI, CPVE, LAPP and so forth) following another without any apparent logic or progression. However, in other respects the political and funding priorities accorded such initiatives have had systematic effects, not least in reducing LEA control of education, introducing free market strategies and supporting differentiation and selection. Thus, far from reducing duplication, waste and repetition in the system, government education reforms have increased competition and overlap between various intermediary bodies (e.g. NCC, NCVQ, TECs), various courses or programmes (e.g. TVEI, BTEC, CPVE, YT, ET) and various types of provision (e.g. CTCs, grant-aided schools, comprehensives, FE, tertiary and sixth-form colleges). In both institutional and curricular terms such haphazard development has atomized provision by increasing division, differentiation and selection, and by making it even more difficult to establish a coherent comprehensive pattern of education and training *for all* across the eleven to nineteen age range (Gleeson 1989, 1991). Yet, despite the then Prime Minister Margaret Thatcher's view 'that there is no such thing as society', and her successor's apparent commitment to a classless society, it is possible to discern an unfolding of Conservative education policy along class rather than societal lines. This is particularly noticeable in the ways government has targeted its various educational projects to specific audiences (notably the assisted places scheme, CTCs and new grant-aided schools) and, elsewhere, has conscripted the less fortunate into sink schools, youth (YT) and adult (ET) training programmes, backed by punitive changes in social security legislation which, for many, further reduce opportunities for post-sixteen earning and learning. This conception of education represents a far cry from the common-sense view held in the 1960s that schools were important both to the individual who attended them and to society at large. Nowadays the contemporary context of education for citizenship has little to do with nurturing the complex relationship between individual and society, and everything to do with sponsoring individuals acting in support of their own sectionalized interests.

If the ERA has significantly influenced the legal, administrative and ideological under-pinnings of schooling, it has not necessarily altered the qualitative base of education, or influenced school effectiveness one way or another. In this respect it is important to recognize that analysis of the noise and heat of reform and the making of national policy still begs questions about the implementation and realization of qualitative reform in the schools and classrooms (Ball 1990). As Ball has noted, 'the struggles over interpretation and accommodation go on', a view which suggests that despite all the rhetoric about market-led reform there still remains all to play for in the debate about making schools more successful. The question remains as to which direction the debate should take.

Although schooling is not strictly compulsory the question arises: is it realistically avoidable and how should we debate the alternatives? Given our analysis, how can we, for example, justify compulsory schooling and the processes of enforcement, containment and control that go with it for certain working-class pupils? The simple answer is that we cannot. On the other hand it does not follow that we support the de-schooling or anti-school lobby, each of which (but for different reasons) views de-institutionalization as an answer to the issues of liberation and contemporary schooling. In answer to both questions, therefore, our position is that the historical and contemporary rigidities associated with schooling, and the failure of market forces to deliver real and lasting educational reform, do not of themselves invalidate schooling. Rather, it has been the political and social context within which schools have had to operate that has continually undermined the ideal that schooling for all leads to education for all. Consequently, the challenge is not simply one of making schools more effective, but also one of changing the criteria and context of schooling in terms of its form, content and control. Anticipating the paradox of this pro-state-schooling dilemma, Johnson (1991) points to the impoverishment of current state education provision and the need for its improvement, rather than its dismantling in the name of radical alternatives which, he maintains, do little more than give up on working-class education. According to Johnson:

> The difficulty is to work out alternatives. A more open, permissive, network-like system, as envisaged by de-schoolers in the 1970s, could increase unfairness still further. Some measures for de-institutionalizing education (reducing the compulsory schooling period for example and extending training) would be gifts to the right and would reproduce the whole historical legacy of anti-education. There would be marvellous opportunities for cutting public expenditure; not 'care in the community' only (without funds) but education on the cheap as well... but the pro-state-schooling strategy is paradoxical too. On the whole I support the plan of expanding public education, into a comprehensive 'tertiary stage' and especially expanding higher education. But if compulsory schooling is extended without changes of its form, content, levels of popular control and social context, what is to prevent the same old forms of resistance emerging, the same unequal outcomes, the same disappointing results?
>
> (Johnson 1991)

There is, as Johnson observes, no quick fix or easy answer to the sorts of alternative educational movements which he envisages. Central to the reform process must be recognition that it is not just policies, structures of access and provision that need to be changed but also the content, context and control of education. This process of reform involves recognition of the central role of education in the personal and social development of the child, and a rethinking of the institutional constraints of school, including the kind of assumptions about care and control, parenting and childhood that underpin them. Without such reform the sentiments of the pupil who, when asked by his former headteacher what he thought of new school buildings, answered 'It could all be marble, sir, but it would still be a bloody school' (British Government Report 1963, referred to by Hamilton 1990) are likely to remain those of future generations of school pupils. It is not simply more of the same, or organizational change that is required now – since new structures can very often serve Old Masters (Tawney 1918) – but a programme of educational reform that is informed by public and political debate, and that seeks to address the corporate needs of society as well as the individual interests of young people. Such a debate must first confront the reality that an education system increasingly driven by market forces is likely to have dramatic consequences on personal, social and economic development in years to come.

Educational selection and differentiation is neither an effective nor an efficient way of distributing talent throughout society. This is not to deny that talent, ability and competition are important preconditions of attainment in society. However, if choice is seen to drive the new market mechanism of education the question remains as to *who* has choice and to what extent parents' demands for what is in the best interest of their children coincides with what is in the best interest of *all* the nation's children. Here the danger is that if education is determined solely by self-interest it will make schools less responsive to local and national needs, allowing the most able and privileged more say and greater access in determining the new arrangements of schooling and society itself. Thus, in accentuating competition rather than cooperation the market principle in education is socially and economically divisive, and fails both to educate young people and to utilize the talents of the widest cross-section of the population. Essentially, the question boils down to whether education should serve the sectionalized interests of elites or cater for the needs and abilities of all pupils. At the moment the competitive ethos of the ERA, supported by the assisted places scheme, CTCs, opting out and open enrolment, is that it fails to serve children of all abilities: in separating off star and sink schools it discourages pupils from experiencing peer support and the influence which such support provides in the learning process. Moreover, differentiation between able and less able pupils doubly disadvantages pupils with special needs, including those in care: they are not only cut off from a comprehensive system involving all their peers, but also receive proportionately less resources to meet their educational requirements under the new formula funding of LMS (Johnson 1991). Accordingly, in such circumstances, where schools become differentiated by the ability of their pupils, it remains unclear how the twin aims of the ERA – achieving universality of choice and uniformity of standards – are to be realized and, perhaps more importantly, whether star and sink schools are actually what parents really want.

In challenging the hegemony of market forces in education it is necessary to recognize that such forces are socially defined and are neither transfixed or immutable. Left to themselves, such forces do not improve learning, schooling in general, or teacher quality and supply. Their strategic application in government social and economic policy has been to serve an ideological purpose, both in deregulating local democracy, services, provision and funding, and in obscuring the redistribution of wealth in favour of the most advantaged. Thus, despite the *Independent* newspaper's 'Charter for change' (5 June 1991), anticipating that local council control needs to be 'clearly and swiftly abolished as soon as schools are ready', the reality is that the demise of local authorities is likely to weaken the power of consumers (parents and local community alike) 'to the benefit, mostly of professionals, but mainly of officials, who will be protected by distance and by time from popular pressures' (Bogdanor 1991). According to Bogdanor, if market forces are to operate effectively, particularly in education and public services, they require regulation, beyond the limitations of the Parents' Charter and self-governance.

> Since there is no clear demarcation between what is policy and what is not, the likely outcome of centralised control of education is a process of buck-passing. Where things go wrong, the minister will say 'Do not blame me, blame the manager [that is, the head or the funding council]'. The managers, on the other hand, will complain that if only they had sufficient resources, they would not have had to take unpopular decisions. The citizen will be unable to determine where responsibility lies. Boards, as Jeremy Bentham noticed, are screens. They serve to protect those working on them from the rigours of accountability. The truth is that we have not yet found a method within the confines of ministerial responsibility of making centralised public services properly accountable. It was for this reason that the Conservative government embarked on its quango cull in the years between 1979 and 1983. It is ironic now to find the Conservatives creating new quangos by the dozen in order to enforce their programme of market regulation.
>
> (Bogdanor 1991)

Viewed from this perspective any consideration of the 'alternatives' must take into account the relations between education, community and labour market in favour of *policies* that emphasize cooperation and democratic partnership rather than competition, and that balance market considerations with the personal, social and economic purposes of education and training. Thus, if concepts such as ethos and atmosphere are to mean anything in the pursuit of school effectiveness, education for citizenship must be viewed as a shared experience; not one in which pupils are arbitrarily separated off within and between schools on the basis of vocational ability, academic aptitude, class or gender characteristics. Notions of quality and equality in education presuppose a model of pupils as active citizens, rather than one which sees them as a product or a problem to be fitted into some pre-ordained slot in society. They necessarily imply an altogether different vision of pupil empowerment and entitlement from that enshrined in the National Curriculum, which is a mechanistic and overly subject-specific curriculum with a central emphasis on testing and performance. It is not, however, our purpose here to argue against the principle of a National Curriculum as such, but to advance a less bureaucratic and market-driven concept of education, one in which active learning, learner support, identification of pupil needs and cooperation rather than competition constitute the central principles. Consequently, in rethinking the institutional constraints of school and the assumptions of experts about parenting and childhood (and the care that goes with it), it is necessary to question the prevailing content, curriculum and experience of schooling and, indeed, to make schooling itself more flexible.

Finally, and specifically in relation to school attendance, our conclusion is that improving pupil motivation, attendance and standards in education involves much more than the present carrot and stick incentive structure allows. This is not to deny the important gains which schools have made in rewarding and encouraging success among pupils, over and beyond the 'Mars Bar' syndrome, involving cups, merit marks, medals and prizes. There is, for example, evidence that a number of important initiatives associated with GCSE project work, link courses, TVEI, LAPP, modular developments, compacts and work-based learning have increased the potential flexibility of curriculum and school organization. Moreover, such initiatives, often associated with IT, flexible learning and community projects, support Meighan's (1988) concept of flexi-schooling, which combines the in and out of school learning experience to which many young people readily respond. The problem remains, however, that such initiatives largely remain peripheral to mainstream education, are inadequately funded and are often only for less academic pupils. Accordingly, if real fexibility is to be achieved it requires greater rather than less investment in such learning opportunities for *all* pupils, combining properly resourced and accredited schemes of study linking school, work and community. Additionally, what is called for at the present time is a curriculum that integrates knowledge, skills and people, and that does not separate off able from less able, sink from star school and academic from vocational student in a divisive fashion. The major starting point must be to define education and training more broadly, to emphasize youth's active involvement in, rather than separation from, mainstream society. This means a rejection of the narrow and subject-specific orientation of the National Curriculum, which reflects the political assumptions about popular schooling and control enshrined in Conservative political dogma. In reality what now accounts for the shrill paranoia about truancy is the emphasis placed in the National Curriculum on the universal delivery of core curriculum, phased assessment, foundation subjects and testing at key stages (ages seven, eleven, fourteen and sixteen). This emphasis puts a high premium not only on attendance, but also on the success of the National Curriculum and the reform process itself – ultimately placing an added burden of responsibility on parents and young people.

What we have argued in this chapter is that the active role of student learning within and outside school and workplace needs to be stressed, accentuating the social and political processes involved in making the link between education, training, work and community a more relevant, critical and meaningful process. This is particularly important in the area of post-sixteen education and training policy, which currently acts as a disincentive for many young people staying on. Despite the apparent rise in full-time staying on rates post-sixteen (to 53 per cent), very little is happening in the sixteen to nineteen curriculum, with many pupils involved in GCSE re-takes or opting for inappropriate A-level, BTEC or YT courses, which accommodate neither their needs nor their interests. On closer inspection it is therefore not surprising to observe high wastage and failure rates from such courses at seventeen-plus, which do not immediately show up in the post-sixteen figures. The real issue is to ensure continuity of provision and progression across school and college, both to counteract overlap in the qualification system (A levels, YT, BTEC, NVQ, CPVE, SEAC) and to encourage more young people to achieve substantially higher qualifications at eighteen, giving access to higher education and skilled jobs (*Guardian* 7 May 1991). In this respect investment in the transition and transmission points between school and college, community and labour market is likely to have a number of beneficial effects, not least in improving motivation, skills and access to further ecucation and employment. Thus, an alternative way of looking at investment and choice in the community is to view them not as something driven by market forces, but as something attained and achieved by individuals in receipt of high quality education and training, which can be translated as useful knowledge in the workplace and community context. It is this type of incentive that will support schools and colleges in their attempts to become effective, both in pursuit of real and lasting reform, and in reducing the incidence of disruption, alienation and truancy experienced by many young people. Not only is this likely to enhance the morale, motivation and skill levels of citizens, parents, pupils and professionals alike, it is also likely to inspire confidence in a future that education and training may bring; a future that transcends arbitrary distinctions between 'winners' and 'losers'.

Bringing education back in will not be an easy task. Yet if we are to challenge the present climate of educational nemesis it is surely time to recognize that standards in education cannot be left to the unregulated effects of market forces which, alone, know no logic or morality and which, contrary to prevailing rhetoric, can actually set no standards independent of human endeavour. It is to this neglected aspect of the current debate about quality and effectiveness in education that this study is addressed. Those who bunked off and never got caught (and those who did get caught) would know what we are talking about, even though it is unlikely that they will ever have the opportunity to say so in quite these terms. However, it has not been our intention to romanticize truancy but to contextualize it as a phenomenon that tells us as much about the system and how it works as it does about the young people and families who purportedly reject it. By giving voice to the latter we have sought to shed light on the former at a time when new systems of education, training, criminal justice and child care are being presented as containing all-embracing solutions to the old problems of education, inequality and social justice. Yet cosmetic change is not enough and, as this study has suggested, recent educational legislation is more likely to increase than diminish social divisions and inequality. That is not surprising. Both truancy and the laws in which it is constituted are rooted in the class and political interests of an increasingly divided society. Not until the politics of compulsory education are driven by a belief that the equal education of all our children is equally in all our interests will more young people believe that they can equally benefit from the goods that schools have to offer.

APPENDIX 1: BIOGRAPHICAL
DETAILS OF THE YOUNG PEOPLE
INTERVIEWED

Biographies of young women (alphabetically by pseudonym)

Alicia (16)

A few weeks short of leaving school, Alicia was planning to take several exams which she hoped would enable her to follow a career as an army nurse. Currently at her third high school, Alicia was used to taking fairly frequent days and half-days off from school, spending this time sleeping or watching television. Largely uninterested in school work, Alicia attended primarily for the social contact it provided. Despite this, and despite her truancy, Alicia managed to make her way through the school system without attracting too much negative attention, and without coming into contact with education welfare.

Anita (15)

Anita had been happy in school until the third or fourth year, and had begun taking time off in her fifth year. Often this was because of a lack of interest, rather than a particular aversion to school. She hoped to do fairly well in her exams and go on to study child care at college. Anita's non-attendance brought her into frequent conflict with her mother and also brought her to the attention of the education welfare officer who, at the time of interview, was threatening to bring legal action. However, Anita thought that the EWO was 'nice' and that she could talk to her if she needed.

Annette (14)

Annette, a resident at Beechwood family centre, appeared to be a disturbed and unhappy young woman. Although she was extremely uncommunicative, a story of dissatisfaction with school and days spent wandering around town centres with her best friend slowly emerged. Annette had come into frequent contact with social workers and EWOs, and was sometimes picked up by the police while wandering the streets, although not for committing any offences. Her reasons for being in care were unclear, but staff had hinted at a history of sexual abuse, and this *may* be supported by Annette's clear reluctance to talk about her time spent in the city's general hospital. However, her evident trauma may have been connected with the family centre itself, which was one of the centres involved in the 'pindown' controversy. Annette seemed hurt or bewildered by most aspects of her life, her only enthusiasm being her ambition to become a disco dancer.

Bernadette (9)

Bernadette was the only primary school interviewee, but she tells an interesting story of parentally condoned absence, in particular the gender-specific 'home duties' expected of girls and young women. Attending the IT programme at Forest Hill because she was 'at risk', rather than because of her own criminal inclinations, Bernadette was clearly defined as coming from a 'problem family', and her truancy was only one of a complex web of problems.

Cynthia (16)

Living in Cumbria Road long-stay children's home, Cynthia had left school several months before being interviewed. Looking back on her schooldays, she attributed her truancy to 'just being one of the gang'. She felt that, because she was in care, her school checked up on her more than was usual, and, under considerable pressure from both the school and the home, she reduced her truancy during her fifth year to certain lessons and the occasional half-day. In her final year, she also decided to work harder because of forthcoming exams, some of which she succeeded in passing. In the near future she was looking forward to moving into a semi-independent flat, and to taking up a YTS placement in child care, and possibly taking a college course in the same subject. Cynthia is one of the seven young people who had been on 'pindown', having been sent temporarily to Church Street (YPA) from Cumbria Road (children's home) for truancy and absconding. She had learnt to 'play the system', knowing which actions to take and which to avoid, in terms of likely responses from those in authority.

Dawn (15)

Dawn was due to leave school in a few weeks, and was clear about her future: she wanted to train as a caterer, whether or not she passed her exams. She often found school irrelevant and brought work home while absent from school. She gave bullying as a second major reason for her absences. Her younger sister, Jackie, was also known as a non-attender to both the school and the EWO, and both were a little puzzled as to why their family had not been taken to court when one of Jackie's friend's parents had been taken to the magistrates' court. Dawn had been threatened with legal action while in the fourth year, but no further action had been taken.

Glenda (14)

Glenda explained that she was in voluntary care at Church Street (YPA), partly because there was conflict with her parents, and partly because she thought that it would count in her favour in her forthcoming court cases (she had already appeared in court on charges of burglary). Residential care workers explained that the conflict between Glenda and her parents was due to her perceived sexual delinquency, and the care workers attempted to control Glenda in this respect. Glenda attributed both her truancy and her criminal activities to being 'just bored': she was prepared to curtail both under duress from various agencies. Glenda had been on 'pindown' for two weeks, but was the only one to describe it as 'not too bad'.

Jackie (12)

At the age of twelve Jackie already had a reputation with the school and the EWO as a persistent non-attender, and reported that her friend – with the same record of absenteeism – had caused her parents to be fined in the magistrates' court because of her truancy. Jackie had been involved in the new system at Hareton High to reward good attendance but, disliking Mars Bars, was unimpressed! She shared fairly strong anti-school attitudes with her mother and older sister (Dawn), often viewing it as an irrelevance to her life on a large council estate. At the time of interview, Jackie was being threatened with court action by the EWO.

Kathleen (15)

Kathleen was involved in shoplifting at around the age of ten, but her only appearance in court was to do with non-attendance. A care order was made, but Kathleen was allowed to remain at home with her parents. She said she would have been prepared to go into local authority care rather than return to school. At the time of interview she was attending the IT programme in Church Street, having been expelled from school for fighting. Although she felt that the atmosphere was tense at times on the programme, she much preferred it to mainstream schooling. Despite an air of bravado, Kathleen said she felt ill most of the time, and reported two suicide attempts.

Kerry (15)

Kerry was living in Priory Road, a long-stay children's home, with her younger sister, and both had experienced foster placements. A charismatic young woman, Kerry was the natural leader in the home. Having truanted fairly frequently earlier in her school career, she became a fairly regular attender in her fourth year, because of concern over exams. Nevertheless, she still found school difficult, and was often absent because of illness, sometimes real, sometimes faked. She talked about periods of depression, and incidents of self-injury. She was on the fringes of a group of drug-takers, but was determined not to become involved herself. Kerry had ambitions to secure a good home and a good job for herself, and not to fall into the trap of early motherhood, as she saw her elder sister as having done. However, at the age of sixteen (about a year after the interview) Kerry, still at school and in care, was pregnant.

Leah (15)

Leah's mother was present during the interview (and was also interviewed separately) and there was evidently little conflict between them over Leah's truancy, although this had led to magistrates' court for the mother, and a forthcoming juvenile court appearance for Leah herself. Leah had also been permanently excluded from her school (for fighting with other girls and conflict with teachers) and was currently having home tuition. Leah attributed many of her problems to the school itself, and thought she would settle down if she was accepted into her chosen school. Leah wanted to be a secretary when she left school, but was afraid she had made the wrong option choices during her fourth year. In the end, no new school was found for Leah, and her EWO negotiated an unofficial pre-YTS secretarial placement for her.

Lesley (15)

Lesley was one of the most persistent non-attenders, beginning to truant in her second year at school and escalating the truancy to the point where she only attended for a few days during her fifth year. She has been in court for non-attendance, and began attending more regularly for a short while after a supervision order had been made, and when she was under threat of a full care order, but had soon started truanting again. Lesley's non-attendance caused a lot of conflict between her and her mother, and on one occasion her mother called the police in an attempt to force her to go to school. Lesley had been on a voluntary care agreement, but was then remanded into care because of a series of charges including assault and criminal damage. At the time of interview Lesley was in Moorland Road (YPA), but had previously spent time on 'pindown' in Church Street (YPA), from which she had absconded. She had also run away several times from Moorland Road. Lesley hoped to do YTS training in hairdressing or child care when she left school.

Mandy (14)

Mandy began to truant in her fourth year at school, when she was faced with changing schools and taking options. She took several weeks off at a time, spending the time walking around the shops with her older sister. She found school boring, but thought she would attend regularly if she could return to her old school. She said she was not too worried about the EWO's frequent visits and threats to take her to court. Mandy attended the IT programme at Forest Hill for one evening per week, as she was deemed to be 'at risk'. As part of the programme, workers tried to encourage her to attend school regularly, but she was only interested if they would offer her a cash inducement. Mandy was interested in a job in child care when she left school.

Michelle (14)

Currently in her third year, Michelle had taken a lot of time away from school during her second year, partly for her own reasons, and partly so that she could help her mother who had been involved in a car accident. Her parents had been taken to magistrates' court the previous year because of her own and her brother's absences, and had been given a conditional discharge. The whole family were grateful to the EWO who had, they believed, prevented the children from being taken into care. Michelle had been frightened by the court case and was attending school more regularly, although she still took some illicit time off. Michelle had experienced a lot of conflict with the teachers, but felt more settled during her third year. She thought that she would attend fairly regularly for the rest of her school career, as she hoped to join the police force on leaving school.

Rosemary (13)

At the time of interview in her second year, Rosemary had had many absences since beginning high school. She reported no particular reason, she simply didn't want to attend school. Her ambition was to be accepted into a special school, as she thought that that would be a much more pleasant experience. Both she and her mother disliked the EWO, who had taken the parents to court where they had been fined £150 and who was also threatening to take Rosemary to juvenile court. Rosemary responded to threats by going to school for a while, but soon began taking time off again. She was part of the incentives scheme for good attendance at her school (Hareton High), but thought it was irrelevant. Rosemary compared herself with her best friend, and others, who had had as many absences as she had, but whose parents had not been taken to court, and felt that the system was arbitrary. However, her approach was lighthearted and she did not seem to be too worried about the various threats. She expressed an interest in bricklaying as a career, but thought there might not be any opportunities for women.

Sarah (15)

At the time of interview in her fourth year, Sarah had stayed away from school a lot during her second year because she was bullied, largely, she thought, because she was in care. During her third and fourth years, she began attending more regularly, not because she was in trouble, but because she thought she was wasting her life. In fact, she felt that because she did not get attention for truanting she wanted to rebel more, which involved her staying out late at night and eventually being taken into care. She had spent some time in Whin Hill House (residential psychiatric placement) and another family centre before ending up in Greenwood Avenue family centre. When she left school she hoped to qualify as a nursery nurse.

Susan (16)

Susan's history was a complicated one, involving many moves between parents, step-parents and care institutions, as well as several changes of school. She had been expelled from one school and was currently refusing to attend another. She explained that she missed school a lot because she wanted to attend her boyfriend's court cases and, later, to visit him in prison. She has been in court several times herself, on charges including stealing and assault. At the time of interview Susan was living at Church Street family centre, and had been on 'pindown' several times, for truancy and absconding, for periods of up to two months. She described this experience as depressing and said it only made her more determined not to go to school. Susan described herself as having 'been through a lot', including sexual abuse as a child, solvent abuse, a spell in Whin Hill House and several moves between her parents. When she had moved into a flat within the young person's accommodation she had felt that she was becoming more settled, only to discover she was pregnant. She said that she had settled down again since her abortion. Her ambitions for the future would include doing something 'unusual for a girl', or something to do with art, but in the short term she intended to train for clerical work.

Tracy (11)

Although defined by teachers and IT workers (Forest Hill) as at least a potential non-attender, Tracy said that she had 'never bobbed', and thought that teachers checked on her attendance because 'I'm naughty and they think I'll do anything'. In her first year of high school, she disliked it very much, seeing it as something she simply had to 'bear'. As she was on an IT programme, Tracy had clearly been identified as potentially 'at risk' and/or as a trouble-maker.

Biographies of young men (alphabetically by pseudonym)

Aidan (16)

Interviewed a few weeks before leaving school, Aidan had been an occasional truant in his final year. On the whole, he liked school, taking time off only when he felt like doing something different: in fact he would prefer to be staying longer at school. His absences had been punished by the school, but there had been no involvement with education welfare, or other agencies. His parents knew about his absences, but left it to the school (Blue Mount High) to deal with. Aidan was hoping to be a mechanic on leaving school.

Campbell (15)

Until a short while before interview, Campbell had been living in Parkhouse Road YPA, charged with various offences, but was then living at home. He still attended the centre for personal tuition as he had been expelled from school (this tuition was provided by the juvenile justice programme). He had also spent some time in voluntary care 'because me mum couldn't handle me'. Campbell had been punished by the school for non-attendance (and for disruptive behaviour), and had been threatened several times with legal action by EWOs, but said he was unaffected by this, and continued doing what he wanted to. He was working in an abattoir at weekends, and hoped to do that full-time when he was officially allowed to 'leave school' (this was to be in January rather than at Easter, as he was excluded from school and receiving some tuition).

Chris (13)

Chris had been in and out of care since he was four, at first because he was physically abused by his father, and later because he was charged with criminal offences, including burglary. At the time of interview, he had been in Church Street YPA for two months, and had been permanently excluded from school four months previously to that. He was receiving tuition while in care, and hoping to be accepted into the local school. He liked his last school and attended regularly, having only truanted in primary school. He came to the attention of the school largely because of his behaviour, which led to agency-induced non-attendance, i.e. permanent exclusion from school. Chris liked staying at Church Street, on the whole, although he disliked his time spent on 'pindown', which led to him 'cracking up' and hitting a member of staff, who hit him back. Chris hoped to be a painter and decorator when he left school.

Dale (14)

Dale had truanted in primary school, and began again in his second year of high school, continuing up to the fourth year, when he was interviewed. He reported staying away only for a few days at a time, but the school, his parents and the EWO perceived him as a serious and persistent non-attender. His mother saw him also as being difficult and disruptive. Dale said he took time off because of difficulties with both teachers and pupils. He felt that the threats of his parents and the EWO that he would be taken into care if he persisted in non-attending were made just to scare him. He had had a social worker at age ten because of his non-attendance. He was unsure whether he would attend school regularly in the future, but was interested in a career in computers when he left school.

Dan (15)

Dan was described by his mother and by his EWO as being intelligent, but someone who just didn't want to work. The EWO described him as devious, judging him to be 'playing the system'. Dan began taking time off during his third year, and took more and more time off during his fourth and fifth years. He disliked school, but said he would make more effort to attend, partly because of pressure from the EWO, and partly to please his mother. Dan hoped to become a car mechanic on leaving school.

Duncan (14)

Duncan had been in care for about a year, dividing his time between young persons' accommodation (Parkhouse Road) and a family centre (Crossroads). The YPA was mainly for young offenders but Duncan had not committed any offences, and was placed in the special unit. Duncan said he refused to return to school because of bullying, and although he had been threatened with care proceedings by the EWO, he was in fact taken into care because of conflict with his family. At the time of interview Duncan was taking part in the new juvenile justice tuition scheme, two days per week, although his social worker was trying to have him accepted by a new school.

Edward (16)

Edward described himself as 'sort of expelled, not properly', although he had in fact been excluded from school during the month prior to interview. He was doing a pre-YTS placement in joinery, and hoped to continue full-time with this after his official school-leaving date, which was to be in a month's time. Although he had spent a year away from Norwest at school in Scotland, he felt he still had a bad reputation on returning to Norwest, and continued taking time away from school and being disruptive when he was there. Edward had been in care for three years, and liked the family centre where he lived (Greenwood Avenue). However, he disliked the time he had spent on 'pindown' at Church Street, where he had been sent because of truancy. Punishments at school had left him unaffected, but he said he would rather go to school than be on 'pindown'. Edward had a series of minor offences (mainly shoplifting), but had only been cautioned, and had not appeared in court.

Geoffrey (16)

Geoffrey had left school a few months prior to the interview – since then he had been working at various labouring and unskilled jobs. Geoffrey had a complicated history involving various care/custodial institutions, including several periods in Brooklands CHE, Moorland Road YPA and a young offenders' institution. He was a persistent non-attender, was expelled from school for disruptive behaviour, and had been involved in various offences, mainly burglary. At his current care placement (Moorland Road), Geoffrey was on a programme of 'independence', and preferred to stay there as he felt he would get back in trouble if he returned to live with either of his parents (divorced and both remarried). He was already on a community service order, and thought that this would be extended after his next court case. Geoffrey was hoping to find a new job, and perhaps go to college to improve his literacy skills.

Ian (15)

Ian at the time of interview was attending school fairly regularly, but had taken a lot of time off during his third year, which he attributed to bullying and generally not liking school. He had also experienced conflict with his parents over his behaviour (including stealing and temper outbursts), and his mother had called the police in at one point, as she felt she could not handle him. Ian had spent a period of time in Whin Hill, and was described by the psychiatric social worker as being one of their successes. Certainly, he was then enjoying school, hoping to pass his exams, go on to university and eventually become a journalist. His parents were impressed with him, and felt that he was doing very well at school.

John (15)

John began to truant while he was in primary school, spending the time 'doing nothing, or hassling somebody', and becoming involved in shoplifting, for which he had been cautioned once. At the time of interview he was in the children's home at Cumbria Road from which he had absconded, staying overnight in an empty house. He had spent time in Church Street on 'pindown' for truancy (up to six weeks at a time). More recently, he had been attending school fairly regularly, largely because he was checked up on by the school. John was waiting for a court case for various offences, and expected a suspended sentence or an attendance centre order. John came into care because his parents did not want him with them anymore, and they subsequently divorced and both remarried; he expected his mother to be soon moving away from the area. They had both become Jehovah's Witnesses, and he felt this had something to do with their disapproval of his activities. John liked his children's home, but had hated his time spent in Church Street.

Kirk (15)

Kirk allowed his mother to do most of the talking in their joint interview. He gave his reason for non-attendance as being a dislike of school and a desire to start work. He was absent frequently during his first year, and was taken into care during his second year, at Church Street, which he liked, apart from being placed on the 'pindown' regime. Later, he spent four months in a detention centre (now known as a young offenders' institution) for burglary. At the time of interview, Kirk was on a care order, but was staying at home and was supervised by staff at Church Street. He was at that time attending school regularly, partly because of his supervision (including incentives for attending school) and partly because he would be able to leave school in three months time, and did not think it was worth getting into trouble. Kirk was keen to go to work and willing to take any job when he left school.

Lenny (16)

Due to leave school three months after the time of interview, Lenny had been expelled three months previously, and was still waiting to be accepted by a new school. He was expelled for misbehaviour, but had also been in trouble the previous year because of his non-attendance. His parents had been taken to court over his and his sister's truancy, and had been given conditional discharges. The whole family were well-disposed towards the EWO but fairly hostile towards the school (Hareton High). The parents conceded that the children misbehaved, but also felt that teachers misused their powers. On the morning of the interview, Lenny had received a letter informing him that he was to be cautioned over an incident of shoplifting, something his mother felt would not have happened if he had not been expelled from school. Lenny hoped to join the army when he was old enough.

Martin (16)

Soon to be leaving school (Blue Mount High), Martin was worried that his absenteeism would affect his exam performance. He did not dislike school, and he only took time off when he was tired or generally fed up. Martin was going through the selection process for the army, and had one more interview to go. He thought he would be accepted anyway, but wanted to pass his exams in order to further his career. His parents did not know about his truancy, and he had not come into contact with any agency outside school. The teachers were not particularly punitive, simply telling him he must 'study harder'.

Michael (16)

Michael was leaving school (Blue Mount High) a few days after interview, and was hoping to take a business or management course at college, and eventually to follow his parents into public house management. He had liked school until the middle of his fifth year, when he began 'to get a bit restless'. He began to take occasional days away from school, either because he was tired or to enable him to catch up with GCSE coursework. He had had some (limited) contact with the EWO.

Mike (16)

Soon to leave school, Mike had been an occasional truant, and still took some half-days off from school, especially if he was late in getting up. He felt that teachers were unreasonable in their extent of checking on him, attributing this in part to the bad reputations acquired by his older brothers. He felt that he was not treated sufficiently as an adult. He had not come into contact with any agency outside school, but had been subjected to internal school discipline – such as detentions and being put on report – because of his absenteeism. This had occurred mainly during the fourth and early fifth years, decreasing as exams approached. Mike was willing to take any job on leaving school.

Mushtaq (16)

Mushtaq had been absent for half-days or particular lessons, but as he attended registration he claimed that he had not been caught. (Note, however, that he had been identified by Kevin Watson, his year tutor at Blue Mount High, as a non-attender.) Mushtaq said he had not been punished by the school for truancy, and also that his parents did not know – 'if they did know, they'd probably hit me'. Mushtaq expected to pass most of his exams, and go on a YTS placement. He hoped that eventually he would get a job in computing.

Patrick (15)

At the time of interview, Patrick had been in care for over five years, four years at Moorland Road, and a few months each at Yew Tree House and Crossroads family centre. Workers at Crossroads, where Patrick was currently resident, said that he had been taken into care because of a combination of factors, including family breakdown and poor school attendance. Patrick had been expelled from Stephenson High School ten months prior to interview and had subsequently been attending the juvenile justice tuition scheme. He was also on education welfare's list of persistent truants. He had refused new places in a couple of local schools, and felt that he was losing interest in attending school again. Before being expelled, Patrick had taken only a little time away from school, which he liked. He had, however, disliked primary school, and had truanted while there. Apart from court appearances concerning his court order, Patrick had also been in court for burglary, for which he received a twelve-month conditional discharge. Patrick was fairly settled in Yew Tree House, but had disliked Crossroads because 'the boss kept beating me up like... 'cos I ran off'. He was unsure whether he would be in care until he was sixteen, or until he was eighteen, but said that he would like to work in a shop when he left school.

Paul (12)

Having attended Roman Catholic schools during his primary and first year of secondary schooling, Paul was now attending the local non-denominational school. Having truanted frequently during his first year of secondary school (for periods up to two months), Paul did so more rarely during his second year. This he attributed not to a change of school, but to the stricter regime in his current children's home (Yew Tree House) as compared with his previous stay in a family centre. Paul had received several cautions for shoplifting and other offences, and was about to appear in court for assault. (About eighteen months after interview, Paul appeared in court on a long list of charges, mostly stealing, burglary and shoplifting, but the outcome is not known.) Paul attributes his recent regular attendance to the officer in charge at Yew Tree House, partly because he was known to hit young people, and partly because he had made Paul realize how important school was in terms of his future plans to join the Royal Navy.

Robert (16)

In care at Greenwood Avenue family centre, Robert was in his fifth year at Hareton High. He had been expelled from one of the amalgamated schools which make up Hareton, and since being taken back he had truanted a lot, up to four months at one time. The school threatened to expel him a second time and this, along with frequent contact with the EWO, persuaded him to attend school more regularly. He had felt more settled lately, and thought he had been in trouble at school because he was unsettled in the family centre. This had led to him running away several times, for which he was 'grounded' by the care staff. He has been in court three times for burglary, for which he was sent to Brooklands CHE and was about to go to court again, on the same charge. Robert was looking forward to leaving school, as he could see no point in attending. He hoped to find work with a Scottish fishing fleet.

Robin (15)

Robin had begun truanting at the age of twelve, for days or weeks at a time. He was in care at the time, and punishment for truancy involved being 'grounded' for one night. Now living in Yew Tree House, he attended school regularly because the officer in charge checked with the school, and hit him if he had been (unjustifiably) absent. Robin still hated school as much as he ever had, but he thought he would continue to attend regularly until he was due to leave school the following summer. His only contact with education welfare was being stopped by an EWO in a public park, while truanting. Robin had received one caution for burglary. He had no idea what he wanted to do when he left school, but thought that the officer in charge would 'get me fixed up with something'.

Tom (13)

In care at Priory Road children's home, Tom had recently been expelled from Hareton High. Because he had been only a very occasional truant, Tom's non-attendance was agency-induced. He had encountered a lot of conflict with peers, being bullied for his perceived homosexuality. Tom had experienced a period in Whin Hill House (residential psychiatric placement) and was currently receiving home tuition. His main ambition was to stay out of trouble and to 'go to a normal school and be a normal boy'. Tom found it difficult to avoid conflict, with both staff and children at the children's home. He had run away on occasion, but thought he would not do it again. Tom wanted to be a doctor when he left school, as he enjoyed biology and first aid in school.

Wesley (14)

Wesley was not a persistent truant, estimating that he had truanted five times, for a few days at a time. At the time of interview he was attending regularly, but said that he would have truanted again if he thought he could get away with it. He felt that this was not possible as he was known as a truant to the teachers, and was 'on report'. The officer in charge of Yew Tree House was also 'very strict'. Wesley had run away from the home several times, and had been 'grounded' as a punishment. He had had no contact with education welfare but had been cautioned several times by the police, for burglary and shoplifting. However, his only court appearances were to do with his care order, which was made because his parents 'couldn't cope'. Wesley thought he would continue to attend school regularly and when he left school he expected to join his parents' small pottery business.

APPENDIX 2: POLICIES ON SCHOOL NON-ATTENDANCE IN BIRMINGHAM, LEEDS AND GLASGOW: THREE AREAS FOR COMPARISON WITH NORWEST

Birmingham's 'Operation Sweeper': police truancy patrols

Interviews took place with a chief inspector and a superintendent, and two police officers were accompanied on a truancy patrol (October 1989).

General background

'Operation Sweeper' was set up in May 1988 and there were several periods when special police patrols took place. In between these periods there was an ongoing awareness for the need to tackle truancy. From 16 October 1989 there was a two-week special initiative to clear truants from the city centre. The reason for this was that there had been a dramatic increase in robberies and the police wanted to clear away the more petty problem of truants in order to mount a special operation against robberies. The Chief Inspector noted that a major problem for him was in keeping media interest alive concerning 'Operation Sweeper', as there was a danger of it becoming routinized. He said he wanted to keep a high profile as he believed that this had a deterrent effect. In terms of numbers they have dealt with around 200 non-attenders in the first year of Operation Sweeper. The reasons given for the patrols were that, first, there were dangers to young people in being around the city centre and, secondly, there was a public perception that the police should be seen to be 'doing something' about truants.

The procedure during the patrols was that a police officer would stop young persons suspected of truancy and ask them to accompany the officer to the police station where their names and addresses and the names of their schools would be taken. There would be no other form of questioning or interrogation, and parents would usually be called in 'to be reunited with their children'. The details of the case would then be given to the education welfare service, who would decide whether or not to follow the case up. This was the limited extent of their involvement, as the chief inspector stated that the EWS did not approve of Operation Sweeper and did not want to be directly involved in patrols (unlike in Bedfordshire, for example, where EWOs and police officers operated joint truancy patrols; see *Times Educational Supplement* 10 March 1989, 21 April 1989).

Truancy–delinquency link

The police officers were of the opinion that there was no direct causal link between truancy and delinquency but that truancy *does* provide the opportunity for delinquent acts to take place. An important point to be made, they felt, was that truants were also potential victims of crime. Robbery was especially common but there was a danger of them becoming involved in drugs, prostitution and gambling in the amusement arcades. They believed that there was no evidence of a reverse relationship, that is that delinquency causes truancy, although of course it is the case that some delinquents are truants.

Effects of Operation Sweeper

They claimed that there was a significant reduction in delinquency in the city centre and that, for example, there had been a two-thirds reduction in shoplifting offences among the school-age population. They said they could not claim to have reduced truancy rates as such, and acknowledged that truants were probably just displaced to other areas of the city: however, they felt that at least they were at less risk in the suburbs than they were in the city centre.

On the legal context of Operation Sweeper they made some reference to the Children and Young Persons Act 1969, but conceded that it was a 'grey area', one on which they would not like to be challenged legally.

Powers of arrest

They pointed out that they would not like to use their powers of arrest, and that in fact they have not been used. They added that they would not like to see truancy criminalized as such and that they would prefer the present vague *status quo* to remain concerning their powers.

When asked about the likely changes following the forthcoming Children Act 1989, they said that they thought there would be no direct changes relating to police activities, but that in any case new legislation would not make much difference to the way in which police officers carry out their jobs. In particular, they would still approach apparent truants in the city centre, whatever legal changes were enacted.

The young people

They said that the truants themselves were usually willing to accompany officers to the station and that their manner was mostly subdued rather than aggressive. However, they did note that some critics would argue that this procedure was a breach of young people's rights, in that few thirteen-year-olds would feel able to refuse a police officer's request.

Comparison with Norwest

Norwest police stated that they had no intention of conducting police truancy patrols. Their contact with school non-attenders was peripheral, consisting only of attendance at juvenile liaison committee meetings, which focused on offenders, but which were attended by EWOs and took into account the school attendance records of the young people under review. Thus, Norwest did not engage in overt policing of school non-attenders.

The 'Leeds experiment': the juvenile court adjournment system

An interview took place with Dr Roy Hullin, who is a biochemist at Leeds University and was chair of the juvenile panel for thirty years, until his resignation in 1987.

The Leeds adjournment system

Dr Hullin gave a chronological account of the development of the Leeds system of dealing with truancy within the juvenile court system.

1970-2: The system at this time was very much *ad hoc* and magistrates felt considerable frustration with the lack of success of social work supervision orders following the changes made under the 1969 Children and Young Persons Act. In an informal way, individuals began to develop what has become known as the 'adjournment system', whereby young people brought before the juvenile court because of school non-attendance would find their cases subject to interim care orders and a series of adjournments until their attendance at school was found to be satisfactory. During this period magistrates held discussions with child psychiatrists and made initial studies of school registers, and found that the system appeared to be achieving its aim of reducing truancy.

1972-87: During this period the system was formalized despite considerable opposition from social workers. Despite different perspectives, Dr Hullin noted that a working relationship was established between social workers and magistrates and he believed that the system thus implemented was very effective. The system operated as follows: only serious truants would be brought before the courts (serious being defined as around 20 per cent attendance over a period of six months). At the juvenile court hearing, interim care orders would normally be made but not implemented in the first instance. The normal practice was for the case to be adjourned, at first for a week and then for longer periods if the young person could demonstrate full, or nearly full, attendance during the given period. If attendance was *not* satisfactory to the magistrates then the young person would be taken into care for a short period, usually a matter of weeks, and then given an opportunity to return home in order to demonstrate improved attendance. Dr Hullin noted that it was rarely necessary to make a full care order, and that if such an order was made, this was usually for social or family reasons additional to the young person's non-attendance at school. In the early years, the juvenile court heard around 400 cases each year, although this number declined in later years. An essential part of the system was that education welfare officers were able to bring cases before the court in a matter of days rather than weeks or months. In order to facilitate the processing of cases, four sessions were held every week in the juvenile courts, solely concerned with school non-attendance. Dr Hullin claimed that the system worked very well for individuals in that they soon realized that sanctions would be made if they continued to be absent from school; he also pointed out that there was a general deterrent effect on other young people once the system began to become widely known.

1987–9: After a period of fifteen years, during which time the 'Leeds adjournment system' operated in a fairly stable manner, there began to be strong pressures for change, particularly from the left wing of the Labour-led council. (Dr Hullin referred to these instigators of change as belonging to the 'loony left' and noted that he himself belonged to the 'old school' of Labour.) He felt that a lot of hostility was directed towards him personally and noted that several attempts were made to remove him from the bench, including an appeal to the Lord Chancellor. In 1987 he did resign from the juvenile bench (although he still sits in the magistrates' courts) and he believed that his opponents took this opportunity to change the system, introducing a policy of no prosecutions for school non-attendance. Experiments with a new system took place in South Leeds and the education committee claimed that a significant drop in truancy rates took place for this area. Dr Hullin strongly disputed this, however, and argued that truancy rates have in fact increased dramatically under the new system (see *Times Educational Supplement* 10 February 1989, 31 March 1989, 21 April 1989, 28 July 1989).

Children Act 1989

The experimental South Leeds system, introduced in 1988, anticipated the provisions of the Children Act in halting court appearances for non-attendance at school, and replacing legal action with a more pastoral approach by both schools and education welfare officers. Dr Hullin believed that such moves in effect made attendance at school voluntary and that one of the main implications of this was that the truancy rate would increase significantly once children realized that there were no longer any effective sanctions against school non-attendance.

Comparison with Norwest

Although it is true that there was no deliberate or systematic adoption of the Leeds experiment in Norwest, there is some evidence to suggest that the system *was* influential on juvenile magistrates' policy and practice. While some magistrates stated that they had not been influenced by the Leeds system, others reported some admiration for the experiment, and commented that they, too, were inclined to make adjournments in a significant number of non-attendance cases. Analysis of court records indicates that adjournments were frequently made: in 1985 and 1988, for example, they were made in 46 per cent of cases, and in 80 per cent of cases in 1990. A breakdown of the reasons given in court records for making these adjournments indicates that a significant proportion were made with the explicit purpose of monitoring or reviewing school attendance: this reason was given in 8 per cent of all cases in 1985, 31 per cent in 1988 and 15 per cent in 1990, giving an average of 18 per cent for these three years. Thus, although Norwest did not adopt such a deliberate and coherent policy as the Leeds magistrates, there were nevertheless significant elements of the Leeds system present within the juvenile court system; in particular, adjournments made in order to review school attendance.

Gorbals truancy project: a community-based approach

An interview took place with Sister Mercedes, the coordinator of the project (Glasgow, May 1989).

General background

The Project has been in operation since 1983 and developed from the work of Catholic Social Services. Funding for the project came from Urban Aid, and the project was overseen by Strathclyde Region Education and Social Services departments. There are two full-time posts. The project deals with six to ten young people, usually aged between twelve and sixteen. The work of the project includes a basic literacy programme, individual and group work, educational visits, role play and group discussion. Although the project workers are trained teachers, there is no strict adherence to a school curriculum. Any or all of the methods mentioned above would be used in an attempt to respond to individual needs. The overall aim of the project was to re-introduce young people to school, to offer them some time out from any difficulties they may have and to equip them with the skills they need in order to attend school regularly. Very often a gradual re-introduction to school was attempted, for example with the child attending school for one or two afternoons per week and spending the rest of the time attending the project. The approach of the project was child-centred, and attempted to cater for the needs of the whole person. Sister Mercedes explained that this involved considering the home and social backgrounds of the young people, which very often included some or all of extreme poverty, high unemployment levels and poor housing conditions. Philosophically, the project was committed to a minimum of discipline, to accepting often difficult behaviour and to being flexible in the approach to working with the child.

Community context

Glasgow is a city with a significant Irish Catholic population, and the Gorbals in particular is an area with a high proportion of Roman Catholics. Thus, a project originating from the work of Catholic Social Services and staffed by workers belonging to religious orders was familiar to, and accepted by, the local community. In addition, the Franciscan ethos of working with the poor to bring about social change was consistent with Glaswegian traditions of self-help, community development and community activism.

Truancy–delinquency link

Sister Mercedes observed that a lot of truants, although by no means all, do become involved in petty crime, which is defined as including car theft, burglary and assault. However, two ex-attenders at the project have been charged with attempted murder, so more serious crimes do also occur. In terms of causes of delinquency, she thought that truancy does give the opportunity for involvement in crime, partly as the Gorbals is geographically so close to the temptations provided by the city centre. However, she also thought that a major factor was that the older gangs of youths attempted to involve young people in crime and would often threaten them with violence if they refused to take part in criminal activities. In her opinion, those young people out on the streets during the day were clearly more vulnerable to this sort of risk.

Causes of truancy

In terms of the causes of non-attendance, Sister Mercedes thought that the blame lay partly with the school and partly with the parents. She emphasized that it was not the young people who had failed, but rather it was the system that had failed them. She noted that parents often had anti-education attitudes, which was understandable as they had received little benefit from the education system themselves, and they saw little point in educating their children within the current context of high unemployment rates. Young people also tended to have these anti-education attitudes, especially in inner-city schools where teachers were seen as authority figures. A major factor here was the culture clash between home and school. She felt that the comprehensive system was partly to blame: the ideal of equality was fine, but not all children were equal, or had equal abilities. In teaching mixed ability classes, a teacher inevitably concentrated on the middle group, thus neglecting those in the higher and lower ranges of abilities.

Liaison with schools

Liaison with the four primary and two secondary schools (Catholic and non-denominational) had not been very successful. Sister Mercedes noted that relations between themselves and the schools have not been very good in the past although they were showing some improvement. A major cause of this had been that the Roman Catholic secondary school had wanted the project to be based on school premises: she thought that this was because they wanted to have more direct control over the project. A further source of conflict was that schools tended to want to see quick results in terms of the turnover of young people attending the project, whereas the project itself preferred to keep the young people for as long as they seemed to need to be there, which might be anything up to a year or more. Liaison was generally with school guidance teachers and most of their referrals came from schools.

Comparison with Norwest

Norwest does not share with Glasgow its history of self-help and community activism, nor its traditions of Church-based community development. Unsurprisingly, then, there were no projects in Norwest comparable to the Gorbals truancy project. All of Norwest's truancy initiatives were connected to the statutory rather than the voluntary sector, and none adopted an approach as clearly child-centred as that espoused by the Gorbals truancy project.

REFERENCES

Abrams, P. (1982) *Historical Sociology*. Shepton Mallet, Open Books.

Alder, M. and Raab, G. (1988) 'Exit, choice and loyalty: the impact of parental choice on admission to school in Edinburgh and Dundee', *Journal of Education Policy*, 3 (2).

Allen, H. (1987) *Justice Unbalanced*. Milton Keynes, Open University Press.

Althussar, L. (1972) 'Ideology and ideological state apparatuses: notes towards an investigation', in Cosin, B.R. (ed.) *Education, Structure and Society*. Harmondsworth, Penguin.

Anon (1955) 'War on absentees', *Education*, 105, 425.

Aries, P. (1973) *Centuries of Childhood*. Harmondsworth, Penguin.

Atkinson, P. and Rees, T. (1982) *Youth Unemployment and State Intervention*. London, Routledge and Kegan Paul.

Auld, R. (1976) *Report of the Inquiry into the William Tyndale Junior and Infants School*. London, ILEA.

Ball, S.J. (1990) *Policies and Policy Making in Education*. London, Routledge.

Banks, O. (1955) *Parity and Prestige in English Secondary Education*. London, Routledge and Kegan Paul.

Banks, O. (1971) *The Sociology of Education*. London, Batsford.

Barton, L. (ed.) (1980) *Schooling, Ideology and the Curriculum*. Lewes, Falmer.

Bash, L. and Coulby, B. (1989) *The Education Reform Act: Competition and Control*. London, Cassell.

Belotti, E.G. (1975) *Little Girls*. London, Writers and Readers.

Belson, W.A. (1975) *Juvenile Theft: The Causal Factors*. London, Harper and Row.

Berg, I, (1980) 'School refusal in early adolescence', in Hersov L. and Berg, I. (eds) *Out of School*. Chichester, John Wiley.

Berg, I., Hullin, R., McGuire, R. and Tyrer, S. (1977) 'Truancy and the courts, a research note', *Journal of Child Psychology and Psychiatry*, 18, 359-65.

Berg, I., Butter, A., Hullin, R., Smith, R. and Tyrer, S. (1978a) 'Features of children taken to juvenile court for failure to attend school', *Psychological Medicine*, 8, 447-53.

Berg, I., Consterdine, M., Hullin, R., McGuire, R. and Tyrer, S. (1978b) 'The effect of two randomly allocated court procedures on truancy', *British Journal of Criminology*, 18(3), 232–44.

Berg, I., Goodwin, A., Hullin, R. and McGuire, S. (1983) 'The effect of two varieties of the adjournment procedure on truancy', *British Journal of Criminology*, 23(2), 150–8.

Berg, I., Goodwin, A., Hullin, R. and McGuire, S. (1987) 'School attendance: visits by EWOs and appearances in the juvenile courts', *Educational Research*, 29.

Berg, I., Brown, I. and Hullin, R. (1988) *Off School. In Court. An Experimental and Psychiatric Investigation of Severe School Attendance Problems*. New York, Springer-Verlag.

Berg, L. (1968) *Rising Hill: Death of a Comprehensive School*. Harmondsworth, Penguin.

Bernstein, B. (1971) 'Education cannot compensate for society', in Cosin, B.R., Dale, I.R., Esland, G.M., Mackinnon, D. and Swift, D.F. (eds) *School and Society*. London and Henley, Routledge and Kegan Paul/Open University Press.

Bernstein, B. (1976) *Class, Codes and Control Vol. 3*. London, Routledge and Kegan Paul.

Blagg, N. (1987) *School Phobia and its Treatment*. London, Croom Helm.

Blytheman, M. (1975) 'Truants suffer more from "disadvantage of life"', *Scottish Educational Journal*, 58, 80–4.

Bogdanor, V. (1991) 'Where will the buck stop?', *Times Educational Supplement*, 14 June.

BMBEC (1977) *Pupil Absence Survey*. Mimeo.

Booth, T. and Coulby, D. (eds) (1987) *Producing and Reducing Disaffection*. Milton Keynes, Open University Press.

Bourdieu, P. and Passeron, J.C. (1977) *Reproduction in Education, Society and Culture*. London, Sage.

Bourdieu, P. (1976) 'The school as a conservative force', in Dale, R. *et al.* (eds) *Schooling and Capitalism*. London and Henley, Routledge and Kegan Paul/Open University Press.

Bowles, S. and Gintis, H. (1976) *Schooling in Capitalist America*. London, Routledge and Kegan Paul.

Bridge, J., Bridge, S. and Luke, S. (1990) *Blackstone's Guide to the Children Act 1989*. London, Blackstone.

Brighouse, T. (1990) *Guardian*, 23 October.

Broadwin, I.T. (1932) 'A contribution to the study of truancy', *Orthopsychiatry*, 2, 253–9.

Brooks, D.B. (1974) 'Contingency contracts with truants', *Personnel Guidance Journal*, 52, 215–20.

Brown, P. (1987) *Schooling Ordinary Kids*. London, Tavistock.

Brown, P. (1991) 'Schooling and employment in the UK', in Ashton, D. and Lowe, G. (eds) *Making Their Way*. Milton Keynes, Open University Press.

Brown, S. (1989) 'Social information and its "usefulness" in the juvenile court: an analysis of magistrates' accounts in organizational context', PhD thesis, Teesside Polytechnic.

Brown, S. (1991) *Magistrates at work*. Milton Keynes, Open University Press.

Cain, M. (1989) 'Feminists transgress criminology', in Cain, M. (ed.) *Growing Up Good*. London, Sage.

Carlen, P. (1987) 'Out of care, into custody: dimensions and deconstructions of the

State's regulation of twenty-two young working-class women', in Carlen, P. and Worrall, A. (eds) *Gender, Crime and Justice*. Milton Keynes, Open University Press.

Carlen, P. (1988) *Women, Crime and Poverty*. Milton Keynes, Open University Press.

Carroll, H.C.M. (1977) 'A cross-sectional and longitudinal study of poor and good attenders in a comprehensive school', in Carroll, H.C.M. (ed.) *Absenteeism in South Wales*. Swansea; University College of Swansea.

Casburn, M. (1978) 'Juvenile justice for girls', unpublished manuscript, Women's Research and Resource Centre.

Casburn, M. (1979) *Girls Will Be Girls*. London, Women's Research and Resource Centre.

Cashmore, E. (1989) *Making Sense of Sport*. London, Routledge.

Centre for Contemporary Cultural Studies Education Group II (1991) *Education Limited*. London, Unwin Hyman.

Chamblis, W.J. (1964) 'A sociological analysis of the law of vagrancy', *Social Problems*, 12, 67–77.

Chartered Institute of Public Finance and Accounting (1990) *Probation Service Statistics, 1990–91 Estimates*. London, CIPFA.

Chiqwada, R. (1989) 'The criminalization and imprisonment of black women', *Probation*, 3, 100–5.

Coffield, F., Borrill, C. and Marshall, S. (1986) *Growing up at the Margins*. London, Heinemann.

Cohen, S. (1985) *Visions of Social Control*. Cambridge, Polity Press.

Coleman, J.S. (1966) *Equality of Educational Opportunity*. Washington, D.C., US Government Printing Office.

Collison, M. (1980) 'Questions of juvenile justice', in Carlen, P. and Collison, M. (eds) *Radical Issues in Criminology*. Oxford, Martin Robertson.

Coolidge, J.C., Hahn, P.B. and Peck, A.L. (1957) 'School phobia: neurotic crisis or way of life', *American Journal of Orthopsychiatry*, 27, 196–306.

Corrigan, P. (1979) *Schooling the Smash Street Kids*. London, Macmillan.

Cox, C.B. and Dyson, A.E. (eds) (1969a) *Fight for Education: a Black Paper*, London, Critical Quarterly Society.

Cox, C.B. and Dyson, A.E. (1969b) *Black Paper 2: The Crisis in Education*. London, Critical Quarterly Society.

Cox, C.B. and Boyson, R. (eds) (1975) *Black Paper*. London, J.M. Dent.

Cox, C.B. and Boyson, R. (eds) (1977) *Black Paper*. London, Temple South.

Croft, I.J. and Crygier, T.G. (1956) 'Social relationships of truants and juvenile delinquents', *Human Relations*, 9, 439–66.

Crowther Report (1959) *15–18: Report of the Central Advisory Council (England)*. London, HMSO.

David, M. (1980) *The State, the Family and Education*. London, Routledge and Kegan Paul.

Davie, R. *et al.* (1972) *From Birth to Seven*. London, Longman and National Children's Bureau.

Davies, B. (1976) *Social Control and Education*. London, Methuen.

Davies, B. (1986) *Threatening Youth*. Milton Keynes, Open University Press.

Deem, R. (1978) *Women and Schooling*. London, Routledge and Kegan Paul.

Deem, R. (ed.) (1980) *Schooling for Women's Work*. London, Routledge and Kegan Paul.

DES (1975) *Survey of Absence from Secondary and Middle Schools in England and Wales on Thursday 17 January 1974.* London, HMSO.

DES (1983) *Police Liaison with the Education Service.* London, HMSO.

DES (1987) 'Good behaviour and discipline in schools', *Education Observed*, no. 5.

DES (1989a) 'Attendance at school: a report of Her Majesty's Inspectorate', *Education Observed*, no. 13.

DES (1989b) 'The Lower Attaining Pupils Programme (1982–88)', *Education Observed*, no. 12.

Department of Health (1984) *Children in Care of Local Authorities at 31st March 1984.* London, HMSO.

Department of Health (1987) *Children in Care of Local Authorities at 31st March 1987.* London, HMSO.

Department of Health (1988) *Children in Care in England and Wales, March 1985.* London, HMSO.

Department of Health (1989) *An Introduction to the Children Act 1989: a New Framework for the Care and Upbringing of Children.* London, HMSO.

Department of Health (1990) *Health and Personal Social Services Statistics for England 1990.* London, HMSO.

Dickens, C. (1848) *Dombey and Son.* London, Bradbury and Evans.

Digby, A. and Searby, P. (1981) *Children, School and Society in 19th Century England.* London, Macmillan.

Donzelot, J. (1979) *The Policing of Families.* London, Hutchinson.

Douglas, J.W.B. (1964) *The Home and the School.* London, MacGibbon and Kee.

Douglas, J.W.B. (1968) *All Our Future.* London, Peter Davies.

Durkheim, E. (1956) *Education and Schooling.* Glencoe, IL, Free Press.

Durkheim, E. (1961) *Moral Education.* Glencoe, IL, Free Press (published in French in 1925).

Durkheim, E. (1972) 'Moral education', in Cosin, B. (ed.) *Education, Structure and Society.* Harmondsworth, Penguin.

Eaton, M.J. (1979) 'A study of some factors associated with the early identification of persistent absenteeism', *Educational Review*, 31 (3), 233–42.

Eggleston, S.J. (1965) 'How comprehensive is the Leicestershire Plan?', *New Society*, 23 March.

Eggleston, S.J. (1977) *The Ecology of the School.* London, Methuen.

Ekblom, P. (1979) 'Police truancy patrols', in Burrows, J., Ekblom, P. and Heal, K. (eds) *Crime Prevention and the Police.* Home Office Research Study no. 55. London, HMSO.

Elton Report (1988) *Committee of Enquiry into Behaviour and Discipline in Schools.* London, HMSO.

Erben, M. and Dickenson, H. (1983) 'Aspects of technical education in France: a consideration of the work of Claude Grignon', in Gleeson, D. (ed.) *Youth Training and the Search for Work.* London, Routledge and Kegan Paul.

Erben, M. and Gleeson, D. (1977) 'Education as reproduction', in Young, M.F.D. and Whitty, G.J. (eds) *Society, State and Schooling.* Lewes, Falmer Press.

Eysenck, H. (1971) *Race, Intelligence and Education.* London, Temple Smith.

Eysenck, H. (1973) *The Measurement of Intelligence.* London, Medical and Technical Publishing.

Farrington, D. (1980) 'Truancy, delinquency, the home and the school', in Hersov, L.

and Berg, I. (eds) *Out of School: Modern Perspectives in Truancy and School Refusal.* Chichester, John Wiley.

Finn, D., Grant, N. and Johnson, R. (1978) 'Social democracy, education and crisis', in Centre for Contemporary Cultural Studies *On Ideology.* London, Hutchinson.

Fitz, J. (1981) 'The child as legal subject', in Dale, R. (ed.) *Education and the State.* Lewes and Milton Keynes, Falmer/Open University Press.

Fleet, L. (1976) 'Some margins of compulsory education', unpublished PhD thesis, University of Bristol.

Floud, J., Halsey, A.H. and Martin, F.M. (1956) *Social Class and Educational Opportunity.* London, Heinemann.

Fogelman, K. and Richardson, K. (1974) 'School attendance: some results from the National Child Development Study', in Turner, B. (ed.) *Truancy.* London, Ward Lock.

Fogelman, K. (1976) *Britain's Sixteen-Year-Olds.* London, National Children's Bureau.

Fogelman, K., Tibbenham, A. and Lambert, L. (1980) 'Absence from school: findings from the National Child Development Study', in Hersov, L. and Berg, I. (eds) *Out of School: Modern Perspectives in Truancy and School Refusal.* Chichester, John Wiley.

Ford, J. (1969) *Social Class and the Comprehensive School.* London, Routledge and Kegan Paul.

Foucault, M. (1977) *Discipline and Punish.* London, Allen Lane.

Foucault, M. (1979) *The History of Sexuality Vol. 1.* London, Allen Lane.

Freeman, M. (1983) *The Rights and Wrongs of Children.* London, Francis Pinter.

Frost, N. and Stein, M. (1989) *The Politics of Child Welfare.* London, Harvester Wheatsheaf.

Galloway, D. (1976a) 'Persistent unjustified absence from school', *Trends in Education,* 4, 22–7.

Galloway, D. (1976b) 'Size of school, socio-economic hardships, suspension rates, and persistent and unjustified absence from school', *British Journal of Educational Psychology,* 46, 40–7.

Galloway, D. (1980) 'Problems in the assessment and management of persistent absenteeism from school', in Hersov, L. and Berg, I. (eds) *Out of School: Modern Perspectives in Truancy and School Refusal.* Chichester, John Wiley.

Galloway, D. (1985) *Schools and Persistent Absentees.* Oxford, Pergamon.

Glass, D.V. (1954) *Social Mobility in Britain.* London, Routledge and Kegan Paul.

Gleeson, D. (1989) *The Paradox of Training: Making Progress out of Crisis.* Milton Keynes, Open University Press.

Gleeson, D. (1991) *Training and its Alternatives.* Milton Keynes, Open University Press.

Graham, J. (1988) *Schools, Disruptive Behaviour and Delinquency: A Review of Research.* Home Office Research Study, no. 96. London, HMSO.

Gray, J. (1981) 'Towards effective schools: problems and progress in British research', *British Educational Research Journal,* 7(1), 59–69.

Gray, J. and Jesson, D. (1989) *Truancy in Secondary Schools Among Fifth Year Pupils.* Sheffield, University of Sheffield.

Gray, J. and Jesson, D. (1990) 'Truancy in secondary schools amongst fifth-year pupils', report of the QQSE Research Group, Educational Research Centre, University of Sheffield.

Gray, J., McPherson, A. and Raffe, D. (1983) *Reconstructions of Secondary Education: Theory, Myth and Practice since the War.* London, Routledge and Kegan Paul.

Green, F. (1980) 'On becoming a truant – the social administrative process in non-attendance', Unpublished MA thesis, Cranfield Institute of Technology.

Grenville, M.P. (1988) 'Compulsory school attendance and the child's wishes', *Journal of Social Welfare Law*, 1, 4–20.

Griffin, C. (1985) *Typical Girls?* London, Routledge and Kegan Paul.

Grimshaw, R.H. and Pratt, J.D. (1984) 'Truancy and delinquency in perspective: a review of their relationship in the light of recent U.K. evidence', University of Sheffield.

Grimshaw, R.H. and Pratt, J.D. (1987) 'Truancy: a case to answer', in Reid, K. (ed.) *Combating School Absenteeism*. London, Hodder and Stoughton.

Grunsell, R. (1980) *Absent from School: the Story of a Truancy Centre*. London, Writers and Readers (formerly published as *Born to be Invisble*, 1978).

Habermas, J. (1976) *Legitimation Crisis*. London, Heinemann.

Hagan, J., Simpson, J. and Gillis, J.R. (1979) 'The sexual stratification of social control: a gender-based perspective on crime and delinquency', *British Journal of Sociology*, 30(1), 25–38.

Hall, S. (1977) *'Review of the Course', School and Society, Unit 32, E202*. Milton Keynes, Open University.

Hall, S. (1981) 'Schooling, state and society', in Dale, R. (ed.) *Education and the State*. Lewes and Milton Keynes, Falmer/Open University Press.

Hall, S., Critcher, C., Jefferson, T. *et al.* (1978) *Policing the Crisis: Mugging, the State, and Law and Order*. London, Macmillan.

Halsey, A.H. (ed.) (1972) *Educational Priority Vol. 1. EPA Problems and Policies*. London, HMSO.

Halsey, A.H. (1980) 'Education can compensate', *New Society*, 24 January.

Halsey, A.H., Floud, J. and Anderson, C.A. (1960) *Education, Economy and Society*. New York, Free Press.

Halsey, A.H., Heath, A. and Ridge, J. (1980) *Origins and Destinations*. Oxford, Clarendon Press.

Hamilton, D. (1990) *Learning about Education*. Milton Keynes, Open University Press.

Hargreaves, A. (1989) 'The crisis of motivation and assessment', in Hargreaves, A. and Reynolds, D. (eds) *Education Policies: Controversies and Critiques*. London, Falmer Press.

Hargreaves, D. (1967) *Social Relations in a Secondary School*. London, Routledge and Kegan Paul.

Hargreaves, D. (1982) *The Challenge for the Comprehensive School*. London, Routledge and Kegan Paul.

Harris, N.S. (1989) 'Truancy and legal intervention in search of the holy grail', *Education and the Law*, 1(1), 19–26.

Harris, R. and Webb, D. (1987) *Welfare, Power and Juvenile Justice*, London, Tavistock.

Hersov, L.A. (1973) 'Truancy and school refusal', *Midwife and Health Visitor*, 9, 258–62.

Hersov, L. and Berg, I. (eds) (1980) *Out of School: Modern Perspectives in Truancy and School Refusal*. Chichester, John Wiley.

Hillgate Group (1986) *Whose Schools? A Radical Manifesto*. London, Claridge Press.

Hodge, V. (1968) 'Non-attendance at school', *Educational Research*, 11, 58–61.

Hodges, J. and Hussain, A. (1979) 'La police des familles', *Ideology & Consciousness*, 5.

Holmes, G. (1989) *Truancy and Social Welfare: Bells Ringing in the Distance*. Cheadle, Boys and Girls Welfare Society.

Home Office (1946) *Report of the Care of Children Committee*, CM 06922. London, HMSO.

Home Office (1949) *Memorandum on Juvenile Delinquency*, jointly with Ministry of Education. London, HMSO.

Home Office (1965) *The Child, the Family and the Young Offender*, Cmnd 2742. London, HMSO.

Home Office (1968) *Children in Trouble*, Cmnd 3601. London, HMSO.

Home Office (1988a) *Punishment, Custody and the Community*, CM 424. London HMSO.

Home Office (1988b) *Tackling Offenders: an Action Plan*. London, Home Office.

Home Office (1989) *Prison Statistics for England and Wales 1988*, CM 825. London, HMSO.

Home Office (1990) *Crime, Justice and Protecting the Public*, CM 965. London, HMSO.

House of Commons (1984) *Second Report from the Social Services Committee: Children in Care, Vol. I, II and III*. London, HMSO.

Hudson, A. (1990) 'Troublesome girls: towards alternative definitions and policies', in Cain, M. (ed.) *Growing Up Good*. London, Sage.

Hudson, B. (1984) 'Femininity and adolescence', in McRobbie, A. and Nava, M. (eds) *Gender and Generation*. London, Macmillan.

Hudson, B. (1987) *Justice through Punishment: a Critique of the Justice Model of Corrections*. Basingstoke, Macmillan.

Humphries, S. (1981) *Hooligans or Rebels? An Oral History of Working-class Childhood and Youth 1889–1939*. Oxford, Basil Blackwell.

Illich, I. (1971) *Deschooling Society*. London, Calder and Boyers.

Ingleby, D. (1972) 'Ideology and the human sciences: some comments on the role of reification in psychology and psychiatry', in Pateman, T. (ed.) *Counter Course*. Harmondsworth, Penguin.

Ingleby, D. (1976) 'The psychology of child psychology', in Dale, R. *et al.* (eds) *Schooling and Capitalism*. London and Henley, Routledge and Kegan Paul/Open University Press.

ILEA (1981) *Perspectives on Attendance*, Research and Statistics Branch, Document RS 749/80. London: Inner London Education Authority.

ISTD (Institute for the Study and Treatment of Delinquency) (1974) 'Truancy in Glasgow', *British Journal of Criminology*, 14, 148–255.

Jackson, B. and Marsden, D. (1962) *Education and the Working Class*. London, Routledge and Kegan Paul.

Jackson, S. (1987) 'The education of children in care', Bristol Papers. School of Applied Social Studies, University of Bristol.

Jencks, C. (1972) *Inequality: a Reassessment of the Effect of Family and Schooling in America*. New York, Basic Books.

Jenkins, R. (1983) *Lads, Citizens and Ordinary Kids*. London, Routledge and Kegan Paul.

Jensen, A.R. (1980) *Bias in Mental Testing*. London, Methuen.

Johnson, A.M., Falstein, E.I., Szurek, S.A. and Svendsen, M. (1941) 'School phobia', *American Journal of Orthopsychiatry*, 11, 702–11.

Johnson, R. (1976) 'Notes on the schooling of the English working class, 1780–1950', in Dale, R. *et al*. (eds) Schooling and Capitalism. London and Henley, Routledge and Kegan Paul/Open University Press.

Johnson, R. (1981) 'Really useful knowledge: radical education and working class culture 1790–1845', in Dale, R. (ed.) *Education and the State*. Lewes and Milton Keynes, Falmer/Open University Press.

Johnson, R. (1991) 'Ten theses on a Monday Morning', in Centre for Contemporary Cultural Studies Education Group II, *Education Limited*. London, Unwin Hyman.

Labour (1990) News Release, 17 August, London.

Lacey, C. (1970) *Hightown Grammar*. Manchester, Manchester University Press.

Lee, D., Marsden, D., Rickman, P. and Duncombe, J. (1990) *Scheming for Youth*. Milton Keynes, Open University Press.

Lees, S. (1986) *Losing Out: Sexuality and Adolescent Girls*. London, Hutchinson.

Levy, A. and Kahan, B. (1991) *The Pindown Experience and the Protection of Children: the Report of the Staffordshire Child Care Inquiry 1990*. Staffordshire County Council.

Lewis, D.K. (1981) 'Black women offenders and criminal justice: some theoretical considerations', in Warren, M.Q. (ed.) *Comparing Female and Male Offenders*. London, Sage.

Lewis, O. (1966) 'The culture of poverty', *Scientific American*, **215**(4), 19–25.

Lloyd-Smith, M. (ed.) (1984) *Disrupted Schooling: the Growth of a Special Unit*. London, John Murray.

Local Government Training Board (1973) *Report of the Working Party on the Training of Education Welfare Officers* (The Ralphs Report). London, LGTB.

Lockwood, D. (1985) *Civic Exclusion*. Mimeo, University of Essex.

McCulloch, G. (1991) 'An alternative road? Problems and possibilities of the Crowther concept', in Gleeson, D. (ed.) *Training and its Alternatives*. Milton Keynes, Open University Press.

Maclure, S. (1990) *Education Re-formed*. London, Hodder and Stoughton.

MacMillan, R. (1977) *Education Welfare: Strategy and Structure*. London, Longman.

McRobbie, A. (1978) 'Working class girls and the culture of femininity', in Women's Studies Group Centre for Contemporary Cultural Studies, *Women Take Issue*. London, Hutchinson.

May, D. (ed.) (1975) 'Truancy, school absenteeism and delinquency', *Scottish Educational Studies*, **7**, 97–107.

Meighan, R. (1988) *Flexi-schooling: Education for Tomorrow. Starting Yesterday*. Ticknall, Education Now Books.

Meyer, P. (1977) *The Child and The State*. Cambridge, Cambridge University Press.

Mills, C.W. (1959) *The Sociological Imagination*. New York, Oxford University Press.

Mitchell, S. (1972) 'The absentees', *Education in the North*, **9**, 22–8.

Mitchell, S. and Shepherd, M. (1980) 'Reluctance to go to school', in Hersov, L. and Berg, I. (eds) *Out of School: Modern Perspectives in Truancy and School Refusal*. Chichester, John Wiley.

Morris, A., Giller, H., Szwed, E. and Geach, H. (1980) *Justice for Children*. London, Macmillan.

Morris, A. and Giller, H. (1987) *Understanding Juvenile Justice*. London, Croom Helm.

Morris, M. and Griggs, C. (eds) (1988) *Education – the Wasted Years? 1973–1986*. Lewes, Falmer Press.

Mortimore, P. *et al.* (1988) *School Matters*. Shepton Mallett, Open Books.

Musgrave, P.W. (1965) *The Sociology of Education*. London, Methuen.

Musgrove, F. (1964) *Youth and the Social Order*. London, Routledge and Kegan Paul.

NACEWO (1975) *These We Serve. The Report of a Working Party Set Up to Enquire into the Causes of Absence from School*. London, National Association of Chief Education Welfare Officers.

Nava, M. (1984) 'The urban, the domestic and education of girls', in Grace, G. (ed.) *Urbanisation and the City*. London, Routledge and Kegan Paul.

Okely, J. (1983) *The Traveller-Gypsies*. Cambridge, Cambridge University Press.

Pack, D.C. (1977) *Truancy and Indiscipline in Schools in Scotland* (the Pack Report). London, HMSO.

Parker, H., Sumner, M. and Jarvis, G. (1989) *Unmasking the Magistrates: The Custody or Not Decision in Sentencing Young Offenders*. Milton Keynes, Open University Press.

Parsons, K. (1990) 'Ideologies in practice: the context of the youth training scheme', unpublished PhD thesis, South West Polytechnic.

Parsons, T. (1959) 'The school class as a social system: some of its functions in American society', *Harvard Educational Review*, **29**, 197–318.

Paterson, F.M.S. (1988) 'Schooling the family', *Sociology*, **22**(1), 65–86.

Paterson, F.M.S. (1989) *Out of Place: Public Policy and the Emergence of Truancy*. Lewes, Falmer Press.

Pearson, G. (1975) *The Deviant Imagination: Psychiatry, Social Work and Social Change*. London, Macmillan.

Pirie, J. (1975) 'Truancy runs in families', *Times Educational Supplement* (Scotland), 4 July.

Platt, A. (1969) 'The rise of the child-saving movement', *Annals of the American Academy*, January, 381.

Pollak, O. (1950) *The Criminality of Women*. Philadelphia, University of Pennsylvania Press.

Pratt, J.D. (1983) 'Folklore and fact in truancy research', *British Journal of Criminology*, **23**, 336.

Prout, A. (1988) ' "Off school sick": mothers' accounts of school sickness absence', *Sociological Review*, **36**(4), 765–89.

Purvis, J. (1981) 'Women and teaching in the 19th Century', in Dale, R. (ed.) *Education and the State: Politics, Patriarchy and Practice*. Lewes and Milton Keynes, Falmer/Open University Press.

Ranson, S. (1984) 'Towards a tertiary tripartism: new codes of social control and the 17+', in Broadfoot, P. (ed.) *Selection, Certification and Control*. Lewes, Falmer Press.

Ranson, S. (1990) *The Politics of Reorganizing Schools*. London, Unwin Hyman.

Reeder, David (1981) 'A recurring debate: education and industry', in Dale, R. (ed.) *Education and the State: Schooling and the National Interest*. Lewes and Milton Keynes, Falmer/Open University Press.

Reid, K. (1982) 'The self-concept and persistent school absenteeism', *British Journal of Educational Psychology*, **52**, 179–87.

Reid, K. (1985) *Truancy and School Absenteeism*. London, Hodder and Stoughton.

Reid, K. (1986) *Disaffection from School*. London, Methuen.

Reid, K. (ed.) (1987) *Combating School Absenteeism*. London, Hodder and Stoughton.

Reid, K. and Kendall, L. (1982) 'A review of some recent research into persistent school absenteeism', *British Journal of Education Studies*, **30**(3), 295–312.

Reynolds, D. (1976) 'Schools make a difference', *New Society,* **37**, 223–5.

Reynolds, D., Jones, D., St. Leger, S. and Murgatroyd, S. (1980) 'School factors and truancy', in Hersov, L. and Berg, I. (eds.) *Out of School: Modern Perspectives in Truancy and School Refusal.* Chichester: John Wiley.

Reynolds, D. and Reid, K. (1985) 'The second stage: towards a reconceptualisation of theory and methodology in school effectiveness studies', in Reynolds, D. (ed.) *Studying School Effectiveness.* Lewes, Falmer Press.

Reynolds, D. (ed.) (1985) *Studying School Effectiveness.* Lewes, Falmer Press.

Reynolds, D., Sullivan, M. and Murgatroyd, S. (1987) *The Comprehensive Experiment.* Lewes, Falmer Press.

Roberts, K. (1984) *School Leavers and Their Prospects.* Milton Keynes, Open University Press.

Roberts, R. (1971) *The Classic Slum: Salford Life in the First Quarter of the Century.* Manchester, Manchester University Press.

Robinson, M. (1978) *Schools and Social Work.* London, Routledge and Kegan Paul.

Robinson, P. (1981) *Perspectives on the Sociology of Education.* London, Routledge and Kegan Paul.

Robinson, P. (1989) *Exploring Educational Issues, Unit 16, Course E208.* Milton Keynes, Open University.

Rubenstein, D. (1969) *School Attendance in London 1870–1904.* Hull, Hull University Press.

Rutter, M. and Madge, N. (1976) *Cycles of Disadvantage.* London, Heinemann.

Rutter, M., Maughan, B., Mortimore, P. and Ouston, J. (1979) *Fifteen Thousand Hours: Secondary Schools and Their Effects on Children.* London, Open Books.

Sayer, J. (1987) 'Why have you come to school today? A pathology of presence', in Reid, K. (ed.) *Combating School Absenteeism.* London, Hodder and Stoughton.

Seabrook, J. (1974) 'Talking to truants', in Turner, B. (ed.) *Truancy.* London, Ward Lock.

Seeley, J.R. (1966) 'The making and taking of problems: toward an ethical stance', *Social Problems,* **14**(4), 382–9.

Sharp, R. and Green, A. (1976) *Education as Social Control.* London, Routledge and Kegan Paul.

Shaw, J. (1981) 'In loco parentis: the relationship between parent, state and child', in Dale, R. (ed.) *Education and the State: Politics, Patriarchy and Practice.* Lewes and Milton Keynes, Falmer/Open University Press.

Simon, B. and Rubenstein, D. (1969) *The Evolution of the Comprehensive School.* London, Routledge and Kegan Paul.

Simon, B. (1960) *Studies in the History of Education 1780–1870.* London, Lawrence and Wishart.

Simon, B. (1988) *Bending the Rules: The Baker Reform Act.* London, Lawrence and Wishart.

Steedman, C. (1988) 'The mother made conscious: the historical development of a primary school psychology', in Woodhead, M. and McGrath, A. (eds) *Family, School and Society.* London, Hodder and Stoughton.

Stoll, P. and O'Keeffe, D. (1989) *Officially Present.* London, Institute of Economic Affairs.

Stott, D.H. (1966) *Studies of Troublesome Children.* London, Tavistock.

Stronach, I. (1989) 'Education, vocationalism and economic recovery: the case against witchcraft', *British Journal of Education and Work*, 3(1), 5-31.

Sutherland, G. (1973) *Policy Making in Elementary Education 1870-1895.* Oxford, Oxford University Press.

Tawney, R.H. (1918) 'Keep the workers' children in their place', *Daily News*, 14 February.

Taylor, L., Lacey, R. and Bracken, D. (1979) *In Whose Best Interests?* London, Cobden Trust and National Association for Mental Health.

Tchaikovsky, C. (1985) 'Looking for trouble', in Carlen, P., Hicks, J., O'Dwyer, J., Christina, D. and Tchaikovsky, C. (eds) *Criminal Women.* Cambridge, Polity Press.

Tennent, T.G. (1971) 'School non-attendance and delinquency', *Educational Research*, 13(3), 185-90.

Thomas, W.I. (1923) *The Unadjusted Girl.* Boston, Little, Brown and Co.

Thompson, E.P. (1963) *The Making of the English Working Class.* London, Gollancz.

Thompson, E.P. (1967) 'Time, work-discipline and industrial capitalism', *Past and Present*, 38, 56-97.

Tibbenham, A. (1977) 'Housing and truancy', *New Society*, 39 (753), 501-2.

Turnbull, A. (1987) 'Learning her womanly work: the elementary school curriculum 1870-1914', in Hunt, F. (ed.) *Lessons for Life.* Oxford, Basil Blackwell.

Tyerman, M.J. (1968) *Truancy.* London, University of London Press.

Tyerman, M.J. (1972) 'Absent from school', *Trends in Education*, 26, 14-20.

Tyrer, P. and Tyrer, S. (1974) 'School refusal, truancy and adult neurotic illness', *Psychological Medicine*, 4, 416-21.

Walker, A. and Walker, C. (eds) (1987) *The Growing Divide: A Social Audit, 1979-1987.* London, Child Poverty Action Group.

Wallace, C. (1987) *For Richer for Poorer.* London, Tavistock.

Waller, D. and Eisenberg, L. (1980) 'School refusal in childhood – a psychiatric-paediatric perspective', in Hersov, L. and Berg, I. (eds) *Out of School: Modern Perspectives in Truancy and School Refusal.* Chichester, John Wiley.

Wardhaugh, J. (1990) 'Regulating truancy: the role of the education welfare service', *Sociological Review*, 38(4), 735-64.

Wardhaugh, J. (1991) 'Absent without leave: state responses to school non-attendance', *International Studies in Sociology of Education*, 1, forthcoming.

Warnock Report (1978) *Meeting Special Educational Needs.* London, HMSO.

Webb, D. (1984) 'More on gender and justice: girl offenders on supervision', *Sociology*, 18 (3), 267-81.

Wells, D. (1990) 'Gleanings', *Social Science Teacher*, Spring.

White, R. (1980) *Absent with Cause.* London, Routledge and Kegan Paul.

White, R. and Brockington, D. (1983) *Tales out of School.* London, Routledge and Kegan Paul.

White, R., Carr, P. and Lowe, N. (1990) *A Guide to the Children Act 1987.* London, Butterworths.

Wiener, M. (1981) *English Culture and the Decline of the Industrial Spirit 1850-1980.* Cambridge, Cambridge University Press.

Williams, P. (1974) 'Collecting the figures', in Turner, B. (ed.) *Truancy.* London. Ward Lock.

Willis, P. (1977) *Learning to Labour: How Working Class Kids Get Working Class Jobs*. Farnborough, Saxon House.

Willmott, P. and Young, M.D. (1959) *Family and Kinship in East London*. London, Institute of Community Studies.

Woods, P. (1976) 'Having a laugh: an antidote to schooling', in Hammersley, M. *et al.* (eds) *The Process of Schooling*. London and Milton Keynes, Routledge and Kegan Paul/Open University Press.

Woods, P. (1979) *The Divided School*. London, Routledge and Kegan Paul.

Worrall, A. (1989) *Offending Women*. London, Routledge.

Worrall, D. (1979) *Gypsy Education*. Walsall, Council for Community Relations.

Wright, N. (1977) *Progress in Education*. London, Croom Helm.

Wright-Mills, C. (1959) *The Sociological Imagination*. Harmondsworth, Penguin.

Young, J. (1971) 'The role of the police as amplifiers of deviancy, negotiators of reality and translators of fantasy', in Cohen, S. (ed.) *Images of Deviance*. Harmondsworth, Penguin.

Yule, W., Hersov, L. and Treseder, J. (1980) 'Behavioural treatment in school refusal', in Hersov, L. and Berg, I. (eds) *Out of School: Modern Perspectives in Truancy and School Refusal*. Chichester, John Wiley.

NAME INDEX

SUBJECT INDEX